# DISCIPLINE AND THE DISRUPTIVE CHILD

*A New, Expanded
Practical Guide
for Elementary Teachers*

Revised Edition

## Muriel Schoenbrun Karlin
## Regina Berger

**Parker Publishing Company**
Professional Publishing
Englewood Cliffs, NJ 07632
Simon & Schuster. A Paramount Communications Company

©1992 by

PARKER PUBLISHING COMPANY

West Nyack, New York

10 9 8 7 6 5 4 3 2

**Library of Congress Cataloging-in-Publication Data**
Karlin, Muriel Schoenbrun.
    Discipline and the disruptive child: a new, expanded guide for elementary teachers / Muriel S. Karlin, Regina Berger.
        p. cm.
    "Revision"—Galley pre.
    Includes index.
    ISBN 0-13-219643-3
    1. School discipline. 2. Problem children—Education.
I. Berger, Regina. II. Title.
LB3013.K35 1992
372. 15—dc20                                    92-6999
                                                CIP

ISBN 0-13-219643-3

**Parker Publishing Company**
Professional Publishing
Englewood Cliffs, NJ 07632
Simon & Schuster. A Paramount Communications Company

Printed in the United States of America

# ABOUT THE AUTHORS

**Muriel S. Karlin** has taught children at the elementary and junior high levels, acted as an educational and vocational guidance counselor, and been active in teacher training for years. She is now retired from her last position as assistant principal in a New York City junior high school but continues to be actively involved with in-service education for teachers. She has taught teachers in the Summer Institute for Teachers of the Disadvantaged and has contributed many articles to professional journals. Mrs. Karlin is also coauthor of several other practical resources for teachers, including *Successful Methods for Teaching the Slow Learner.*

**Regina Berger** taught for many years in the New York City school system, specializing in the development of high-interest activities to spark students' involvement in learning. She coauthored, with Muriel S. Karlin, *Successful Methods for Teaching the Slow Learner, Experimental Learning,* and *The Effective Student Activities Program.*

# DEDICATION

To the troubled and consequently troublesome children, and to their teachers and parents, with knowledge and confidence that many of these youngsters can become worthy adults because of the love-filled labors of those who sincerely and whole heartedly work with them.

Regina Berger
Muriel S. Karlin

On a personal note, I dedicate this revision to my beloved and very wise coauthor, my aunt, the late Regina Berger, and to my very dear husband, Emanuel Trachman.

Muriel S, Karlin

# HOW YOU WILL BENEFIT FROM THIS BOOK

This is a book to help you with your discipline problems—the problems encountered in every grade, even as low as kindergarten. In fact, the sooner the need for wholesome discipline is realized, the better—for the children's sake as well as for the teacher's.

This is not a book of philosophy or psychology, but of methods and techniques. It will aid you by placing in your hands the ways and means of working with your disruptive youngsters. You will find procedures with which to experiment, if you are to reach these boys and girls, and consequently teach them. It will also help you, we believe, understand them—comprehend their needs, and make yourself aware of their problems. It is the awareness of the sad fact that almost every child who is a discipline problem is a troubled child that will enable you to help and to teach him or her.

The format of this book has been chosen to aid you in finding the information you need quickly and easily. Chapters have been devoted to the major types of troublesome children—to understanding them and to coping with them in your classroom.

First, you will find material to help you see yourself as the leader of the class, the teacher. Next, you will be given some insights into the problems children may be faced with (and all too often are) in their daily lives. You will then find many suggestions that will help you work on solutions to these problems—whenever possible—or live with them when the solution is impossible. We cannot go into a child's home and rectify all of the evils we might find there, but we can offer that child a place of refuge and comfort for five to six hours a day. Since it is to be hoped that you can work with the parents of the disruptive youngster, we point out ways in which you can work, to win their confidence and cooperation.

Next are chapters on working with the child who has learning problems, or who is quarrelsome or openly aggressive in his or her behavior. No theory here, but good, solid steps for you to take. You may be plagued by attention seekers; in the chapter on this subject you will find ways and means to satisfy the needs of this particular type of child. The problems dealing with the hyperactive youngster, with the underachiever, and with nonmotivated boy or girl are discussed.

Another chapter is devoted to the child who has a phobia about coming to school, the one who is a truant, and the one who isolates him- or herself from other youngsters. The next chapter is concerned with the physically handicapped youngster and the child of poverty, of which there are too many. The chapter devoted to youngsters who abuse drugs, sniff glue, or drink alcohol has been enlarged because abuse is prevalent.

In the years since the first edition of this book appeared great changes have occurred in our society and have had a profound effect on the youngsters in schools throughout the nation. We have added chapters dealing with these situations. Many youngsters are abused, are the children of alcoholics or substance abusers, or are "crack kids." All of these children have special needs requiring your understanding and knowledge. The same is true of children whose families are in a state of disruption due to separation, divorce, death, or homelessness.

The two-parent, two-child family, with mother at home with the children while dad brings home the family income is difficult to find today. Many children are living with single parents, with stepparents, or in foster homes. We have included material to use in any or all of these situations.

There are a large number of youngsters, more than ever before, who simply don't care about their education or their future, and we have devoted a separate chapter to methods for working with them. Dealing with the child who is seriously disturbed or mentally ill is tremendously difficult for any teacher. These children must have special attention and care, and the methods to use are here.

The penultimate chapter of *Discipline and the Disruptive Child* is one that is of great importance. It is titled "Negating some of the Violence All Around Us." and offers methods you will find of interest.

At the end of this book you will find a questionnaire that will help you look at yourself objectively. This self-examination is usually difficult to do, but here it is simplified to the extent that you can examine the specific steps you have taken in working with the disruptive youngsters in your class.

Every method, every technique put forth in this book is based on our experiences in dealing with children— as teacher, counselor, and administrator. My coauthor, Regina Berger, taught for more than forty years in elementary schools in the Harlem section of New York City. I was a science teacher, a guidance counselor, and an assistant principal in elementary, intermediate, and junior high schools of Staten Island for over twenty-six years.

Ms. Berger passed away in 1984, and the revision of this book fell to me. She is sorely missed, for in addition to being my coauthor, she was my dear friend and my aunt.

The following were her words, as she wrote in the original introduction to this book:

"Every method, every technique is based on love and understanding. We try to help you to peer into the child's mind, into his life and into his environment. We try to help you to create a situation in which the troubled child— and every child—can learn. As a physician diagnoses a case, so we ask you to try to help the child to solve his problems by diagnosing them first, and then by treating them."

Perhaps the words that should reverberate through the mind and heart of the teacher as he or she deals with all children, and particularly with the troubled and consequently disruptive child, are these:

> Hostility breeds hostility.
> Respect commands respect.
> Love awakens love.

Muriel S. Karlin

# ACKNOWLEDGMENTS

We are indebted to many more people than can be acknowledged in here. However, we wish to thank particularly the following individuals for their assistance:

Mr. Maurice Wollin, Community Superintendent, District 31, Staten Island, New York.

Mrs. Helen Harris, Educational and Vocational counselor, Public School 82, Manhattan, New York.

Mr. Norman H. Harris, Principal, Anning S. Prall Intermediate School, Staten Island, New York.

The office of Education Information Services and Public Relations, Board of Education, City of New York, and special thanks to Superintendent Jerome Kovalcik.

Our thanks, too to our typist, Mrs. Mary Davies, of Public School 39, Staten Island. Proofreading was done by Mr. Henry Karlin and Ms. Lisa Karlin.

We are also grateful to the many teachers whose work and experience are chronicled here, and to our friends who offered help and suggestions.

Above all, we are indebted to the children we are privileged to work with and who are, really, the reason for this book.

Regina Berger

Muriel S. Karlin

In doing the revision of this book, I am very much indebted to Mr. Arnie Magenheim, Principal of Public School 39, Staten Island, for his many ideas and suggestions. His school might well serve as a model of the best in public education.

I appreciate the material supplied to me by Ms. Emilie Streis of the New York City Teacher Centers Consortium of the United Federation of Teachers.

I am most grateful to my mentor, in regard to my computer, Mr. Vincent Frizziola, of Intermediate School 72, Staten Island. He is an excellent science teacher and a really true friend.

My sincere thanks to my husband, Mr. Emanuel Trachman, a chemist and educator, for his many hours of work proofreading this manuscript and for making comments and valuable suggestions.

No book can come to fruition without the aid and advice of the author's editor. I have been most privileged to have worked with two of the very best, Mr. George Parker and Mr. Winfield Huppuch. I cannot possibly thank them enough.

Muriel S. Karlin

# CONTENTS

## Chapter Three
## BASIC METHODS OF WORKING WITH
## YOUNGSTERS WITH PROBLEMS • 38

## Chapter Four
## GETTING PARENTS TO COOPERATE
## WITH YOU • 56

# Chapter Five
## THE CHILD WITH LEARNING PROBLEMS • 71

# Chapter Six
## WORKING WITH THE FIGHTER OR THE QUARRELER • 86

## Chapter Seven
## THE ATTENTION SEEKER AND THE
## HYPERACTIVE CHILD • 102

## Chapter Eight
## THE UNDERACHIEVER AND THE
## NONMOTIVATED CHILD • 114

## Chapter Nine
## THE SCHOOL PHOBIC, THE TRUANT,
## AND THE LONER • 125

## Chapter Ten
## THE PHYSICALLY HANDICAPPED CHILD
## AND THE CHILD OF POVERTY • 138

# Chapter Eleven
# THE YOUNGSTER WHO ABUSES ALCOHOL, DRUGS, OR INHALANTS • 150

# Chapter Twelve
# ABUSED CHILDREN, OF SUBSTANCE ABUSERS, AND CRACK KIDS • 165

## Chapter Thirteen
## CHILDREN WHOSE FAMILIES ARE DISRUPTED BY SEPARATION, DIVORCE, DEATH, OR HOMELESSNESS • 178

## Chapter Fourteen
## CHILDREN LIVING WITH SINGLE PARENTS, STEPPARENTS, OR IN FOSTER HOMES • 195

## Chapter Fifteen
## WORKING WITH DISRUPTIVE STUDENTS
## WHO JUST DON'T "GIVE A DAMN" • 209

# Chapter Sixteen
## THE SERIOUSLY DISTURBED CHILD • 225

# Chapter Seventeen
## NEGATING SOME OF THE VIOLENCE
## ALL AROUND US • 239

## Chapter Eighteen
# A SELF-ANALYSIS QUESTIONNAIRE FOR EVERY TEACHER • 255

# INDEX • 262

# 1

## ESTABLISHING YOURSELF AS THE TEACHER

This is a book about children and teachers and the interpersonal relationships between them, relationships based on communication and respect, love and understanding. It discusses the art of teaching and the art of helping children learn. It is concerned with class control and class structure, with discipline and working with disruptive children. All of these factors are interdependent, for one cannot possibly teach without communication and respect, without love and understanding; and one cannot have these without developing the ability to control one's class and subsequently teaching the children self-control.

We believe that loving and understanding children is as necessary to teaching as the oxygen we breathe is to life. The chapters that follow will help you understand your youngsters and work with the difficult ones—the disruptive ones. The young people who become problems in the classroom are the ones who always have problems of their own.

We hope to give you insight into the lives of some of your boys and girls so that you can see the connection between the events shaping their characters at home, and their behavior in school. Hostility bred at home causes a young person to be hostile in the classroom. An angry boy or girl may be furious with a parent yet take out his or her rage on a classmate or a stranger. The problems your children have may be, and often are, deep rooted and difficult to solve. But you can understand them, and from this understanding comes empathy and love.

The successful teacher has deep empathy for people: people en masse and people as individuals. There is no substitute for this. If you do not enjoy being with people, if they make you feel vaguely uncomfortable much of

1

the time, if you realize you are afraid of them, teaching will be just a job for you, and possibly an unpleasant one. However, if you truly care about young people, your work can be the source of great joy. Certainly this joyousness does not happen every day, and not all the time, but it can happen many days and many times.

*I Honestly Like You.*    If you can honestly say to a child who has been disruptive—not at the time, but later—"I really like you. How can you disappoint me by behaving this way?" you are communicating with this youngster on a most important level, by showing care and affection. The need for caring and affection is so great that infants who are physically cared for but not loved, not held, not cuddled, not spoken to, are unable to develop normally. This need continues throughout life, and your students will respond to you in a far different manner if you show them that you really care about them.

Caring is different things to different people. A smile, a pat on the back, a wink are all significant gestures. They are signs of approval, such as the gold star pasted on a child's paper, or the words "I'm proud of you. This is fine work" written on a tenth-grader's composition. It is the comment "Very good" made after a student answers a question correctly, or the comment "That's a good try" if it was, or simply "Not quite" when he or she is incorrect that makes the difference in the way a student feels. How different this is from using the cold word "Wrong!"

But caring and affection are simply not enough. One must also have a knowledge of the skills of one's profession. As a teacher you must know how to teach. You must be able to hold the children's attention, how to establish a climate for learning, and how to teach the children not only academics but also self-control.

We have seen young teachers enter our profession, directly after graduation from college, filled with love for the children but lacking training. And we have seen them leave the profession five months or a year later, disillusioned, or worse still, considering themselves to be failures. Love and skill are both necessary. One without the other is just not enough.

It is our aim to assist you in understanding your girls and boys and to show you how to establish a structured situation in your classroom so that they can and will learn. This can be called class control, or it can be called discipline, but you must have it to teach effectively. This is true on whatever level you teach, applying as much to high school students as to first graders.

In these pages you will find many specific suggestions for establishing this structured situation. They may have to be adjusted to the level on which you are teaching. However, they are basic to good class control and to good teaching, whether it be on the elementary, the intermediate, or the high school level.

The basic concepts you will find in this book are more important today than ever. It is obvious that young people are growing up in a very chaotic world. They need structure and exposure to good interpersonal relationships. Your classroom, with its climate for learning and your vital, interesting teaching, can show them that they can create for themselves a better environment, a better personal world.

## UNDERSTANDING THE ROLE OF THE TEACHER _____

Your success in achieving discipline and creating a climate for learning in your classroom is a direct result of the image you have of yourself and your role as a teacher, for these concepts govern the manner in which you function. Let us examine these concepts, therefore, in the light of teaching in the elementary, intermediate, or high schools. They differ considerably from those of the college professor and others working with adults rather than children or young adults. The role of the teacher, specifically what he or she does, will not be identical for every teacher, but certain defined areas have proved of importance to us and will for you too.

Since the earliest schools, the prime function of the teacher has been to transmit knowledge to his or her pupils, to impart skills and to help the pupils learn to solve problems. This basic aspect of our work has not changed. When we use the verb *to teach*, it is these procedures that are implied, for it is these methods that our society and every society since the Egyptians with their hieroglyphics, and the Greeks, Romans, and Hebrews, with their alphabets have utilized. We are dealing with the transmission of knowledge that one generation has received or developed to the next generation. Traditionally the teacher is the adult, the pupil the child. This is as true today as it was thousands of years ago.

However, teachers have developed many new methods to transmit knowledge and to meet the needs of the children of today. It has been found, for example, that the lecture method of old is highly ineffective. If we substitute questioning, even to develop new ideas, the lessons are far more stimulating and more problem solving in nature. Class discussion evokes thought. We can, and must, develop techniques that will cause our students, no matter their ages, to think. This is far better than spoon-feeding them at every turn.

In the schools of previous generations, the teacher was an autocrat, ruling by domination and certainly not above the use of physical or psychological punishment. The whip was not uncommon nor the dunce cap rare. Fortunately we have left this pattern of behavior far behind us and have substituted other means of influence over the children. These other means are the ones we shall discuss throughout this book.

***You Must Be in Charge.***   No teacher today can rule with an iron hand. The day of the despotic teacher is long gone. Nevertheless, every teacher must have control of what is going on in the classroom. You are responsible for teaching children, which is impossible when the climate is chaotic. You must have the situation under your management (one of whose elements is discipline) by being in complete control. You must be the captain of the ship, or the ship will founder and possibly fail to reach its destination.

Yours is a very sensitive situation. You cannot be "buddy-buddy" or a pal to your students. Nor can you be a member of the group, a peer or contemporary of the youngsters. You can certainly be their friend and, at times, their confidante. And you can certainly share experiences with them—and it is to be hoped that you will. But if **you do not feel you are in charge, you can rarely, if ever, be a truly effective teacher.** It's your task to structure the situation to see to it that you are in charge.

This is not to say that you will dominate every lesson. Nor do you need to. You will establish routines, show the children there is work to be done, and get them started. You will transmit your expectations to them, such as the expectation that you know they can do good work and will do it. You, in short, will start the intellectual ball rolling. You might sit on the sidelines and have the children have a panel discussion, or you might have a youngster actually teach the class. Or you might have one write on the board or actually lead the class discussion. But your presence, and the climate for learning you have created, will serve to structure the situation in your classroom.

You may know of highly successful teachers who never appear to be working hard. Their students are, instead. In fact, these teachers give the impression they are relaxed and enjoying themselves—and in reality they are. But this is only possible because they have established the climate for learning. They have laid the groundwork and conveyed to their young people the concept that the teacher is there to teach, and, more important, the students are there to learn. Their presentation of material is such that they keep the young people interested from the first day of the year to the last.

This ease, this climate, is not achieved overnight. A great deal of work is required to arrive at this point. How does the teacher achieve it? He or she may work with the children to plan the actual lessons and determine the methods to be utilized. The teacher may suggest alternative activities to the class, activities that he or she has already planned, and allow the class to choose among them. But he or she will set up routines and consult with the youngsters to set up the "rules of the game." He or she will ask for the children's suggestions and opinions and take them into consideration.

One of the words teachers hear all too often is the word *boring,* for youngsters are used to being entertained. They have grown up watching television, an impassive, non-thought-provoking activity. Realization of this very important factor must affect one's teaching. A teacher must vary his or her methods to get the youngsters to actively participate. Lecturing often falls on deaf ears.

If there are boys or girls in the class who are preventing the others from working, the teacher must work with them. But it is the teacher who sets the stage, who creates the manuscript, and who directs the production.

No teacher who cannot assume responsibility for creating a climate for learning can be a successful teacher. No child can ever approach his or her potential if discipline is nil. A class must function as a team and as with every team there must be a leader. In the classroom situation the leader must be you, the teacher.

*Your "Bag of Tricks."*  You are, after all, trained as well as educated for the task. You must know methods and techniques (a "bag of tricks") and you must have an understanding of and a feeling, an empathy for the children. You must be able to work with them. You must be able to control them so that when they are presented with work, they will do it. You might be surprised to learn that many times girls and boys (mostly girls) will complain to a supervisor, "That teacher can't control our class." It is said sometimes wistfully, and sometimes in indignation, with angrier words; "Can't you do something?"

We know of one young substitute teacher who misguidedly allowed her class of one day to "do anything they wanted to do." She thought if they wanted to read, they would read. She put arithmetic examples on the board and suggested any child so inclined might do them. She took out art materials and gym equipment. Even with these second graders chaos ensued. At dismissal time one of the little girls said to her, "I have an awful headache. Our teacher is coming back tomorrow, isn't she?"

When a person feels inadequate to the task he or she assumes, be it teaching or practicing medicine, sewing a dress or repairing an automobile, he or she will have to work hard to overcome that feeling, and to build a positive self-image. However, to instill confidence in others, one has to appear adequate and give the impression one knows what one is doing. In no field of endeavor is this more important than in teaching. To help you feel adequate, we offer you what appears to be a rather simple suggestion, but one we have found works extremely well: Planning.

Plan your lessons carefully and completely. Leave absolutely nothing to chance. If you are not sure of the amount of time a lesson will take, plan more material than you will need, but plan, plan, plan. We promise you these plans will be tremendously valuable to you. However, do not consider your plans to be inviolate. They should not be.

Plans must be regarded as flexible tools to be varied whenever necessary. Do not hesitate to change them as the situation dictates. For example, you might decide to have a debate. You introduce the topic. The class, however, seems very uninterested. You try to motivate them further, but it isn't working. Your best procedure is then to change the topic or the technique.

Perhaps if you had presented more material, questioning the class as you developed it, you might have generated more interest. Perhaps your motivation was faulty. Try to determine why that particular technique failed and keep that in mind when you do more planning. But in your mind, *establish lesson planning as a law and flexibility as an amendment.*

There is no reason in the world not to use plans you have developed for one group with another. Of course, you should vary the plans to suit the particular class you are teaching, but if the plans are good, they can be used again and again. There is no need to keep reinventing the wheel.

In your role as teacher you need to wear many hats. To gain and hold the children's interest requires you to use as much dramatic ability as you possess and can develop to present your lessons.

*Youngsters Want to Be Taught.*    Make no mistake, children want a structured classroom where things of interest to them are going on. They feel more secure in a structured situation than in a nonstructured one. Unfortunately, many youngsters do not have a feeling of security in their homes, for reasons we will go into later. They are comfortable in the classroom.

Boys and girls want teachers who really teach them. They resent those who do not, and they can spot a phony after twenty minutes of exposure to him or her. They know we are paid to teach them, and they want us to do so. Of course, on some grade levels this is not obvious, but it is true nevertheless.

We are speaking of young people who are not strung out on drugs and who have not been under undue pressure from peers who might be. But we have seen the "toughest" youngsters respond to structured classrooms with good teachers in a very satisfactory manner. They won't behave that way in every classroom, but they will for the teacher who is in control.

It has been our experience that the students' favorite teachers are those whose classes are structured, who feel comfortable and unthreatened, and who can relax with their students. These teachers are warm and interested in the youngsters, but this in no way means the boys and girls will be able to waste their time in their classrooms. Their teachers have something of value to give them, and it is presented in as palatable a fashion as possible. This is where dramatic ability comes in. The teacher who feels he or she is adequate to the task becomes creative and innovative.

We are all familiar with how deadly dull a class can be with a teacher who drones on and on, without modulating his or her voice or modifying his or her ideas. We have all sat through what seemed like eternity waiting for the bell to ring. But no one wants to be a teacher like that! A person who is interested becomes interesting; if one is intellectually stimulated one becomes stimulating. Therefore, you need to know a great deal about the subject you are teaching. Even a simple topic can gain new appeal if you find something in it to interest your students.

It is necessary for you to have your students' respect so that you can respect yourself. You earn this by being a professional, by considering your profession to be one of the most important and critical in today's world, as it was in previous civilizations. You can never allow yourself to go down to the youngsters' level; rather, you must work to raise them to yours.

In the matters of vocabulary, for example, some educators feel children should be allowed to express themselves as they wish, using the vocabulary they have learned in the streets (and possibly in their homes). It is our fervent hope that you feel as we do, that when a child is entrusted to you, you will try in every way you can to educate him or her in every aspect you can. Surely choice of language is one.

If we adopt the philosophy we need do nothing other than allow the children self-expression, we find we are teaching them very little and preparing them even less for their adult lives. How will they ever improve their vocabularies if we do not teach them by example and help them learn new and appropriate words?

We surely do not mean to give you the idea that self-expression is not to be encouraged, for it definitely is! Every child needs outlets for his or her emotions, and we can and should supply those outlets. Drawing, composition, and discussion are but a few ways to foster this. But self-expression need not imply four-letter words. Is it not our task to teach young people how to convey their ideas in socially acceptable terms? They will learn to convey them in other ways outside our walls, but if we do not teach them the traditional words, who will?

How do you see the role of the teacher? This is a most important matter, and we suggest you give it serious thought. Our concept is that of a person who creates the climate of learning in the classroom, who achieves discipline through firm leadership, who feels adequate to his or her tasks, who is interested and therefore interesting, who is a professional in his or her approach at all times, and who understands and loves children.

## CREATING A CLIMATE FOR LEARNING

### Establish Routines

The first step in achieving discipline and creating a climate for learning is to establish routines, your system of doing things. Children want and need routines because routines give them a feeling of security, which fulfills one of their basic psychological needs. There are a number of ways in which establishment of routines can take place:

- You may have set up your routines long before you meet your class in September. (This is true for many experienced teachers.)
- You may decide on some of the routines in advance and work out the remainder with your class.
- You may work out all of the routines with your class, based on the philosophy that any rules and regulations made by those on whom they are to be imposed will be more effective than rules and regulations dictated by others. (Other experienced teachers have found this to be preferable.)

It is best to establish routines at the beginning of the school year. However, it is never too late and is always well worthwhile to add routines at any time in the year. If you are having difficulty in the middle of the term, institute the routines immediately. They should help you.

Following are some examples of procedures that can be routinized. The suggestions will obviously not work for every grade level. It is up to you to decide which are of value to you. Surely if you are teaching on a grade level where you meet a different group every hour, your routines will of necessity be different from classes in which the children are in the same room for most of the time. *However, the concept of setting up routines still holds. It's just that the routines will be adjusted to your situation.*

- Entry: Delineate exactly how the children should enter the classroom. Do they go to the closet to hang up their coats, or do they sit down first? Is conversation to be permitted? We have found it works well if conversation is allowed, until a specific indication from you that that time is over.
- Hanging up clothing: Designate a specific place for every child's coat. Be sure to give the taller children the hangers that are highest up.
- Seating: Assign a permanent seat and be sure it is accepted as permanent. We have found it worthwhile to reassign seats every ten weeks—putting the youngsters who were in the back up front and vice versa.

Determine as many actions as possible that can be routinized and then stress the method decided on. Giving out materials, collecting them, getting on line, leaving the room, or fire drill procedures are some examples.

Having work on hand for the class to do—*at all times*—should be part of your routine. This is fundamental to establishing a climate for learning.

We are not talking about busywork, which is deadly. We refer to work with a value, work that the youngsters will find interesting. You need a stock in trade of exercises and devices that you can use.

A favorite, for example, is "Unscramble." Girls and boys seem to enjoy this activity over and over again. Give them a list of scrambled words and have them figure out what the words are. (You have to give a designation, or the game will be too difficult.) For example, the following scrambled words are all names of U.S. states. Which are they? ZONRIAA, KYNOWER, BALMAAA.

Or, using a dictionary how many words can the children find with the ending "-ology"? Have them list the words with their meanings (a good way to build vocabulary).

You might start discussions of current events, sports, or personalities. Discussions, however, require more of your attention than written work of some kind. One teacher found her sixth graders reacted well to keeping a journal, in which they wrote during the early morning or after completing their work.

Not all methods work for all classes, and you have to find those that are good for your students. However, it's a fact that the children of today will not sit still or be quiet if they have nothing to do. They need, indeed almost crave, intellectual stimulation. A bookshelf with magazines as well as books can also supply this and should be available to the children when they have completed the assigned work or even before the day's work has begun.

If your students have nothing to occupy them, don't expect them to "behave." They can't, and they won't. It is too much to expect of healthy youngsters, who are full of life and energy and who are used to being entertained. Although the activities we have used as examples may not entertain each and every child, they do hold the interest of many young people.

It is well worthwhile to keep a record of those activities that you find work well and to use them from month to month, but not more often.

## Establish Rules and Regulations

As we have said, children need a structured situation. They seek the security that structure offers, in the classroom as well as in the home. One reason divorce causes youngsters to be so upset is that it shatters this necessary sense of security. (The behavior problems shown by children in school often reflect upheavals of one kind or another in the children's home life.)

To have structure in your class, you need rules and regulations. The school administration undoubtedly has established some, and these should be discussed so that they are understood by each youngster. This is particularly important for a boy or girl who is new to the school or when the class is an entering one.

It is our belief that young people should have some voice in the establishment of these school rules and regulations. This voice is usually through the General Organization or through some form of student government. We are of the opinion that the thoughts of the youngsters deserve careful consideration and should never be ignored or regarded lightly. The same is true in the classroom.

Have your youngsters suggest the rules of behavior they choose to live by. Have them elect class officers to help in the enforcement of these rules. Try not to override or dominate them, but do attempt to have rules and regulations established that will make life in the classroom more pleasant for everyone.

It is simple to set up regulations that make life easier for everyone. For example, have a rule that requires a monitor to pass the basket around the room five minutes before dismissal. Have the youngsters discard any papers from their desks or from the floor around their seats. This provides a clean classroom with a minimum of effort. (In the intermediate school, this can be done several times during the day. The custodial staff will be grateful!) A rule such as the following is helpful to teachers and youngsters alike: "Any member of the class involved in littering will be required to give up his or her opportunity to be a monitor for one month." This leads to the subject of establishing a monitorial system.

## Make Every Youngster a Monitor

By establishing an effective monitorial system you can accomplish a great deal. You will be relieved of many chores, which your children are anxious to do. We know of one teacher whose desk was always neat. "When do you get a chance to put everything away?" we asked. "Oh, I don't do it. My monitor does," was her reply. She had used the system we are outlining here very successfully.

Every one of us needs to feel he or she is worthwhile and important, and a monitorial job gives a youngster that status. The youngster can go home and tell his or her parents, "I'm the blackboard monitor. Mrs. Jones needs me." The parents are usually impressed, even though this is the same child who refuses to do any chores at home. The key to this system, though, is that **every child must have a job.** No child should be allowed to feel left out and become a malcontent.

Realize too that by giving children monitorial jobs you then have a very powerful weapon. You can threaten to take the job away. However, this deprivation is extremely serious. *Never* remove youngsters from their position without first warning them that you are being forced to do so. The threat is often enough to keep the youngster in line.

If you must remove a youngster from his or her job, do it with obvious reluctance, because you have lost some of the control you were able to exert on this girl or boy, and because this can be hard on the student's self-esteem.

Here is a listing of some of the many monitorial jobs you can establish in your classroom:

1. Class officers, including a president, vice-president, secretary, and treasurer. Their duties will be outlined below. Have the class elect these officers.

2. Representatives to the school's General Organization. If your school does not have one, work to get one established. This is an important way to teach the democratic process.

3. One attendance monitor, who checks for absence and lateness and gives this information to the secretary.

4. One chalkboard monitor who erases the work on the board every day.

5. One chalkboard monitor who washes the board daily.

6. One window-shade monitor, who adjusts the shades daily.

7. One clothing closet monitor, who is responsible for locking and unlocking the closets.

8. Two monitors in charge of distribution, who give out paper, books, or anything else that must be distributed.

9. Two wastebasket monitors, who pass the baskets around the room five minutes before the end of the day.

10. Two fire drill monitors, who help the class officers keep order during fire drills and when the class is in line to go somewhere.

11. Two housekeeping monitors, who dust the windowsills, keep the teacher's desk neat, and keep the closets tidy.

12. One bulletin board monitor, who will put up and take down displays.

13. Two library monitors, who take charge of the class collection of books and magazines.

14. Two plant monitors, who take care of the plants and who plant bulbs and seeds.

15. One fish tank monitor, who cares for fish, turtles, or other animals you have in your classroom. Choose a youngster who is knowledgeable in this area and who is responsible.

16. Two supply-room monitors, who report for supplies and carry them back to the classroom.

17. One audiovisual monitor, who transports and operates audiovisual equipment.

18. Two collection monitors, who collect books, papers, and so on.

19. A class host and a class hostess, who greet visitors whenever they come into the room.

20. A money-collecting monitor, who collects money whenever necessary for charity drives, and so on.

There are many other possibilities, but this listing gives you a wide base from which to work.

The tasks of the class officers are more involved than those of the monitors. The president should take charge of the class when the teacher is not in the room and assist when the teacher is busy. When a monitor is needed to leave the room, that job should be the president's. He or she should also lead the class when it moves in and out of the room to the auditorium or to the cafeteria and during fire drills.

The vice-president should notify the office if a teacher is absent. He or she takes the place of the president when the latter is absent. During a fire drill or during regular dismissal he or she is the last person to leave the room and is responsible for every youngster leaving it.

The secretary writes notes on the board so that the teacher can do other things. (It is essential that the person chosen for this position can write legibly on the board.) He or she lists the names of the absent students on the chalkboard and also has the responsibility of telephoning those pupils to give them the work they have missed and the homework assignments.

The treasurer collects all monies—for trips, "milk money," and charitable contributions. He or she is responsible for keeping financial records.

**Making the Monitorial System Work.** If you establish this system, make sure you give the youngsters as much to do as possible. This is excellent training for their future lives, and it also serves very valuable purposes in the classroom. You may find it difficult in the beginning to give so much authority to your students, but the results of doing so make your efforts to do so worthwhile.

One of the important things an extensive monitorial system accomplishes is it makes the children feel needed. Use every bit of enthusiasm you can muster to sell the importance of each task, and it will be done well. Your life will be easier, and the students' far richer.

The monitorial system can easily be enlarged. For example, you can have class artists to assist other youngsters who have difficulty drawing. In the same vein, class writers, mathematicians, readers, and spellers are all possibilities. An excellent job for a bright child is doing research—looking up information that is needed. As you can see, the variety of monitorial positions is great, depending only on your creativity.

One of our fourth-graders had the job of decorating the room. This child amazed everyone with her intuitive good taste and imagination. She relied on the seasons and nature for her sources, and from September through June made the classroom attractive by using leaves, shells, pictures, and even small branches of trees. Her mother was thrilled with this aspect of her child's education and so was I. The decor was so clever and unusual that other teachers came in to admire it.

## Explain Your Expectations

Often teachers are surprised when their youngsters do not pay attention or do poor-quality work. The teachers lower their sights and accept poorer and poorer quality work instead of raising the sights of their children. Call it faith, call it confidence, or call it expectations, but if you expect your youngsters to behave in an adult manner and to do their work conscientiously, they will. This has been proved time and again in educational experiments. If, on the other hand, you expect your boys and girls to do poor work and you accept it, that is exactly what you will get.

Be sure your class knows exactly what it is you expect of them. If young people are aware of the type of work you anticipate they will do, you can get very good results. Be sure, however, that the youngsters are capable of handling the work, that it is on their level or just above it, and that they are reasonably interested in it. No one wants to read dull material if given a choice. Nor should they be compelled to do so. But if your assignments are of interest to the youngsters, and if your attitude is helpful and understanding, your students will reflect this.

If you expect good work and you get it, it's an excellent procedure to reward the youngsters by praising them and giving them good grades. These must of course be deserved and must take into consideration what you know the boy or girl is capable of. If you feel a child could do better, return the paper with comments to that effect. The youngster has to know why he or she did not do well the first time. Have him or her then revise and return it to you. *Make constructive suggestions, never derogatory remarks.* Always build up and never, ever, tear down.

This same basic principle works in regard to pupil behavior. If Johnny is told, "You're bad," not necessarily in those words but with that intent, he will be disruptive to prove what you say is true. If on the other hand he is told, "I know you're trying, but I'm sure you can do better," he has your expectations to work up to.

*Never label any child.* As we shall discuss later at great length, you will be trying to find out why he or she is misbehaving to help him or her change that behavior.

Find something every youngster in your class can do well and build on that. Not one or two children, but each and every one. There are always one or two talented girls or boys who do everything well. All of the others seem to fall into the shadows, which is not desirable. Every child should do one task—whatever that may be. Be sure all of them feel your expectations for them and watch them try to exceed them.

One class of ours, when asked to raise money for a project, was told, "I know you can do it." They made plans themselves, executed the plans and raised three times the amount needed. This device, high expectations, is not foolproof, but it does work a great deal of the time, and with youngsters with whom you might least expect it.

## Teach on the Students' Level

If your teaching is to prove rewarding to your students, it must start at their level, and progress upward. At times this progress will be rapid, at other times slower. Without progress, without that moving forward, however, their attention will disappear, they will become bored, and our great enemy, apathy, will appear. Apathy—an unawareness, a lack of caring, and a refusal to take part in the learning process—can make your youngsters virtually unteachable. The new material you cover, the unknowns you explain, the pleasure in learning you create can dispel apathy and turn your children into interested individuals, really seeking to learn.

However, if you do not have them "with you" from the start, you take a chance on turning them off, and the result, too, can be apathy. How can you determine your children's level?

This is best done by diagnostic testing. Simple skills tests, for instance, can show you the deficiencies in your pupils' knowledge and the point at which to start working with them. These tests need not be long or involved. Have the youngsters correct these tests themselves—after you explain why they are taking them. The reason is simply for finding out what the class knows and what they need to learn. Then state specifically how you will use the results.

A diagnostic test may be used before every unit of work. For example, the questions in Figure 1 might be used before you begin teaching a unit on the government of the United States.

The responses to questions such as these will give you and your students a starting point for their study of the government.

## Figure 1

The United States Government

Diagnostic Test

1. We elect a president once every _____ years; the vice-president every _____ years.

2. The laws of our nation are made by _____.

3. The judicial branch of our government decides whether or not a _____ conforms to our Constitution.

4. The Senate and the House of Representatives of the United States together form the _____.

5. We elect two _____ from each of the fifty states.

6. The seat of our government is in _____.

7. The number of members of the House of Representatives from each state is determined by the _____ of the state.

8. The president and vice-president are members of the branch of government called the _____.

9. A person must be _____ years old to vote.

10. When we refer to the "federal government," what is meant?

## Make Your Teaching Exciting

Using the test in Figure 1 as a starting point, here are some of the activities you might use:

1. Take a trip to Washington, D.C., including tours of the Capitol, the White House, and the Supreme Court building. Difficult? Of course. Worthwhile? Of course. Impossible? That's for you to decide. We have found this trip to be one of the best of any we have ever taken, for one very good reason. Many of these youngsters would otherwise never visit their nation's capital. (Sad, but true.)

(Incidentally, any trip can be used to motivate your disruptive youngsters to improve their behavior. While we hate to see any child excluded, there are times when this may be necessary, but it should not be done without warning the youngster.)

But there are many reasons why this trip would be out of the question as far as your situation is concerned. Why not show a video of these places? You might choose to take the trip yourself and film it, or you can obtain a commercially made video.

2. Divide your class into three committees, each one representing one of the branches of government. Have the entire class "elect" a president and a vice-president. These persons will then outline their duties. Do not rule out a young woman for either of these positions. The others in the executive branch can be members of the president's cabinet.

There are many senators and representatives and Supreme Court justices, so having all the children participate poses no problems. You may have the youngsters be specific individuals, in which case the youngsters can write to those persons, asking for their opinions and telling them of the project in which the class is involved.

Make these presentations come to life by helping the boys and girls obtain as much information as they can on the subject.

3. Show a film such as *Mr. Smith Goes to Washington*. While of yesteryear, this film is still relevant and will appeal to the youngsters.

4. Invite your Congressperson to speak with the class, either in school or at his or her office. Members of Congress generally respond favorably, especially in an election year.

5. Have your class put out a publication called "The Government of the United States." It could contain an outline by each student of the position (see activity 2) he or she had held.

6. Create an assembly program based on this unit.

If you find that your students know the material on this diagnostic test and it is not necessary to teach the material, you can go on to units on state and then local government. We have discovered that young people have little, if any, knowledge in these areas.

We've illustrated the use of the diagnostic test as it might be used in social studies.In language arts you can determine much about your students' ability to write by a device as simple as this: Duplicate the paragraph in Figure 2 and have the youngsters rewrite it, correcting all of the errors.

### Figure 2

Deer granmother

when i cam home momy sed to me there are a packaje fram your gramma. i wuz happy i hopped it waz a toi or a radio i shock it and tought befor i openned it. i yeled and skreamed. wuz i wuzited. thank yuz four de nis pajamis.

your granson
Timmy

There are 45 errors to be corrected in this paragraph. However, give the youngsters three points for each one they find. This means they can get a total of 135, but explain to them that this is a diagnostic test to determine where they make their mistakes, not a test based on 100 points.

**Using Textbook Material for Diagnostic Testing.** Most texts contain material at the end of each chapter that is suitable for diagnostic testing. You can also find out how well your students can do the work you have planned for them by asking questions orally. We ask the girls and boys to nod their heads when we question, "Do you understand? If so, nod yes, and if not, no." To make them feel comfortable, we add, "If you don't understand, there are others in the class who don't either. You will be helping me with my work if you are brave enough to tell me you don't understand what I am teaching." It is, however, easier to be misled by answers to oral questions than by those obtained through written testing.

In addition to teaching reading skills, as soon as your class is capable of handling it, we believe you can accomplish much in your teaching of reading with an individualized reading program. You may use texts, although books from the library are preferable, but in either event allow the children to select the books they wish to read and vary the selections to allow the children a fair amount of choice.

While the youngsters are reading, you have time to work with each child and discuss the material he or she is reading. Most teachers also require the child to write a short summary of one to three sentences about the material he or she has read. The child also keeps a list of every book read, and the teacher may keep a master chart of this. (A possible job for the class secretary.)

In Public School 39, Staten Island, New York, every person in the school reads for twenty minutes, from 1:00 until 1:20 in the afternoon. This program, introduced by Principal Arnie Magenheim, has proved to be very successful. "We all enjoy it," he comments, "and the youngsters see adults reading, too."

If you see to it that the reading material offered is of real interest to the youngsters, they will read it. Some texts are far better than others in this regard, and it is up to you to choose carefully, so that reading them is pleasurable in addition to being a requirement.

Dr. Jerome Bruner, a well-known authority on education, some years ago pointed out that we can teach any material as long as it is at the youngsters' level. Many of the topics that are usually reserved for adults are fascinating for children as well. The fields of archeology and anthropology, for example, and even sociology and psychology, can be delved into with children. Youngsters can learn to read by reading about prehistoric people or about the early Egyptian civilization rather than reading dull, insipid material.

Bring in subjects you find stimulating and share them with your students. One successful teacher traveled during vacations, took loads of pictures, purchased many items such as clothing and handicrafts, and used them as the basis for much of her teaching during the school year. She had many stories to tell of her experiences, and her classes were enthralled!

A class can do research and write compositions about the possibility of life on Mars and will enjoy that far more than writing about "My Pet," or "How I Spent My Summer Vacation," and they will also enjoy reading their compositions aloud to their classmates.

"This is a far cry from improving discipline in my classroom," you might be thinking, but in reality it is not. The more intellectually compelling your topic, the more attention you will note among your children.

We once invited a guest who was going to show a film to our assembly of 500 eighth graders. There was a buzzing, and I called for "absolute silence."

"Don't bother," my guest told me. "When this film starts you'll be able to hear a pin drop." And you could. The film dealt with a young man's search for his parents and his identity, and there wasn't a sound in that auditorium.

## Make Your Teaching Interesting

The best means of achieving a climate for learning is to make learning as fascinating as possible. Here are just a few suggestions to start you thinking about how you can do this:

1. Try to link your lessons directly to the youngsters' lives. When the curriculum seems unrelated to their concerns, it becomes your task to make it meaningful. To do this, you have to be aware of what is happening in the immediate world in which your students live.

One relevant topic, and one that must be covered, is the use of narcotics and drug addiction. Lessons in this should be given to every grade, starting with first grade. This topic can be considered in every subject area, not simply in science or health classes. It is of importance in every school and in every community, for drug pushers are everywhere and may be the most innocent appearing of boys or girls.

If your school board permits it, the topic of AIDS can be introduced to the children, of course on their level of understanding. Youngsters need information, and they need it from a reliable source, and one that they trust.

2. Always be willing to learn from your students. Listen to them. They can really educate you in terms of their world, a world that may be, and

often is, very different from yours. How many teachers grew up in single-family homes or in homes in which both parents work?

Your most disruptive child can probably teach you a great deal in terms of his or her lifestyle. Knowing about that lifestyle will make you a better teacher and more able to teach that child self-control.

3. Make your teaching experiential. Instead of telling your children facts, have them do things. If you are able to make your lessons such that the girls and boys can be physically active, you will find an improvement in their behavior. For example, don't discuss the "how to take one's pulse" without having your pupils work in pairs taking each other's pulse. This should be done before and after they do some exercise such as running in place for a minute. (Be sure no physician has ruled out the exercise for a particular child.)

When a class project has been decided on, it works well to have the youngsters complete as many aspects of it as they can handle. For example, you might choose to do a play. Have the youngsters write it, stage it, and act in it. Even have them create and execute the stage settings, advertise the play, invite parents and other classes to see it, and then review it. This can be done in social studies as well as in language arts classes.

4. Make your teaching as timely as possible. Have your class read and discuss articles from newspapers and magazines. Young people should be aware of the happenings in the adult world around them. So often they are not. Using this type of reading material they can be taught such skills as reading for specific information, finding details, and skimming. The amount of important information they will gain quickly cannot be overestimated.

5. Take the class on trips. The interest you can develop in connection with a trip is surprisingly great. Boys and girls love to go places with their classes. Shouldn't a first grader who lives in the city learn what cows and chickens really look (and smell) like? Or a seventh grader see ships being loaded or planes taking off? The selection of trips is almost infinite—if you open your eyes to the possibilities.

As we have already mentioned, trips can help greatly with your teaching of self-control. Even an unruly class will behave if promised a trip. Used wisely, this device can be an excellent one for helping the young people develop self-discipline.

Be sure you stress the rules of behavior before the trip. We were once asked by a bus driver as we returned from a class expedition, "What did you do, lady, chloroform them?" Of course not, but we had told these sixth graders that they were responsible for their own behavior. If anyone did not follow all of the rules, he or she would never go on another trip again. This incident took place some years ago, but the basic premise still holds true.

Youngsters must know exactly what is expected of them. This has to be spelled out and reiterated time and again.

6. A factor you may not have thought about but that is very important is the effect of television on young people. They often watch for hours and hours each day and as a result have become passive. In our classrooms that passivity is the last thing we want. Not only that, but because these youngsters have lived all of their lives being entertained in their homes, many of them expect that to continue in the classroom.

You have to plan to have your students actually working, really working, as much of the time as possible. If they have to do something that seems as insignificant as copying the material you put on the chalkboard, they are still doing something. Surely you want them to do more than that, so you ask questions and have them provide answers—again in writing. You are teaching them that there is more to life than watching a screen.

## THE FIGURE OF AUTHORITY

At a time in our history when we, the adults, are suspected of being overly permissive, at a time when there is upheaval all around us, the teacher, we believe, must represent authority. This is a very difficult task, we believe, for you must be the figure of authority in your classroom without being authoritarian. You must represent to your youngsters the strength and the understanding of a person dedicated to your task and unafraid of its responsibility. Yet you have to do this so that they do not see you as an adversary.

It has been our experience that this type of teacher is what youngsters want and need. Otherwise, the youngsters lose their sense of security. Many times youngsters have come to us requesting a change of class. Perhaps three or four times this has been "because the work is too hard." Most of the other times, children have stated their reason using words to the effect, "That class is too noisy. I'm not learning anything." On occasion they will add, "That teacher can't control the class."

If you do not give this matter thought, you can lose your status with your class, and your control, without even being aware of it. It slips away, and you wake up to the fact that you can't teach this class. There are, unfortunately, some teachers who never admit this, even to themselves. They are having a terrible time, for they are ineffective and, even more important, so is their teaching.

If a teacher is willing to admit that he or she has lost control, then he or she can do something about it. *The will to be the figure of authority and to put the energy into it contributes much to a person's becoming the figure of authority.* It is what the young people really need and want, and should have!

As the figure of authority, you structure your class—the work to be done and the time to do it. If you enter your classroom and find the youngsters noisy, get them started on written work *at once.* You must do this with firmness and purpose in your manner.

At the beginning of the school year, most of the boys and girls will proceed to do as you say. If one or two do not, say to each one of them, "Come on, let's get started." Say it with a smile, but so that the youngster knows you mean business. If any student is permitted to get away with not working, the fat is in the fire. The next day there will be another slightly rebellious child, and the number will increase as the term progresses.

If when told to work a child refuses, immediately find out why. At least 50 percent of the time the response is, "I have no pen" or "I have no pencil." Or no paper, or no book. It saves a great deal of time and effort to supply the missing item, but do so with the words, "I'll lend you one today. Promise me you'll try to remember to bring one tomorrow." Say this pleasantly, lovingly, but with firmness. Be sure the youngster returns the pencil or pen before he or she leaves your class. If not, the giveaway becomes expensive. Yet it is far better to have some supplies on hand than to have some youngsters not working and disruptive because they lack their supplies. Note, too, that it is invariably the youngsters who have no supplies who cannot afford to miss the work being done in class.

You may wish to build up a stock by having a "Pen and Pencil Contribution Day" at the very beginning of the term, if your school does not supply these items. Ask the class to bring in any pens or pencils they can spare. This is very worthwhile.

Some youngsters will forget what one teacher has named "their tools" (pens, pencils, notebook, and textbooks) daily. You have to keep after them. As an alternative, you can keep their pens and pencils for them in a drawer of your desk.

What of the child who tells you, "I can't do this work. It's too hard for me." Immediately give him or her another assignment, one he or she can handle. We recall one boy (of supposedly normal intelligence) who had not learned by the seventh grade to write his name. It is sad, but he had been consistently promoted, probably because he never presented a discipline problem. A wise language arts teacher gave him the assignment to write one letter of his name at a time, and in that class he finally managed to master writing his name, but not much else.

Then there's the child who says to you, "I don't feel like it," when asked to do the assigned work. If he or she were to say it quietly it probably wouldn't be so bad, but he or she usually shouts it. Or a child says, "I ain't gonna." How do you handle this youngster? The best technique is to take the youngster aside and ask him or her in a quiet voice, "Why?" If he or she refuses to answer, press it. "Can't you handle the work?" you ask. "Is it too difficult?" (If the answer is yes, alter the assignment.) If it is no, pursue the matter further. "Are you bored with it? Is it too easy?" While this is doubtful, if the answer is in the affirmative, again, change the assignment. Still negative? Then inquire, "What seems to be the problem? Can you tell me?" If the youngster doesn't reply, then say, "Are you feeling well?" or "Is everything all right at home?"

If after these inquiries the answers indicate no reasons for the child's refusal, say "I would be pleased if you would start to work. Shall I give you a different assignment, or will you try this one?" It has been our experience, and that of many teachers, that in 90 percent of the cases, the youngster will cooperate. If he or she does not, then say, "I hope you will feel better soon, and I think working will help you." It is a rare boy or girl who doesn't respond to sincere caring.

The key, however, is communication between you and your young-sters—learning from them wherein the problems lie. A patient approach, a friendly smile, and an understanding heart can do wonders.

A good example of this is the following, which happened to one of us. One day, during my first year of teaching in the intermediate school, I noticed a boy sound asleep at the back of the room. I walked over, intending to blast him. I vividly recall thinking, "Who does he think he is, sleeping in my class?" But something, and I shall never know exactly what it was, stilled my tongue.

Instead, I quietly woke the child up and told him to see me at the end of the class. The subsequent discussion brought forth the information that the boy had been out of his home all night. He lived with his mother in a one-room apartment, and she sent him into the streets whenever she wanted him out of the apartment. He had wandered around for hours the night before. On this particular day, the child just couldn't keep his eyes open. How could he possibly be blamed?

## CONCLUSION

Teaching is too often perceived to be a one-way street. Teachers must, of course, convey knowledge, but they must be willing to learn as well. They must peer into the children's lives and problems, for the knowledge they gain will make their work more effective.

Most teachers come from "normal" homes. (We've put this in quota-tion marks because the concept of the normal American home having a father, a mother, and two children is rapidly changing.) Most teachers have had sympathetic parents, and they surely have had college educations. They've had the advantages of attending the theater, of going to museums and concerts, and of intellectual stimulation. Rarely have they endured the physical, intellectual, or spiritual poverty that so many of their pupils experience on a daily basis.

The unsympathetic attitude of an arrogant teacher stands between him or her and the education of an unfortunate child. It was Rabindranath Tagore, the Indian poet and freedom fighter, who said, "The great walks with the small. The middling stands aloof."

Your compassion and your understanding are vital to your success as a teacher. Yet you must be firm. You must be the figure of authority and yet not be reluctant to show your affection for the youngsters, for this in turn will awaken their love and respect for you. It is this love and respect that fosters the wholesome discipline for which every teacher strives.

Firmness and lovingness may seem to contradict each other, but in actuality they do not. Many successful teachers have shown this to be true. We recall one teacher, Mrs. Mae Peck, who was called "Eagle Eyes" by the youngsters because she seemed to have eyes in the back of her head. She was very firm but also very loving. Yet her students felt unbounded love and respect for her. Many times she was considered to be the best teacher in the school because while she required her students to work very, very hard, she combined this firmness with great affection.

# 2

# IDENTIFYING THE PROBLEMS UNDERLYING DISRUPTIVE BEHAVIOR

The child who wants the limelight all the time might be one of ten in the family and often be told, "You keep quiet" or "Shut your mouth." The hostile youngster who fights at the drop of a hat or a word may well have had lessons of brutality right in his or her own home from a drunken father or mother, or a sadistic brother or sister. Often "uncles" are abusive, as are the boyfriends of single mothers. Youngsters may be unpleasant because they are hungry, actually physically hungry. The variety of problems that can involve children is, unfortunately, unending and seems to be increasing with each passing year. These problems may be physical or mental, social or economic, or any combination of these.

The purpose of this chapter is to acquaint you with a sampling of the myriad problems facing some of your youngsters in their daily lives. We believe it is of prime importance that you become aware of these problems. They may affect the behavior of the girls and boys in your classroom, causing them to be disruptive or disinterested, diffident or discouraged.

We want to educate you to try to see with understanding eyes the boy or girl who is disruptive. As a physician must first find the cause of a malady before he or she can treat it, the teacher must seek to find the cause of the child's inability to adjust to the school situation before he or she can work toward helping to solve the problem.

We do not mean to mislead you. Many times you cannot do so, but you *can* show understanding, sympathy, love, and affection for the troubled youngster. As a result, his or her behavior will often improve. Have you ever spoken gently to a child who is very upset? You can almost feel the anger drain out of him or her, and gradually, if you are successful, a smile may even appear—almost as if by magic. It is as the Bible tells us: "A soft answer turneth away wrath."

In discussing the various problems that all too often beset our children, we shall for the sake of clarity divide the problems into various categories. You must keep in mind, however, the fact that the categories almost always overlap. In subsequent chapters we will discuss specific ways in which you can work with your troubled, disruptive youngsters.

## GENERAL TYPES OF PROBLEMS _____

### Physical Problems

One of the most common problems is poor vision. Can the boy or girl who is being disruptive see? A youngster who cannot see clearly may not be able to read. A case in point: A little girl was asked to read the first line on the Snellen chart (the eye-testing chart most frequently used). When asked what she saw, she replied, "I know there is a chart on the wall. I can see it, but not the letters."

Another child with very poor vision developed into a severe discipline problem as a result of her frustration. She couldn't keep track of her eyeglasses, without which she was practically blind. She would become angry and aggressive, and engage in constant fighting. Her teacher contacted her parent and obtained an additional pair of glasses, keeping them for when the child needed them. Her behavior improved immediately. Such solutions to problems are rare, but not as rare as one might think.

Does the child have a hearing problem? Often when children are unable to hear, they become disinterested in their work. They "turn off" completely, and easily become disruptive.

Does the child have a heart abnormality? Some youngsters with this type of problem become extremely fearful. However, at other times they ignore their condition. We were told of an incident involving two boys playing "Open Chest," a game in which one calls out these words, and the other has to cover his chest immediately—or he receives a punch. In this case, the boy who was the recipient of the punch was known to have had heart surgery. Fortunately, he managed to divert the blow sufficiently so that no harm was done. However, the teacher who witnessed the incident almost fainted. It happened so quickly she did not have time to separate the boys.

There is a very sad case on record of an adult who spanked a child. While the punishment was being administered, the child died. The adult did not know the child had a severe cardiac condition. *Of course no reader of this book would ever beat a child.* However, the very real danger inherent in striking a child even once must never be overlooked. The old fashioned "boxing the ears" often resulted in deafness. There are many ways to reach and teach a disruptive child. Corporal punishment must never, ever, be used. Under any circumstance it does more harm than good.

A youngster may have an epileptic or other type of seizure. Should you encounter this situation, immediately send one of the other children in the class for the school nurse, doctor, principal or even a neighboring teacher. You may have to take the initiative in calling for an ambulance. Epilepsy is not uncommon today among young children and may well be more prevalent in the future because it is common among "crack babies," many of whom are now of school age.

Diabetic seizures, viral attacks, and other illnesses are also sometimes encountered by the classroom teacher. By perusing the health records of every child in your class, you should be forewarned of these possibilities. Knowing of a child's problems, you are prepared to handle any emergency resulting from the child's condition as well as being able to empathize with the youngster, helping him or her to avoid becoming frustrated by the condition.

We knew one boy, a fighter and a bully of sorts, who had an artificial leg. It was obvious that by indulging in outbursts of hostility he was compensating psychologically. By showing him that we understood his problems, by discussing his behavioral problems, and by talking about his future aspirations with him we found he could be reached, and we were able to really communicate with him. We asked him to do a number of physical tasks, tasks that we were sure he could handle. This gave him feelings of adequacy. It worked wonders for his behavior and his feeling about himself! You would agree if you could have seen the look of gratification on his face while he was complying with our requests. How often emotions that are destructive can be channeled into acceptable behavior!

## Mental Problems

The statistics are—sadly—almost incredible: One out of every ten persons in the United States is, has been, or will be in need of attention for a mental disorder. The most severe discipline problems that arise in the classroom are usually caused by mental illness.

Often teachers will note, "So-and-so behaves as if he is mentally ill." Often they do not realize they have hit on the truth. One manifestation of mental illness is bizarre behavior, which may be self-destructive in nature. We've seen children walk on hot radiators, for example. Repeated bizarre actions on the part of such a child make it imperative that the teacher seek the advice of a trained person, usually the school psychologist, as soon as possible. Hallucinations are another manifestation of mental illness. Usually the youngster does not reveal them voluntarily, but sometimes when the teacher has won the child's confidence, he or she is more likely to speak of them, and then it is possible to obtain help.

Many mentally ill children are more difficult to help. At the age of fifteen, one handsome young man constantly drew pictures of guns, knives, and daggers whenever he doodled. His books, notebooks, and desk were always filled with these sketches. He was even consciously aware of his desire to kill: his ambition was to become a "mercenary," a soldier who fought for the nation offering to pay the most for his services. In school, he was, for the most part, withdrawn, and it was obvious to every teacher who can into contact with him that psychiatric care was very much needed. This care was instituted; however, how much it could have helped him can only be speculated on, because he met a violent death at the age of eighteen in an automobile accident.

These are examples of the mental problems that might plague some of the youngsters you teach. They live with these problems twenty-four hours a day, including, of course, the five or six hours they spend in school. They cannot possibly banish the problems from their minds as they enter the classroom. Much of the misbehavior we may see results from the troubled state of mind of such girls and boys. Yet most of the time the teacher is unaware of the turmoils with which the child is living. Such youngsters may try to work at the tasks assigned, but their thoughts are often focused on problems or events that have occurred in completely different times and places.

## Psychological Problems

Psychological problems can sometimes be incredibly severe and dismaying to a child. We learned of one mother who sometimes forced her child, Bernadette, to sit in an ice-cold tub of water for fifteen minutes. This was a disciplinary measure the mother took because the little girl often "lied." This mother also hung on the wall of her living room, for everyone to peruse, a booklet she called "Bernadette's Lies." The "lies" consisted of harmless fabrications that this imaginative child created to enable her to endure the cruelties perpetrated on her by her sadistic mother.

In later years it became quite evident that Bernadette had a talent for writing, but she forever procrastinated in settling down to do serious writing, although she was anything but lazy. Is it far-fetched to suppose that the cruelties inflicted on her in her early childhood had left profound psychological scars that prevented the young woman from developing her literary talent? One is reminded of Macbeth when he said challengingly to the doctor, "Canst thou pluck from the memory a rooted sorrow?"

We have no way of knowing which of our girls and boys are living in homes or attending schools where they are being damaged psychologically. If a teacher or a parent emphasizes a child's weakness or holds the child up to ridicule or censure, that youngster is not merely hurt at the time, but the psychological harm done might well be permanent. If the adult is a teacher, there is every chance the child will develop a hatred for teachers, for school, and for learning. Wouldn't the youngster in this situation be justified in considering becoming a school dropout? Who, then, would be responsible?

Another case comes to mind. Denise was the daughter of a commercially successful model who thought herself an authority on beauty. Denise did not look like her mother, and once heard her mother describe her as homely. Unfortunately, the youngster believed her mother. For a long time she actually avoided mirrors, and when all of her friends began using makeup, Denise shunned it. Her hair was a mess and her clothes showed a lack of caring. Her mother became more and more annoyed with her.

One day in an art class in school, a sculptor was invited to demonstrate to the class how he worked. He selected Denise as his model. After class she asked him why he had chosen her. "Your face is beautiful, my dear," he told her. "You have classic features, and your eyes are particularly lovely."

Denise was a different person after that day. The sculptor had changed her life. Is this not a profound example of how seriously damaging even a casual remark can be, for the remark Denise's mother had made was just that. And here too is an example of how a school situation can be tremendously beneficial to a youngster.

## Problems Caused by the "Generation Gap"

Centuries ago William Shakespeare wrote of the generation gap and the problems it causes that lead to tragedy. Neither Romeo's nor Juliet's parents had ever won their children's confidence. If they had, the saddest of all catastrophes—the death of a beloved child—might have been avoided. In the classroom you, the teacher, take the place of the parent.

If you can befriend your youngsters, make them feel that you are really their friend, they can appeal to you for advice and counsel. If not, they may well turn to others whose influence might damage their lives and turn them into unending nightmares. Let your girls and boys feel that you, their teacher, will never violate their trust and confidence. It is impossible to overemphasize the dangers that can beset your youngsters, if, for example, they become the victims of dope peddlers.

One outstanding woman, Gladys Campanella Johnson, who taught in Intermediate School 27, Staten Island provides a perfect example of a teacher who had her youngsters' love and respect. Scores of youngsters called her "Mom," and when she was asked about a particular child, usually a disruptive one, she would ask to talk to him or her. Then she would add, "We're very close," and they were. She was "close" to hundreds of youngsters.

Incidentally, she took her mother role very seriously. One day a girl asked me, "Where's Mrs. Johnson? I have to see her."

I replied, "I don't know. Can I help you?"

The child said no and kept repeating that she needed to see Mrs. Johnson.

I became curious and asked her several times why this was so necessary. At long last, she said quietly, "I want to show her these shoes." She looked at me and said even more quietly, "She gave me the money for them."

This is not unusual, for there are many teachers who will help youngsters when the need is one such as this.

## Gaining Their Trust

How can your youngsters be made to feel that you are their friend and that you will never violate their confidence and trust?

• First, by your manner toward them. It should be warm and friendly but not that of a peer. Remember, you are the adult in this situation—but a friend nevertheless.

• Second, by letting them know that whatever misdemeanor they may be guilty of, you do not sit in judgment of them. Although they may be punished for infractions of the rules, make them aware that you do not bear grudges. We heard one excellent teacher, in speaking of a disruptive child, say, "I don't want him to think that I am angry at him forever."

• Third, by peering into the children's lives and becoming familiar with their problems and difficulties. This action may change your entire view of the situation. During a conversation in the teacher lunchroom, one teacher told of the time she wanted to pretend (note: *pretend*) to give a child a spanking. She put the little boy across her knee, and when she did so she saw the threadbare clothing in which the child was dressed. It was January. She said she decided against even pretending to spank the boy and then went out and bought him a warm pair of corduroy pants.

You can bridge the generation gap by listening with respect to what the children tell you. In this way you can learn of their set of values, which often differ from yours. One area in which there are usually vast differences is in music. People tend to like the music that was popular when they were young, and this surely applies to teachers. It's hard to believe, but few young people today are fans of the Beatles, even though many teachers are. The same is true of television programs and of films.

Open honest discussion of such differences of values will enrich both your youngsters and you, and bring you closer together.

## Home-Oriented Problems

We have referred in our other writings to school as the "great leveler." Looking at a group of children, it is virtually impossible to imagine the problems confronting some of them. Yet, invariably, there are a great many, for the difficulties besetting a family affect each member.

We know of one fourth-grade boy who refused to leave the school building day after day. The custodian informed his teacher that the boy was always there until closing time at six o'clock, Monday through Friday. The teacher discussed this with the child. He was reluctant to tell her the reason, but finally the truth emerged.

The child admitted that his parents fought bitterly. He could avoid some of the battle scenes by remaining in the school building because his father worked nights and left home at five in the afternoon. The teacher of course understood and arranged with the custodian for the youngster to do some small tasks and thereby be permitted to remain in the building.

Parents may fight with their children or with one another. They may drink and become abusive. Older siblings might be bullies. (One older boy, by his own admission, threw knives at his younger brother—"Whenever I wanted to show him who was boss," he reported.) Families may be broken up, or fathers desert them; financial problems may cause untold difficulties. You can, we are sure, add to this list, ad infinitum. But the point we must make is that you consider the children in your class carefully. If a child is acting up, try to find out what is troubling him or her. Speak with that child privately, making sure you show him or her that you are trying to find out what the problem is.

Youngsters may be able to confide in you, but if they are unable to do so, don't feel hurt. Young people, particularly boys, are often unable to express themselves, or they may be ashamed to. We have found, frequently, that if a child misbehaves, especially if this is not his or her usual behavior pattern, there is something "bugging" him or her. Unfortunately, we as teachers cannot always help solve the problems, but we can try, and we should!

## School-Oriented Problems

Some children suffer from problems that we, as teachers, inadvertently have caused.

How is a child to react if he or she is made to feel inadequate? Yet this does happen, although no teacher does this intentionally. If youngsters are repeatedly given assignments that they cannot do, they lose self-esteem and self-confidence. Since virtually every teacher was a good student while in school, this concept is one he or she has never, or rarely, experienced.

But think about a boy or girl who cannot write a paragraph well or who is unable to read at a sixth-grade level and is in the eighth grade. How can he or she possibly feel but inadequate? These youngsters do not have to be told they have low reading scores—they are well aware of it. Because they experience this feeling of inadequacy time and again, they think, "What's the difference? Why should I even try to do the work?" They then proceed to go in any direction they choose—by misbehaving, by becoming a truant, or by becoming apathetic and just biding time. Our task as teachers is to help these youngsters do the necessary work so that their feelings of inadequacy about themselves change.

If children enter a class in September and the teacher is unpleasant, they develop antisocial feelings by early in October. Up to that time they have given the teacher a chance, but after a few weeks have passed, they can surmise what the year will bring. Just unpleasantness is enough to turn the boys and girls off; some, invariably, will become behavior problems.

We sometimes give this situation the dignified title "personality clash," but frequently this is just a euphemism. One example of such a situation can be created by a teacher who refuses to discuss students' grades with them. Antipathy is immediately developed and with it un-happy youngsters and possible problems. It is our belief that youngsters are entitled to question their marks; indeed, their interest is commendable. And why should a teacher reject this opportunity to communicate? The request is not out of line—the teacher's handling of it is.

## PREVENTING CHILDREN WITH PROBLEMS FROM MAKING PROBLEM CLASSES

### Start Work Immediately

Many classroom problems can be prevented by having the youngsters start work as soon as they enter the classroom. How many teachers will say, "I'm waiting for you to quiet down." This usually doesn't work. But having a written assignment on the board and establishing the rule that the assign-ment has to be done as soon as the boys and girls enter the room can make a big difference.

Such an assignment must be written. Telling youngsters to study usually doesn't quiet them down. But a multiple-choice series of the kind in Figure 3 is valuable because it enables the class to review material while getting them started. Have the children write the question as well as the answer.

## Figure 3

1. When you have a group of words that give you a complete thought you have _____.

   (a sentence, a question, a phrase, a preposition)

2. A sentence that asks you something is called _____.

   (a statement, a question, an exclamatory sentence)

3. A sentence that expresses a command is called _____.

   (a statement, an imperative sentence, a question)

4. A sentence that expresses strong feelings is called a _____.

   (a statement, an exclamatory sentence, an imperative sentence)

5. We put a period at the end of _____.

   (an exclamatory sentence, a sentence, a question)

6. A word that is the name of a person, place, or thing is called _____.

   (a verb, a noun, a pronoun, an adjective)

7. A word that takes the place of a noun is called _____.

   (an adverb, an adjective, a noun, a pronoun)

8. A word that describes a noun or pronoun is called _____.

   (an adjective, an adverb, a verb, a pronoun)

9. A word that shows action is called _____.

   (an adverb, a verb, an adjective, a noun)

10. A word that describes a verb is called _____.

    (an adjective, a noun, a pronoun, an adverb)

---

While the youngsters are doing this work, you have the opportunity to do yours. When they have completed the work, it should be discussed. Next, each child should be called upon to give an example of every item. If any area needs reteaching, you will know from this exercise which it is, and it should be taught again and again until every child masters it.

What can be accomplished by exercises such as this?

- The class is quieted down and set to work quickly, so that no time is wasted.

- Having each youngster contribute makes each one feel adequate.

- This exercise serves as a diagnostic tool, showing which work needs reteaching.

Encourage each child to strive to get 100 percent by recording the results and using them as part of his or her grade, but only if he or she has gotten that 100 percent.

If you see that some children need additional help, you can give it to them, since you have learned in which areas they are weak.

## Take the Positive Approach

Another way to preclude problems is by avoiding derogatory remarks that will antagonize the youngsters. For example, it is effective if you say to a youngster, "Jim, you could contribute a lot to our work if you put your mind to what we are doing." This is surely preferable to saying, "Jim, it's about time you got started working. You've really done nothing all year long." The disruptive or noncooperative youngster is often seeking attention, and if we can awaken some interest in him or her, we may be able to help him or her get started.

Does praise work? We believe it does, and that it pays big dividends. One excellent teacher of language arts in the intermediate school was Mrs. Edith Horowitz. She made the students she taught feel good about themselves. She constantly used the word *superb*, even with classes that other teachers felt were difficult.

For example, if all a youngster could do was write short sentences but they were correct, he or she was told his or her work was "superb," and then encouraged to try to expand his or her range. Her classes adored her, and even the most disruptive boy or girl rarely behaved badly in her class. (She was also one of the best-prepared teachers, from the very beginning of each class period until the end. She had the youngsters working from the minute they entered her classroom until the final bell.)

## Awaken Social Consciousness

It is our feeling that as educators we must do all we can to awaken a social consciousness and positive feelings for their fellow human beings in the mind of each of our youngsters. We can do this effectively by living it—by being actively interested in every youngster and attempting to give him or her the help he or she needs.

Another facet of this type of education might be through the printed word. This includes reading selections that promote social awareness. It might include having posters in your room that carry the same message. For example, the "Golden Rule," "Do unto others as you would have others do unto you," is extremely appropriate. So are the following words:

Hostility breeds hostility; respect commands respect; love awakens love.

Or perhaps you might like your class to see these words in front of them:

Politeness is to do and say
The kindest thing in the kindest way.

In keeping with this you may choose to quote from the newspaper column written by Miss Manners.

These suggestions may seem old-fashioned, but if we do not try to teach such values, we miss an excellent opportunity. Our young people are surely not going to learn them while watching television or playing video games.

We should also consider the fact that we are living in a time when violence seems to pervade popular culture. and when our girls and boys are virtually surrounded by it. If we can show them another side, a side in which people are concerned for one another, we are doing work of tremendous importance. Sadly, this "other side" is not promoted in the homes of many of our youngsters, and this type of education is very badly needed. President George Bush spoke about a "kinder, gentler nation," but the entertainment industry has not heard his message. As educators, shouldn't we?

As a nation we have lost sight of much of our history. By placing pictures of great men and women on the walls or bulletin boards of your classroom, you can call attention to them. For example, your children should become familiar with George Washington and his words in his Farewell Address: "I hold the maxim no less applicable to public than private affairs, that honesty is always the best policy."

And Abraham Lincoln and his famous words, "Four score and seven years ago our fathers brought forth on this continent a new nation, conceived in liberty, and dedicated to the proposition that all men are created equal."

And Eleanor Roosevelt, who was married to President Franklin Roosevelt. She later served with the United Nations for many years, some of them as chairman of the Human Rights Commission. She helped write the Universal Declaration of Human Rights. "It is better to light one candle than to curse the darkness," she said.

And Dr. Martin Luther King, Jr., and his statement, "I have a dream that one day this nation will rise up and live out the meaning of its creed: We hold these truths to be self-evident; that all men are created equal."

Of course, there are many more Americans whose memory should be kept alive, and by discussing them, their lives, and their contributions you can develop in your youngsters feelings of respect for their fellow human beings and for themselves.

After a class discussion of the sixteenth president, we once heard a young man say, in his own idiom, "Hey, that Lincoln was a poor dude, and he made it to be president." It seemed to be a revelation to him, and he was a disruptive child. Did it change his behavior? Perhaps a bit, but it gave him an awareness he had not had before, and it might possibly have changed his life.

## EARLY IDENTIFICATION OF CHILDREN WITH SERIOUS PROBLEMS

From time to time, not too often we hope, you will have in your class youngsters with serious behavioral problems. (It has been forecast that, unfortunately,there will be many more problems in the future as the children of crack cocaine addicts reach school age.) You will, sad to say, have no difficulty identifying youngsters with serious problems. It's necessary that you keep anecdotal records of their behavior to refer them for special help. If they receive this help, the results can be excellent. It's your task, however, to document the behavior of such children and to call it to the attention of the guidance counselor, the assistant principal, or the principal.

Parents may be aware of the child's problems, but they often try to push them under the rug. They may have noted that Mary goes off and sits by herself all the time but thought nothing of it. Many times teachers will ignore this, and yet the child should be referred for help.

We are aware of one family that ignored the sadistic tendencies of their son as he perpetrated cruelties on animals, such as electrocuting them. The boy was six years old at the time, and his parents were sure he would outgrow this behavior pattern. He did not. In kindergarten he removed tacks from bulletin board displays without being observed and stuck them into other children. The matter reached a head when he seriously hurt another child, and it was only then that the family was receptive to the recommendation that psychiatric help be obtained for him. It was, and it helped change the child's behavior.

Any unusual behavior is worth noting and recording. So is aggression and hostility. Be aware, too, of the isolate, the child who removes him- or herself from the group. Another indication worth watching is the young child who clings to you. Of course, actions that are seriously disruptive must be noted if you are able to get help for the youngster and for yourself. In short, we suggest you keep a card file of youngsters who may become, if they are not already, serious behavior problems. If the problem does not improve, consult the parents or the person with whom the child lives. Often this is a grandmother or other relative. Also alert the guidance staff so that when you make a detailed referral, they will already be alerted to the problem with a particular child.

## Keep Anecdotal Records

Many teachers neglect the task of keeping anecdotal records of disruptive youngsters, yet this is extremely important. If you feel a child's behavior is antisocial, it is well worth your time to note it. In this way you can show the parent, the guidance person, the administrator, and perhaps the youngster him- or herself what the problems are.

On one occasion an anecdotal record disclosed a youngster who got into very serious fights on Mondays. She was slightly disruptive the rest of the week, but on Mondays she was extremely agitated. When this was discussed with the girl and her grandmother, it was discovered that the child's mother visited them every Sunday. Because the girl was so angry at her mother for leaving her with her grandmother, she reacted violently on Mondays.

Another child made a huge scene whenever he was asked where his homework was. An anecdotal record revealed this situation seemed to happen over and over again. The parent was called in, and in the presence of the child the situation was discussed. Finally the boy admitted he was very lonely when he went home and said he could not concentrate. His teacher arranged for him to do his work with another youngster, and the problem was solved. (Not all problems are solved quite as easily, but some are, and it's always worth a try.)

In keeping anecdotal records, the form in Figure 4 is simple but is usually accepted by the principals and guidance personnel. It consists of the date, the child's name, the incident (stated briefly), the action taken by the teacher, and his or her signature.

## Figure 4

| 5/12 | James Jones | James tore a bulletin board display off the wall and refused to replace it. We discussed his action, after which he did replace it, but with rancor. |

Signed _____

If you speak with a parent, that should certainly be noted, with a fuller description of the conversation.

It is definitely worth your taking the time to write simple statements such as this one of each incident in which a child is involved. Your records will be very valuable if this disruptive youngster shows he or she needs assistance from the guidance staff. You will note that the action depicted in Figure 4 is not a capital offense. However, it is actions such as this one that should be recorded to help build an understanding of the situation by persons not directly involved.

When there are several notations of this type, they should again be discussed with the child privately so that he or she is made aware of his or her pattern of behavior. Often there are youngsters who at the beginning of the year have frequent notations but who as the year goes on have fewer and fewer.

## CONCLUSION

We have indicated some of the problems that may confront the youngsters you teach and that may cause them to become disorderly or downright menacing. The root of much classroom disruption often lies in the home situation of the disruptive child, or he or she may be difficult to teach because of a physical or mental problem. Youngsters' lack of cooperation may stem from something that happened to them in school years before or from an uncomfortable situation they are now in. Children may be plagued by deep psychological troubles or difficulties caused by society.

When you have youngsters who are misbehaving, try to determine the causes of their behavior. Try to understand their troubles and to empathize with them. A child who has temper tantrums has them because he or she has so much inner rage he or she cannot cope with it, and it spills out.

Yet an understanding teacher can help that child handle those feelings and can reassure him or her so that the child learns to cope with his or her emotions. Children are rarely mean. They do things for reasons of their own. It helps us as teachers if we can become aware of these reasons. Whenever there is a problem we can help solve, without exception we should try to do so.

But even in situations where there is little we can do, we can prevent the child from "taking it out on the people in school." We can listen sympathetically, accept the child, and show him or her love and affection. Easier said than done, you may think, but still necessary, and still extremely gratifying. In dealing with troubled children, we often take two steps forward and one step back. Sometimes it's two forward and three back. But eventually, except with the very ill, with the really sick youngsters, we do make progress. We can help troubled children be less troubled and less troublesome. With affection and empathy, we can be effective disciplinarians.

# 3

# BASIC METHODS FOR WORKING WITH YOUNGSTERS WITH PROBLEMS

In this chapter we are going to outline some methods for working with troubled youngsters. In the years we have spent working with young people we have found these methods to be most effective. There are some children with whom there is virtually no technique that will work, for these children are seriously ill and cannot function in a classroom situation. Fortunately, however, these youngsters are relatively few in number so are not too frequently encountered. The vast majority of youngsters you will have as students will not fall into this category.

This is surely not to say that all of your girls and boys will be easy to work with, but they will be "reachable," and if you have a number of methods at your disposal you will be able to teach them. These techniques are not tricks or gimmicks but procedures based on sound psychological principles. Many are obvious, yet we know from experience that they are not utilized by some teachers.

But following a method is not enough. You must be a humanitarian, interested in your fellow human beings on a philosophical basis and interested in their offspring on a practical and affectionate basis. If you hate children, as the late comedian W.C. Fields used to profess, you really should not be a teacher; and if you are indifferent to them, you do not belong in teaching. Ours is a profession that must be based on affection, for without it our efforts become unproductive.

In dealing with a troubled child, one who annoys or harasses you or others, one who is hostile and aggressive, one who takes up an inordinate amount of your time and attention, we ask you to try to understand that

38

youngster, to feel affection for him or her, and to try the methods we shall outline here.

## DEVELOP RAPPORT

When we speak of rapport, we are referring to a close, sympathetic relationship, and it is just such a relationship that a teacher should seek to develop with each of his or her students. This is possible if one teaches thirty or even thirty-five youngsters but difficult when, in the upper grades, one has a hundred or more girls and boys in his or her classes. However, most of the time there are troubled (and troublesome) youngsters in every class, and establishing rapport with them is one of the most important methods for helping them improve and achieve self-control.

How can you develop this rapport, this closeness? We suggest you arrange to sit down and talk to, and, more important, listen to, this youngster. Not while the rest of the class is working, but at a time when they are not around. Perhaps you can speak to the youngster privately during his or her lunch hour or after school, or you might meet with such a child during your unassigned period.

"What?" you are asking. "I'm supposed to spend my free time talking to *that* child?" Yes, that is exactly what we are saying—for this is absolutely the most effective method for reaching troubled children. They are aware of the fact that you are giving of your own time to speak with them. (Don't arrange this immediately after a child has misbehaved though, because he or she will think his or her bad behavior is being rewarded. Instead, make time for this talk between incidents.)

When you have set up the situation, you can open the interview by saying quietly, "We seem to be having our ups and downs, don't we? Why is it we can't get along? What can we do to improve things?" Some children will open up and talk to you immediately, but others won't. But keep trying. Give the youngster time to think and to answer your questions.

"Is there something troubling you?" you ask. Again, maybe the boy or girl will answer you, but possibly he or she will not. You would continue, saying, "I can't understand it. I like you. Don't you like me?" You can imagine how effective this can be, because the chances are great that this type of youngster has never heard a remark of this sort from a teacher.

Then continue, "We're both here to work. You are here to work, aren't you?" (What is a child going to say to you, "No, I'm not"?) Add, "Why do you spend our valuable time, yours and mine, disrupting our class? I guess you don't realize what you're doing."

Always give the child an out, a way to gracefully back away from the situation. Show him you aren't angry but perplexed. "You're an intelligent person," you say to the child. "Is there something you're having trouble learning?" If the answer is in the affirmative, either help the child yourself or arrange for the necessary assistance.

Your next question would be, "Is there something bothering you, here in school? Another boy or girl, perhaps?" If, again, the child doesn't respond, ask, "Is there something wrong at home?" Should the youngster tell you there is, suggest that the guidance department could be asked to help, but only if the boy or girl gives you permission.

By asking your questions casually, by showing troublesome children that you really want to help them, you can very often win over even the most hostile youngsters. We have seen many youngsters react favorably to this type of treatment. They don't become angelic overnight, but their attitudes do change. It is human nature to be favorably disposed to someone who professes to care for you and behaves as if he or she does. Before the interview is over, it is crucial that you get the youngster to promise he or she will try to cooperate.

Does this mean you will then permit this boy or girl to "get away with murder" in your classroom? Certainly not. But when this youngster misbehaves, you can call him or her up to your desk and whisper, "Are you letting me down?" This is often enough to get the youngster to stop what he or she was doing, and frequently the child will apologize. You will, we hope, be able to say without rancor, "Please try again, but this time try harder to cooperate."

For some teachers affectionate names are a secret weapon. One of the incidents that stands out in my memory is of a young boy, seriously disturbed, who had with a knife menaced another student. The knife wielder was sent to my office, for, as assistant principal, I dealt with those youngsters whose offenses were serious, and this one was extremely so.

The youngster was so agitated he could not sit down. He paced around the room. "Hank, please sit down," I said to him. No response. "Hank, come on, just sit down so we can talk." He kept pacing, and I could see the anger in his face. I continued trying to get him to settle down a bit. "Hank, all you have to do right now is sit down," I repeated again and again, but the pacing increased.

Suddenly I said to him, and I could never tell what made me say it, "Hey, Pussycat, will you sit down!" Hank looked at me, smiled, and repeated, incredulously, "Pussycat?" That did it. He sat down, and very shortly thereafter this knife-wielding boy began to sob. Hank was a very troubled and troublesome boy. He was referred for, and received, psychological help. When the psychiatrist who was treating Hank decided it was safe for Hank to return to school, he did so, but it was decided that another environment would be better so he was sent to another school.

If you can say "son" or "dear" affectionately to a child and mean it, you have it in your power to reach many girls and boys—even those with severe problems. If it sounds artificial, don't do it. If you are very young and there is not much difference in age between you and your students, don't do it. If you are a male, be extra cautious, for adolescent girls can have fertile imaginations. But in many situations, where it feels right, this type of endearment can break down boundaries and make children reachable.

Now let us consider rapport between children. To develop this type of rapport in your classroom, set up situations in which the youngsters work together. Before you do this, arrange the groups so that there will be no personality clashes. If you know that Denise doesn't get along with Marie, don't put them in the same group. However, don't put best friends together, either. Rather, try to determine which youngsters might become friendly but haven't already done so.

Have boys and girls work together. This will help them learn how to behave with members of the opposite sex in a comfortable setting. While they may be embarrassed at the beginning, this will disappear shortly.

Trips away from the school building can be useful in developing rapport, but here too structure is important. You can divide the class into groups of six youngsters whom you instruct to stay together. There is a fringe benefit to this: Each group should elect a person to report to you. In that way you don't have to count heads constantly but just ask the five or six group leaders.

## SHOW THE CHILDREN LOVE AND AFFECTION _____

"The origin and commencement of the malady is neglected love!" So said Shakespeare's character Polonius in speaking of Hamlet's illness. How many of our disruptive children suffer from neglected love? How many of them see lessons of cruelty and injustice perpetrated at home? How many of them suffer blows and harsh words that damage their character and personality? If these children come to a classroom where the teacher is kind, gentle, and understanding, this is the antidote he or she can give them; this is the lesson he or she can teach them that will in some small way counteract the lessons in sadism they might be learning or have learned elsewhere.

Psychologists have shown that love given children can bolster them and make them sturdy throughout their lives. Ideally it should come from the parents, but here we are acting as parental substitutes, and any love is better than none.

Again we quote from the work of the Bard of Avon, "Love is an ever fixed star, that looks on tempests and is never shaken." You, as a teacher of today, probably must endure some tempests. However, the love you feel and give to your children will help them, and it will also help you remain unshaken. Kind words, smiles, a gentle voice, your sympathetic reaction when a child is in distress, lavish praise when he or she is endeavoring to do his or her work well, and a thousand other little gestures can make all the difference in the world.

One very successful and happy teacher, on the first day of school, asked each child to bring in a photograph of himself or herself. When a child was unable to do this, she brought in a camera and took the photos herself. They were then mounted on a large chart, with room for every girl or boy to sign his or her name below the photo. This chart had a place of honor on the bulletin board, and the youngsters enjoyed looking at it all year long.

A party now and then, for reasons such as birthdays, but also as rewards for excellent work or behavior; your ingenuity in converting a drill lesson into a delightful game; a walk in the park on a lovely day—all of these events will show your children that you care for them, and they will respond in kind.

(Birthday parties can be held once a month, to celebrate the birthdays of all of the youngsters falling within that month. When the birthdays are in July or August, you can use "half birthdays and thereby celebrate in January and February.)

Make no mistake. Children are aware of things many adults never think of. A second grader, for example, told her mother one day, "Our teacher really likes us." When her mother asked, "How do you know that she does?" the little girl answered, with great certainty, "She always wears red dresses to cheer us up!" Think about that. It isn't so far-fetched, after all. In the era when men wore ties, the youngsters would frequently comment on them to other teachers.

## TREAT EACH CHILD FAIRLY AND EQUALLY _____

Young teachers are sometimes confused that love and firmness are conflicting concepts. Nothing could be further from the truth. You must be firm, and as long as you are fair there will be no problem. You must be strong and adhere to your position! *If you say you are going to do something, you absolutely must do it.*

Children respect firm and fair treatment. They will not think you don't care for them. Outward signs of affection and warmth will not make you lax. If children can take advantage of you, there are often times when they will. But they will not like you for it—in fact, they will be more likely to resent you for being "too easy." (Honestly, this is true. We've seen the contempt some youngsters show for teachers who do not keep their classes in control.)

Make demands of your students. Demand good work, demand cooperative behavior and you will get them. Love and respect your kids and they will love and respect you. Show them affection and they will return that too.

We would be remiss if we said every teacher can easily show absolute fairness. Some children are so capable we get to depend on them. These are rarely the troubled children. The latter are usually undependable and rarely are asked to do any tasks, to be "monitors," yet this is what every child craves. Therefore, try not to show favoritism, and use the monitorial system we have outlined in Chapter One. Give every child tasks for which he or she is responsible. Then, when a child is disruptive, threaten him or her with removal of his or her assignment. Don't take it away too quickly—unless the crime is enough to warrant severe punishment, for it is a loss of status in the group as well as the deprivation of the actual job.

This is quite an assignment for you, the teacher, to create thirty or more meaningful jobs, but you can do it using the positions already suggested and your own ingenuity. *Try to give each child a number of tasks to do daily.* Even if you rack your brain to do this, you will find it worthwhile, for these same tasks can be done by youngsters in every class you teach in subsequent years. Make a child feel needed and he or she becomes far less of a problem. Many children have never had the "privilege" of being monitors, and the honor really influences their behavior. The work the children can accomplish is worthwhile as well.

For example, we have seen many classrooms that are messy. Two children passing around the wastebasket cures this and helps make them responsible at the same time. Or, your classroom can be made colorful and attractive by the work of bulletin board monitors. There is literally no end to the amount of work children will do if their energy is channeled.

But remember, every child should have something to do every single day. If you train the youngsters during the first month to do their jobs, your work is infinitely lessened, and you have this powerful tool for control. Incidentally, change jobs around once a month and have each child train the next child. This will heighten interest, provide opportunities for children to work together, and will thus be good training for their future lives. Class artists, class poets, class writers, and class mathematicians can assist you with the actual teaching if there are boys and girls in the class who are sufficiently proficient to do so.

By making each child a monitor, you give feelings of self-worth to every youngster. I recall sending one particularly disruptive boy on an errand. I had walked into a classroom and asked a teacher if I could select a child to send out of the room. She readily agreed, and I pointed to this boy because I knew him. He had often been referred to me for discipline, but here I had an opportunity to give him a chance. As he rose from his seat his almost automatic comment was, "Are you sure you mean me?" When I said yes, he squared his shoulders and came up to me—with very obvious pride. I can guarantee this was the first time he had ever been chosen to be a "monitor."

## UNDERSTAND CHILDREN: EXUBERANCE AND MISBEHAVIOR

At this point, let us discuss the rather uninhibited children who will sing or make noise, dance or "fool around" in the halls or when no work is going on in the classroom. For some teachers this is difficult to understand. Yet it may be nothing more complex than *joie de vivre*, which, thankfully, these children have. If they are singing or dancing at an inappropriate time, they should of course be stopped, but this activity should then be scheduled for a better time. Why not the last half hour on an occasional Friday afternoon?

Should you find your youngsters behaving in this fashion, think before you take them too seriously. And "play it cool." Are they hurting anyone? Or are they just using up some youthful energy? Are they hostile or happy? There is a world of difference. They do not set out to thwart you, the teacher. They are not necessarily aggressive.

The way to handle this is to find the proper time and place. Tell the girls and boys calmly and quietly, "We have work to do now, but we can sing and dance later." This will often get them to stop the unscheduled activities. But who would not rather be happy than sad, dancing rather than working? Speak to them in a whisper, gently and firmly, and, above all, without hostility. Don't erase the smiles from their faces. You might even ask if they would like to sing the song for the class. (Make sure the lyrics are suitable.) After that, a resumption of work is usually far easier and you, the teacher, have taken a giant step toward winning over the youngsters. This is not to be done on a daily basis, but neither does it have to be a once-in-a-blue-moon event. Most often, however, they prefer not to perform publicly, and you have made your point.

If you encounter youngsters singing, dancing, or fooling around in the halls, treat it in the same manner—lightly. Some see themselves as budding Michael Jacksons. Don't make a federal case of minor transgressions. (We are not even sure these are transgressions, unless a crowd gathers, and then there may be difficulty in dispersing it.)

Remember, boys and girls are young, healthy, and full of energy and life. They are not our adversaries. Why should we make ourselves theirs? "It's time to get to your room, now," you say with a smile. They will often smile back. If on the other hand you shout at them, they will frequently shout back, and everyone becomes upset. *Judge what a child is doing and react accordingly.*

A case in point: One winter day a serious, dedicated teacher, whom we'll call Mrs. X., came to the office of the assistant principal to complain. "I just can't handle the situation," she admitted, perspiring visibly. "I need help. Immediately." The assistant principal went with her to the "situation."

About a dozen youngsters were standing in the hall, talking. They had been dismissed from class and told to go home. They were not being disruptive, but they refused to leave the building, and Mrs. X. had gotten frantic. When asked why they wouldn't leave, they said they were waiting for their sisters and brothers—and the temperature outside was 14 degrees. Mrs. X. was so insistent on her "duty" as she saw it, that she had lost her feeling for the children. The assistant principal sent her for a cup of coffee. He remained with the children until they left voluntarily. There was no reason to send them out into the cold.

The next day Mrs. X. told the assistant principal, "You know, I can't understand what got into me. I don't know why I behaved the way I did. Those kids weren't doing anything to cause me to get panicky." She realized, herself, that she had reacted unthinkingly.

Today's children are far less repressed and more inclined to give vent to their exuberance than ever before. When it is out of place, it is our task to show them why. But we must talk to them with patience and *without hostility.* Let us not make mountains out of molehills. Determine the cause of the behavior, and if it is youthful happiness we're sure you would not want to extinguish it.

As teachers, we, above all, must think of the children as human beings, judging each situation as it arises. Children's actions should not be seen as threats to us. The youngsters are, or should be, our friends, our co-workers, and our partners in the process of education, and they should be treated as such. They can be a source of great joy—if we allow them to be. But if we do not understand their actions, if we take them personally, if we are threatened by their youthful exuberance, we lose the pleasure they can bring to us. How often do we react to such situations because we ourselves are upset, "uptight"? A bit of self-appraisal can really help us judge ourselves. We recommend it.

## BUILD A SUCCESS PATTERN WITH EVERY CHILD

A child who is succeeding in his or her work is rarely disruptive. Try to build a success pattern with each girl and boy in your class. We are sure these few suggestions will prove helpful in that regard. Of course you will vary them to suit the needs of your youngsters.

1. Have the youngsters draw or bring in pictures and charts to make the classroom enjoyable. Let it abound in colorful, attractive pictures and books (which should be changed from time to time). Have displays in all parts of the room. *Show the work of every child and be sure each child is represented.* Each child's talent should be recognized and given full expression. The perceptive teacher can discover talents that the children did not know they possessed. Literally cover the walls with the activities of your youngsters.

In one prominent place you might have a poetry corner. (Many girls and boys can write poems if encouraged to do so, and they enjoy working on them.) In another place have a small art gallery where the accomplishments of your children who can express themselves in pencil, crayon, paint, charcoal, or whatever medium they choose can be displayed. In still another area give places of honor to test papers that reflect high achievement.

Be sure that in one form or another the work of your troubled children is on display, for it is their work that is rarely in the limelight.

2. Be sure your lessons are of value to every child. This may mean you will have to individualize instruction some of the time, but it is vitally important that you do so, for very often a youngster will be disruptive because he or she cannot follow the lesson you are teaching.

3. Encourage your children to voice their opinions, for freedom of thought and expression is much to be desired. It goes without saying that cruel opinions should be labeled as such, but the opinion, not the child, should be adversely criticized.

4. You can foster friendships that may be of help to the troubled child. By seating the youngsters wisely—a disruptive child who is a slow learner with a bright child who is not—there is a strong possibility that the slow child will be helped.

Even if it were the bright child who was disruptive, the presence of a nondisruptive boy or girl with a disruptive one has proved to be a calming influence. By experimenting with this method you can determine its value in your class. You may decide, for example, that a frequent change of seats is worthwhile.

5. There are many ways to say the same thing, and you have probably already learned that derogatory remarks don't work. It is so much better to say to a youngster, "This work is all right, but I know you can do better work than this," than to say, "This work is poor. You aren't trying very hard, are you?" Encouragement gets good results, while discouragement can actually cause failure.

6. Encourage the youngsters to ask questions and also to tell you of anything they do of which they are proud. While the youngsters are working, walk around the classroom, glancing at every child's work and complimenting those deserving of compliments. One hopes that this will include the disruptive girl or boy.

7. Discuss the children's progress with them in such a way that they know when they are doing well and when they are not. No report card grade should come as a shock to a youngster.

After you give a test or a quiz and the results show either positive or negative change in the type of work that the child has been doing, talk about that change with him or her. If the work has improved, praise the child, or use the talk to discover where a learning problem exists. For example, has the child understood the concept of the complete sentence, or does he or she need more work on that topic?

8. Be extremely approachable to the children, their parents, and other members of their families. Often it may be an older sister or brother who shows an interest in the child's schoolwork.

As soon as a youngster proves to be disruptive, try to speak with the parent, grandparent, older sibling, or other person with whom the child lives. Try to determine wherein the problem lies and ask for suggestions for how to get the youngster to cooperate.

You will find that you will have to give more of your time, your attention, and your patience to the disruptive child if you are to change his or her behavior. This can be worthwhile, however, for if you succeed in stopping the disruption, teaching your class will be far more pleasant.

## HAVE ACTIVITIES FOR EVERYONE

Feelings of inadequacy can make children misbehave more quickly than anything else. If you put an assignment on the board and a child cannot do it, what is there for him or her to do? He or she may talk to a neighbor or find other things of interest. Such youngsters often become frustrated and resentful. If they feel the work is too difficult, they won't even try to do it. What can you do about this?

1. Plan work in advance for every child, particularly for your potentially disruptive youngster. The work must be geared to his or her level. If the class is reading, find material each child can master. For example, you may be teaching eighth grade, but there may be youngsters reading on the fourth- or fifth-grade levels. This situation should be taken into account in every subject area, not just reading.

There are times when everyone in the class may be given the same work, in which case individual planning is unnecessary. But at other times preparing work specifically for each youngster is essential.

2. Find ways in which each child can contribute to the class work. This is most important with the disruptive child, who needs to make this contribution.

3. Put the material you wish the youngsters to remember on the chalkboard and have them copy it in their notebooks. Do not expect them to take notes from what amounts to your lecturing. Most often the disruptive children are the ones who will retain the least from your spoken words. If you place the material to be copied on the board you accomplish several things:

- You emphasize the important points you are teaching.
- The youngsters have notes to study.
- They have a notebook to show to their parents.
- You have one of the bases on which to give grades.
- The boys and girls get practice in using writing implements, which are still important in this age of computers.

You do not have to write on the board yourself. If you have youngsters in the class whose handwriting is legible, give those children the monitorial jobs as class secretaries. They can use your notes to put the work on the board, or you can dictate to them. This job is usually one of the most sought after, but the ability to write clearly is a necessity.

## TRY TO DETERMINE THE CHILD'S BASIC PROBLEMS _____

When a child misbehaves, there is a reason for this behavior. If we are able to discover what is troubling him or her, we can be of far greater help than if we are unaware of the problems. We can also then help the other youngsters in the class, for the disruptive child takes time and attention away from them. What can be done to find out what problems are causing the child to be disruptive? Here are some steps to take:

1. When children misbehave, talk with them and give them time to answer you. They may not be able to tell you directly what is bothering them, but you may be able to discern where the difficulty lies, possibly by "reading between the lines."

Say to the child sincerely, "I don't mean to pry, but you seem to be having problems cooperating in class. Can you tell me what's bothering you?" (You will probably have to explain the meaning of the word *pry.*) Tell the youngster, "I hope you'll cooperate in the future. I need you to participate in our class, and I know you can do it." Continue in this vein. Ask a child what you can do to help him or her work along with the rest of the class.

You may decide to have this type of talk more than once or twice. Whether you do would depend on the seriousness of the youngster's disruptive actions.

2. If after such conversations there is no improvement, contact someone from the child's home. Here too the information may not come to you directly, but indirectly. Furthermore, you must not appear to be prying.

Whenever you have to deal with parents or family members, we suggest you always use the approach, "I know you want ———— to get the most out of his or her education. What can we do, working together, to help this child?" We have found this approach to be eminently successful, and we have dealt with hundreds of parents. Among them were some whose hostility was very evident at the beginning of our interview. It is rare to find a parent whose attitude will not change and who will not really seek to help the child in question when he or she sees that you mean what you are saying.

3. Review the disruptive child's records, all of them. This includes health, achievement, attendance, behavior, and any special services, such as guidance, that the child has received.

We discovered one severely troubled youngster who had been "seeing double" and getting headaches for years. "I didn't know you weren't supposed to see two things," she said. Glasses corrected the problem, and the child's behavior improved dramatically.

4. Speak to the child's previous teachers and to the assistant principal or principal. Find out if they were aware of problems. Has the youngster manifested this type of behavior in his or her earlier school years?

5. Consult with the guidance counselor, describing the child's behavior pattern. Working together, it is possible you can develop a method for getting this child to control him- or herself.

6. In extreme cases, you may wish to bring the disruptive youngster's behavior to the attention of the assistant principal or the principal. Either might be able to suggest approaches that you could use with this youngster. The principal may also wish to be made aware of such cases if the need for exclusion from school is a possibility.

7. You may wish to discuss the fact that a youngster should be given an intelligence test. At times there are youngsters who should be placed in special classes for retarded children but who have not been so identified.

When you have in your class a child who is inordinately slow and who does not seem to be capable of learning, it is worthwhile to request such testing.

8.  If you have social workers on the staff of your school, you may turn to them for help if the child has a family problem—or a financial one. If such services are not available, perhaps one of the school administrators can be of assistance.

## LISTEN CAREFULLY TO YOUR CHILDREN

Be aware of your youngsters' reactions to situations. For example, there was a look of sheer misery on a third grader's face right after the teacher had given out report cards. It puzzled the teacher, because the little girl's ratings were not poor but were merely passing grades. Touched by the look of desperation on the child's face, the teacher called her up to the desk.

"What's the matter, dear?" she asked. She had already established excellent rapport with the youngsters in her class.

The child burst into tears. The teacher spoke to the girl very quietly and affectionately. After a short time, the child repeated what her mother had said: "If you don't get high marks, don't come home." The child was terrified.

The teacher assumed the parent, whom she had met at Open School Week, did not mean what she had said, but the youngster had taken her words literally. The teacher telephoned the mother, and they had a lengthy discussion, after which she could assure the child that it was safe for her to go home. It is entirely possible that a tragedy had been averted because of the sensitivity of the teacher. She had won the confidence of her little pupil and, incidentally, of the child's mother. How often, though, are children's problems in one way or another created by adults? In this case it was a matter of a foolish remark that caused the little girl a great deal of distress.

## WORK ON SOLUTIONS TO PROBLEMS TOGETHER

If a disruptive child's problem is of such a nature that you can help him or her solve it, you are in a fortunate situation. For example, if misbehavior stems from learning difficulties, it is indeed possible for you to work with the youngster. Diagnostic testing is necessary to determine wherein the difficulties lie, and then special academic help is essential. This help can be provided by you, by family members, by tutors, or even by the child's classmates. If you find, as is often the case, that this child is poor in many areas, select one or two areas in which to concentrate your efforts. We would suggest reading and written English, because they are the most necessary for a person to function in our society. We would follow this with arithmetic help as well.

When a child does not get along with other children, do your best to physically separate the youngster from those with whom he or she gets into arguments. If Debbie and Michael fight, put them in opposite corners of the room, after discussing the situation with them and extracting their promise to stop fighting now that they are no longer neighbors.

You may try and get to the root of their disagreement, but often this is very time consuming. You will find that separating them will help the situation immediately.

When children are disruptive, it will help if you can find out what is bothering them. This, however, is easier said than done. Children have a hard time revealing their feelings. This is especially true of boys, for they are accustomed to bottling their feelings up. If you encounter a difficult situation that you cannot improve, it's wise to seek help outside your classroom.

## SEEK OTHER AID IF NECESSARY

There are many sources to which you can go for help with a disruptive child. It is important that you and the child view this in terms of what it is—seeking help—rather than as discipline. We have already outlined a number of sources of help—the child's parents, your supervisors, the guidance counselors, and social workers.

If the problem is a physical one, the school nurse and the school physician might be the personnel to call on. Use your own ingenuity in helping these youngsters. They are often grateful, for they are more used to punishment than to understanding, more familiar with vituperativeness than with compassion. Seek assistance for them, and you in turn will be helped, for quite often these youngsters will show improvement in the classroom.

## STIMULATE THE CHILDREN'S INTEREST

Your class has a number of disruptive children. What do you do? For one thing, your teaching techniques have to be particularly interesting if you are to hold their attention. These are the youngsters who will not listen to you just because you are the teacher. They will go their merry way—unless you are able to intrigue them—and make them sit up and take notice.

Here's just one idea you might like to try: You realize your youngsters need practice in arithmetic—but how many of them will work at it? If you convert the drilling into a game, they have another reaction entirely. Why not set up a "World Series" and keep the games running—while you get a great deal of work accomplished? Divide the class into teams, *each with its share of bright and slow children.* Have the youngsters wear caps, make banners, decorate the room, and keep score on the board. You will find you can reinforce learning in every arithmetic skill in this way. Such games are often the answer to involving every child in a lesson.

Trips are another method, which we've already mentioned, for holding the children's interest. "But," you are surely saying, "how can you take disruptive children on trips? They'll spoil it for all the others." This will depend on the youngsters. We have taken hundreds of children on trips, including many disruptive ones. We've had children with many problems on trips of all kinds and have never had a child do anything to spoil a trip.

We talk to the class beforehand, really convincing them that if they misbehave there will be no more trips for them, and we've found they cooperate beautifully. We know this from our personal experience and that of many other teachers as well.

The disruptive children want very much to be included. Tell them you are willing to give them a break but that they must not let you down. Give this message to each one, individually, and extract the promise that he or she will not cause any problems. If you feel apprehensive, keep the disruptive youngsters close to you and you'll find the situation will work out well.

Do all you can to find unusual approaches to use in your teaching. If you find your troubled children are disrupting the lesson, speak to them, explaining that you are trying to make their schoolwork interesting. Show them they are preventing you from doing this. "Do you want to do this experiment," you might ask them, "or would you rather not?"

It's easy to guess what their answer will be, for there is scarcely a person alive who is not intellectually stimulated when the word *experiment* is mentioned. Science is an area that can become highly motivational by virtue of the number of such experiments and also demonstrations that you can include in your curriculum.

## DISCOVER NEW INTERESTS

Jonathan was the class nuisance. He was a bright child but undisciplined. After his teacher spoke to the child's parents, she understood the origin of Jonathan's problems. No one had ever said *no* to him. What was she to do?

The solution to this problem came to her quite unexpectedly. She was introducing the concept of the electrical circuit to the class, and Jonathan lit up, figuratively. It was as if there were a new world for him. Seizing on this interest, the teacher asked the boy if he wanted to make a model of a house, showing the various circuits. Of course he did. She negotiated with him. If Jonathan learned to show self-control, he could make such a model, working on it during the last hour of class every day.

The youngster was thrilled. He suddenly seemed to become aware of how disruptive he had been and managed to work quietly for most of the day. Long before the project was completed, his teacher had several new ones planned. Jonathan made doorbells and electrical games, burglar alarms, and "electric eyes."

This work was done with the help of a knowledgeable tutor, so that all the necessary safety precautions were taken. Jonathan was asked to explain each project to the class and did so very clearly. He was transformed from an imp into a cooperative youngster as a result of his teacher's ingenuity.

But Jonathan was bright. What do you do with a slower child who presents problems? The answer is to find something he or she will enjoy. It might be woodworking or making model airplanes. (These do have a place in the classroom. A history of aviation through models is a most effective exhibit. Include rockets and the space shuttle and you have the past, present, and future.)

Several girls presented a problem in class until their teacher, recognizing that they were very interested in fashions, broke this vast topic into segments and began with one assignment, fashions in hairstyling. The girls were fascinated and from then on became, for the most part, very cooperative in order to be given time to work on their "projects."

Assignments of this type require the ability to read and write. If necessary, allow the youngsters to work with someone capable of assisting them. This might be other pupils in the class, or a parent or friend outside of school.

## MAKE A CHILD FEEL NEEDED

If youngsters get the idea that they are pests, they come to school, but unenthusiastically. If they feel they are valued human beings, their attitude is entirely different. If they feel needed, they have a real reason for going to class. How can you make children feel needed?

We've already suggested establishing a monitorial system involving every child in the class. Another is teamwork. By setting up academic teams, you can give each youngster an important place in the class. However, the slow child will probably feel at a disadvantage. If the team takes into consideration athletics, art, music, and every other skill, every child can contribute something.

One enterprising teacher developed a type of competitive team activity that she repeated for many years because it was so successful. The class was divided into six teams. Each afternoon the teacher would announce the activity for the following day. For example, one week, on Monday, every child who brought in a picture earned two points. (It could come from a newspaper or a magazine, or it could be a personal snapshot.)

On Tuesday, every youngster who brought in a library book earned four points for his team. Wednesday, a perfect score on an arithmetic quiz earned three points. Thursday, three points were given for a leaf or flower brought into school. On Friday, six points were given for a perfect spelling paper.

Charts had been made, scores kept, and the excitement mounted. At the end of the month the teacher made a "pizza party" for the winning team. The next month the PTA president invited the winner to lunch. This continued all year and was completed by the awarding of prizes to the team that had the most winning months.

The success of this team activity was based on the fact that the teacher thought up projects that involved every child. No youngster gave up, because while the activity for Monday might be academic, on Tuesday there was sure to be something entirely different. When a drawing of a butterfly was asked for, almost any drawing was acceptable.

There was a fringe benefit too, because of the enthusiastic pupil involvement. If a student was absent, he or she couldn't earn any points, so attendance was excellent. One mother telephoned the teacher to ask if she could please bring in her child's picture. The boy had a sore throat and couldn't talk but insisted on going to school.

Should you try this technique, plan it carefully and plan it for one month. It can always be extended, but only at the insistence of the youngsters. It may pall, in which case you would need something new.

## CONCLUSION

Certain basic methods have proven to be effective in working with disruptive children. First, one must be aware of the cause-and-effect relationship. Children misbehave for reasons, and if you can determine these reasons, you can sometimes eliminate the poor behavior and help the child develop self-control. We believe the first thing any teacher must do to help a troubled child is establish a warm, close relationship with him or her. We use the term *rapport* to describe this.

After you have developed rapport, you can sometimes determine the cause of the child's problems. Perhaps you can help solve them; perhaps you cannot. But you can show the child love and affection and treat him or her fairly and firmly. You can attempt to structure situations that will give the child some measure of success in school, and you can make that youngster feel needed and wanted. You can approach disruptive children with a view toward stimulating them intellectually and introducing them to new fields, new interests.

Your entire approach should be a positive one, for with troubled youngsters far more can be accomplished with understanding and compassion than with punishment. Youngsters misbehave because they have not mastered the art of self-control. When we as teachers lose our tempers, we show the youngsters we have not mastered self-control either. The young people have words for this—they say, "Keep your cool." It behooves us to do the same and to work with our disruptive, troubled children, not against them, to show them we care for them and are truly anxious to help them succeed in this battle for survival that we call life.

In subsequent chapters, we will consider in detail the various types of disruptive children and suggest some specific procedures that we have found successful in working with these troubled, troublesome youngsters.

# 4

# GETTING PARENTS TO COOPERATE WITH YOU

When the first edition of this book was published, the majority of children lived with their two parents. The situation has changed dramatically in the past decade, with many variations in the home situations in which youngsters find themselves today.

Since parental cooperation is extremely important, particularly in regard to the disruptive child, we will begin with the assumption that the youngster lives with his or her mother and father. This may well not be the case, and that will be discussed in subsequent chapters, but we begin with what used to be the typical American home.

In our previous writings we have referred to the parent as the "essential ally." We suggest you adopt this phrase—or at least the philosophy underlying it—for with parental cooperation far more learning can be achieved by most children.

## MEETING PARENTS FOR THE FIRST TIME

The concept of making parents your ally is taken into consideration and acted on by many school systems. Parent-teacher conferences are scheduled early in the school year—usually in October or November. These conferences give you the opportunity to meet the parents, and, under reasonably good circumstances, it should be possible to establish an element of understanding with them. You might begin with these words: "If we work together, you and I, the parent and the teacher, we can do a great deal toward helping your child reach his or her potential. Our goals are the same. Both you and I want your child to do well in school, and by working together, we should be able to reach that goal."

Try to use this parent conference time, if your system has it, to talk with the parent of each child in your class. (If you are in an intermediate school or in a departmental set-up, this is, of course, virtually impossible.) However, it is essential that you make the attempt to personally meet the parents of any youngster who has not learned self-control or is not showing the ability to work independently.

The parents of these children are most often the ones who do not attend such conferences. In that case, invite them in by writing a note or telephoning them in advance of the conference. (You will probably find it easier to reach them by writing than by telephone in these days when both parents work outside the home.) Stress the fact that this is the first conference of the year and that they and you ought to get to know each other.

Discuss with every parent you meet the concepts you are trying to develop with his or her child. Emphasize the fact that you are working with the youngsters to teach them good work and study habits. These will, in turn, enable the girl or boy to benefit a great deal more from every class he or she is ever in, from every teacher he or she ever encounters.

Make every interview, even very brief ones, very personal. Know some facts about every child and his or her work. "Nicole is very quick to grasp relationships between numbers," you tell her mother, as I recall doing. Her parent's reply was, "I've noticed that too. I'm so happy you mentioned it. I've told her father many times, but he says it's only me being a proud mother."

Nicole's mother realized the teacher did, indeed, understand her second grader's penchant for arithmetic, and a bond was established between them. When the teacher added, "But she likes to talk to her neighbors while we are working on reading skills," the mother's quick reply was, "I'll talk to her about that."

It may be difficult, but try not to start any interview with a negative comment, for you will turn the parent against you, personally, and against what you say. Even words to the effect, "David is doing an adequate job, but I know he is capable of much better work because I have seen glimpses of it" is better than "David gets by. He's just passing." Follow up the first statement with "David wrote a one-paragraph description of his favorite toys that was very fine. Did he show it to you? But his next efforts at composition weren't as carefully thought out." By showing appreciation of the child's efforts, you make a friend, an ally, of the parent.

In this interview try to learn about the child. Has he or she ever been seriously ill? (This information may not appear on the health card, yet, for example, a child who has had rheumatic fever may suffer from its effects for years.) Has he or she had problems with his or her brothers or sisters?

(In some families the siblings fight constantly. Often the children, especially the younger ones, come to school very upset.)

What are the parents' attitudes toward the child? (Not all parents love their children—contrary to one of the great myths of all time. Child abuse is an extremely serious problem and has been on the rise for years.) Obviously, you can't ask a father or mother, "Do you love your child?" but you can listen to the parent, and if he or she does not it will come out in your interview. I was once told by a mother in these exact words, "I can't stand that brat. When I tell her I'm going to send her away, I mean it." And this mother did—four times—to elderly relatives a thousand miles away, because the child "did not obey." (Children with such home lives usually respond to any love or affection from the teacher like a kitten lapping up milk.)

During the first interview, ask the parent if he or she knows of any difficulty the child has had in his or her schoolwork and, if so, in what areas. Surprisingly, these difficulties may not show up on the record card. Ask about the child's interests, hobbies, and pastimes. One teacher found the answers to many questions he had when he learned an eight year old in his class delivered newspapers before he came to school in the morning. (Was it any wonder the child tended to fall asleep around 10 A.M. in the comfortably warm classroom?)

This meeting with the parents should, in actuality, be a learning session for you, the teacher. However, so often (we might even say most of the time) the parents we really want to see don't come in voluntarily. It's necessary to send for them. Let us suggest ways to do this. Compare the two notes in Figure 5.

If you were the parent, which letter would you rather receive? The question is unnecessary, of course. But let us analyze these short notes. In the first one the teacher says, "I *must* see you in regard to the behavior of your son, Edward." She goes on to say, "He has been impossible," and then confesses, "I am at my wit's end." She shows her anxiety and her frustration. She then makes an appointment for the next day—giving the parents no alternative—and no recourse.

Suppose they cannot keep this appointment—which is really a summons—to appear. They feel uncomfortable, annoyed or angry, and threatened. What has Edward done? They conjure up pictures in their minds. Or they ask Edward, who immediately answers, "I didn't do nothin'." Their anger or anxiety increases and they, psychologically, get ready to take on this adversary—the teacher.

Contrast this with the second note. Parents receiving it immediately will think, "Isn't Mrs. Smith nice?" Why? She made them feel important. They have an idea there may be some difficulty, but the teacher is obviously a pleasant person who is not threatening them or their son—and they need

**Figure 5**

Dear Mr. and Mrs. Jones,

I must see you in regard to the behavior of your son, Edward. He has been impossible, and I am at my wit's end. Please be sure to see me tomorrow morning at 10 A.M. in our classroom.

Sincerely,

Dear Mr. and Mrs. Jones,

I would like to discuss Edward with you. Could you possibly join me for a cup of coffee? I would be able to talk with you next Monday at 10 A.M. in our classroom. If that isn't convenient, would you please telephone our office, 123–4567, and our secretary will make another appointment for you. I'm looking forward to meeting you.

Sincerely,

Jane Smith

not be on the defensive. The tone of this letter and the welcome that is assured in it will do much to achieve the aim—to bring the parent into the school. Should you need to write a letter to a parent, make it an attractive one, for never before in the history of education has there been so great a need to bridge the gap that has come into being between parents and teachers.

The same is true of telephone calls. Your voice, your attitude, your words all reflect the feeling or lack of feeling you have for the child. As soon as a parent realizes that you do feel for his or her child and that you are interested in the youngster's welfare, that parent is at least partially won over, and his or her cooperation is possibly enlisted. (Time is a factor here, for many parents, while desiring to work with their children, haven't got the time to do so.)

Nevertheless, there is the possibility that there will be not one person teaching the child but two, the parent and the teacher. Try to meet with parents face to face, rather than discussing matters on the telephone, for the latter is rather superficial. This personal meeting should bring you and the parent closer together. It gives you the opportunity to learn more about the child, his or her homelife, and any kind of problems that exist.

For example, there was Jason, age ten, who was a very disruptive child. He did little work in class, finding interests everywhere but in the work at hand. A discussion with his mother disclosed the fact that Jason was constantly being compared with an older brother who was extremely bright. Jason had revealed his feelings. He simply would not compete with this "intellectual giant" and refused to enter into any sort of academic situation where a comparison would be made.

From the interview, the teacher learned Jason played the piano by ear, while his brother could not. She arranged to have Jason play often in the assembly. The recognition he gained, plus the fact this privilege would be removed if his misbehavior continued, caused a marked improvement in both his conduct and his attendance. The boy felt needed, and this brought out the best in him.

Please check with your supervisor to be sure you are permitted to write to or telephone parents. In some school systems this is approved of, whereas in others the supervisor must communicate with them.

## CONDUCTING THE INTERVIEW _____

In any interview your first task is to put the parents at ease. Often parents come into school in a highly emotional state. Part of this is a carry-over from their own childhood, when they were afraid of this figure of authority—the teacher. Part of it is with dread, wondering, "What did Junior do now?"

Be as nice as you possibly can be. You cannot, after all, *demand* parental cooperation; you must *request* it. Be as charming, as tactful, as interesting as you can possibly be. If you are upset or angry you will quickly convey this to the parent. If in actuality you are, it is so much better to say, "Mrs. Jones, I'm afraid I'm upset today. Please forgive me if I may seen a bit harsh, but I did want to see you about Cindy." Then try to be as calm as possible.

Take a positive approach throughout the interview. Begin by telling the parent as many good things about the child as you can truthfully say. Perhaps the child is warm and friendly. Does he or she enjoy life? Is he or she neat and clean, and does his or her appearance reflect the devoted care of his or her parent? (How heartening it is for the parent to hear this!)

Is he or she helpful? Does he or she wish to help the other youngsters in the class? Does he or she have leadership ability? Any or all of these qualities can be pointed out to the parent, but only if they are true of the particular boy or girl. Mention as many of these qualities as you can honestly cite, and do this with warmth and enthusiasm.

Then call the child in and bring up the specific reason the parent was called in. If the youngster is disruptive, ask him or her in the presence of the parent, not in a derogatory tone, but in an honestly inquiring one, why he or she doesn't cooperate. Questions such as these might be asked of the youngster: "Adam, I feel you could contribute a great deal to our learning in the classroom. Is there something bothering you?"

Adam will most probably answer no. Next, cite his good points and ask, "Don't you feel you want to do your best and help our class be one of the best in the school? Let's see how you can do this. You tell me—what can you do to achieve this?"

If Adam can't answer this, and he probably won't, continue in this vein: "Your mother and I both know you can be a leader. Now wouldn't it be nice if you could influence the other children to work hard?"

Before the parent leaves, extract the promise from Adam that he will do all he can to help.

You may wish to give him a daily report card, which both you and his parent will sign. Assure Adam that when he does his best he will be marked accordingly.

Whenever you deal with parents in any way, it is best to minimize the faultfinding, and emphasize what the child can achieve for him- or herself. In this way he or she is encouraged and the parents heartened. Their cooperation is much more likely to be achieved in this way than by invectives, criticisms, and name-calling.

Put yourself in the parents' place. Wouldn't this positive attitude on the part of the teacher be much more likely to gain your confidence and cooperation?

One very successful teacher in a school in a very poor neighborhood approached parents in this way: "I can tell by looking at your child how hard you work to keep him so well dressed and looking as nice as he does. Your boy must be very proud of you. Of course, we want you to be just as proud of him. By working together, I know we can achieve this. I know Darren will cooperate with us, won't you, Darren?"

Such words as these can be just the thing to obtain the cooperation of the parent, and many times of the child too.

Regretfully, we've heard teachers complain to parents, enumerating the child's disruptive actions and never mentioning any of his or her strong points. This puts the parents and the youngster on the defensive; antagonism is born, and often the parents leave upset and angry.

## IF CHILDREN NEED EXTRA HELP _____

There are instances when youngsters' disruptive behavior is caused by their inability to do the work asked of them. If this is the case, you may wish to ask the parents to work with them. However, the parents do not have to do this. You are the teacher, not they. Therefore, if you make this request, be sure the parents realize it is a request.

Tell the parents you will give specific assignments and then do so. These need not be very complex, but they should be highly detailed, and they should leave no doubt in the parents' minds just what you wish covered. For example, "Read and study pages 110–18" is a poor assignment. A better one would be, "Read pages 110–18, and answer the following questions:

1. Why did these events happen?
2. How could they have been avoided?
3. What were the results?"

Please note: Only three questions are asked, but if a youngster is able to answer them, he or she has grasped the meaning of the material he or she has read.

You can suggest to the parent that an older sister or brother might work with the youngster instead of, or as well as, the parent. This serves another purpose too. It channels the energy of both youngsters, gets them working together, in a situation that can possibly prove beneficial to both. As a fringe benefit, it takes them away from video games or television programs.

When a child is disruptive or is not learning, start working on this by having a private conversation with him or her. If this doesn't work, then request that a parent see you. But try to avoid this unless you feel you cannot influence the child yourself. You can probably accomplish far more by talking privately with the child. However, if you feel it necessary, write a note or telephone the parent. This is especially worthwhile if by doing so you can prevent the child from falling behind in his or her work.

## CONFIDENTIALITY

Before you contact parents, be sure to tell the disruptive youngster that you plan to do so. Sometimes just the warning may be enough to cause an improvement in self-control. However, once you have made the statement, if there is no *noticeable change*, you must go ahead with the message to the parent. *Never threaten to do something and neglect to follow through.*

By taking the action of contacting the parent, you are using one of your "big guns." You have already tried speaking privately with the child, we are sure, not once but many times. While he or she may have promised to cooperate, this has not happened, and you've decided that now is the time to get in touch with the parent.

Assure the youngster you will not reveal anything he or she has told you. This may be very important to the boy or girl, and your very mention of it serves to increase the child's respect for you. Needless to say, you would keep this promise. For example, let's consider the case of Michele.

Michele's father was an alcoholic, a fact she had confided to her teacher, Mrs. X., early in the school year. In spite of her sympathetic manner toward the girl, Mrs. X. could not persuade Michele to lower her voice, and Michele tended to shout in the classroom, disrupting the work being done. She was boisterous in the halls and had been talked to many times about these problems.

Mrs. X. had, indeed, discussed Michele's behavior with her over and over again, but to no avail. In fact, the shouting became worse and worse. The day arrived when Mrs. X. told Michele that her parents would have to come in to see Mrs. X.

Michele's face flushed and she became abusive. She appeared to be in a state of near panic, and she could barely speak coherently. Mrs. X. had not, of course, expected this behavior. When she took the girl aside to try to calm her down, Michele burst into tears. Further conversation revealed Michele was terrified lest the teacher reveal to the parent her knowledge of their family secret—that the father was a heavy drinker.

Once Mrs. X. realized what the problem was, she promised Michele she would not mention this fact, and Michele gave her word that she would try to control her behavior. However, she could not, and when the parents were interviewed, the confidentiality of the father's problem was respected. Mrs. X. was shocked, however, when she met him. It would have taken a very poor observer not to notice his red face and the odor of alcohol, which was so evident. Incidentally, the visit did help, possibly because the child's respect for her teacher had increased.

## DO NOT MAKE VALUE JUDGMENTS

If you must tell a parent something, be sure it is a fact, not an opinion. Teachers sometimes state their ideas as if they were undeniable truths—and this is surely not the case.

One ex-teacher told a parent, "Your son is lazy. He doesn't do a bit of work in school." Thereupon the parent took from her purse some writing the child had done and asked, "What do you call this?"

How much better it would have been if the teacher had said, "Your son has not been completing his work lately. He sits and looks out of the window. Has something happened recently that has disturbed him?"

Youngsters who appear slow may not be so at all. Telling their parents they are can cause unnecessary pain. Instead, be specific. "Jeremy won't do his arithmetic. He plays with his baseball cards instead, while the rest of the class is working."

The parent's reaction to this may very well be, "Take the cards away," but that doesn't solve the problem. One of our tasks as teachers is to make the work as interesting as possible. Bright children often become bored by some of the methods and materials we use. It's up to us to try to supply them with work that will challenge them.

## TALK WITH IRATE PARENTS

How do you react when an angry mother or father comes in to see you (usually at your request but possibly on their own)? Do you respond by getting just as angry? That is, of course, the worst thing you can do. Let's discuss how you should handle the situation.

1. *Respond as calmly as you can.* Say to the person, "Mr. Green, I'm glad you came in to discuss this problem. It's really important that I see you so we can talk about it." Speak softly and do not react to the person's anger.

2. Listen carefully to the parent's words and then state his or her viewpoint in other words, reviewing what has been said. Show that you understand what the parent has told you. For example, you might respond in this manner: "As I understand you, this is the situation." Then proceed to paraphrase what the parent has said.

3. Then give your version of what happened.

This is an actual reply made by a teacher: "As I saw the situation," he said, "Kevin was hit by a spitball, but he was shooting them too. I had to put a stop to it as soon as I became aware of what was going on. I reprimanded both boys."

The most important part of dealing with angry parents is to *not react to hostility with hostility.* When parents are unpleasant or nasty, try to be particularly nice to them. Invite them to sit down, and discuss the situation as quietly as possible. Even if they are upset, you have to stay calm. You are the teacher, and your self-control and poise are your most valuable attributes.

If charges are made, give them due consideration and then refute them carefully. Can you imagine how strongly you might react if you were complaining about something that you thought was very serious and the person you were speaking to made light of it? With parents this reaction might well be even stronger.

If you need records to back up your position, have them on hand or get them—but use impartial, documented evidence whenever you can.

Your tone of voice can act as a balm or as an irritant, and with an upset person, the balm is obviously infinitely preferable.

I recall one case that made me lose a night's sleep. Marilyn was a young lady who constantly got into difficulty. One day she was really chastised by the dean. "Don't you touch me," she shouted. (The dean had not the slightest intention of "touching" her, but she was in a fighting mood.)

Her parents were asked to come to school. Not only did her mother arrive, but her grandmother did as well. They were furious at the way Marilyn had been treated—according to the girl's story. The dean requested my assistance and together we spoke with both ladies, but we seemed to get nowhere, particularly with the grandmother. We could not placate them, nor would they accept any of the anecdotes we recounted about Marilyn's behavior. They left, still furious.

Several weeks later, an incident occurred on the school bus at dismissal time. Marilyn was leaning out of an open window. I called to her to move back from the window. She refused, saying, "You can't make me." (She was playing to an audience of her friends on the bus.) I shouted again, and again she remained, her head, as well as half of her body, out of the bus window.

I knew there was no time for this shouting match. I ran into the bus and yanked Marilyn in by her ponytail, just as the bus started to move. She was furious, screaming at me, "Wait until my mother and grandmother get you."

Since I had had the "pleasure" of meeting these ladies, I was, I confess, more than a bit anxious. The next morning nothing happened. Then in the afternoon there was a phone call. Sure enough it was Marilyn's mother. Her first words to me were, "What did that impossible kid do to get you to pull her hair?"

When I explained the situation, she said to me, "You know, after I spoke to you the last time I knew it had to be something. I'm not educated, but I know you wouldn't hurt any kid. Marilyn won't give you a bit of trouble any more."

And there was a big improvement in Marilyn's behavior after that. Her mother had understood what we were trying to do after our interview. Grandmother, on the other hand, certainly had not. Marilyn, meanwhile, is now a young woman. She comes back to the school to visit us about once every year.

## USE THE TELEPHONE EFFECTIVELY _____

We know of one young gentleman, D.G., who started teaching in a vocational high school when he was twenty years old. He was actually younger than some of his students and was certainly the youngest member of the faculty. It was expected that he would have a very hard time. Instead, he became the most respected teacher in the school, and he made this happen in only one month.

D.G. spent hours on the telephone that first month and for a time thereafter speaking with parents. If a youngster so much as called out, there was a phone call home. "Sometimes it was necessary for me to call from home, and sometimes late in the evening," he recalled. "But I knew I had to do something radical. Parents want their kids to cooperate, and I felt they could help me get that cooperation."

In one month even the most difficult youngsters were no longer disruptive. This continued for all the time D.G. taught at that school, but the number of phone calls he had to make became less and less. Once he had established this pattern, which was eminently fair, the students came to respect and then to like him. He was also a very creative science teacher and did many exciting experiments with his classes, but he needed to establish a climate for learning, which he did in that first month.

Even today, with the busy schedule most parents have, when you need parental cooperation, it's worth phoning for, although you may have to make several calls to find someone at home. There are those who believe this method to be an extreme one, but for this particular teacher with his unique problem it worked. In many classes, five or six calls may suffice. However, be sure you ask for parental cooperation, and do not demand it.

"Mrs. Doe, this is Mr. Smith, your son Tommy's teacher," you say to the parent. "I am sure you are anxious for Tommy to learn as much as he can while he is in school. I find he is not getting to class on time and is missing some valuable work. Could you speak to Tommy about this, please. Thanks so much for your cooperation." (The name of the boy or girl is extremely important. It shows the parent you are talking about his or her youngster and not about the class in general.)

## REFERRAL TO THE GUIDANCE DEPARTMENT _____

In speaking to parents you will very often find that just as you are having difficulty with the child in school, they are having difficulty with him or her at home. In this type of situation, the family may be helped by the school guidance counselor or possibly by a social worker, who may be on the school staff or belong to an outside agency. There are many situations with which trained personnel can deal quite effectively.

One such case concerned a fifth-grade boy named Carl. Carl was a poorly adjusted boy who at times would do the work required of him while at others would do nothing at all. He would sometimes run around the classroom almost uncontrollably, yet at other times he'd sit and work beautifully.

Carl's family was referred to a social service agency by the school guidance department. An almost miraculous change took place in him. (It is devoutly to be desired that this happens every time a case is referred, but it doesn't.) Then about six months later Carl reverted to his disruptive behavior. On questioning him, it was discovered his social worker had gone away on a month's vacation. There was no one at home to control the boy. The social worker "father" has disappeared.

In homes where there is no male figure with whom a boy can identify, there is often a problem in school. Such boys will sometimes seek out male teachers or supervisors with whom they ally themselves. These alliances are good ones, for the emerging man must learn from someone how to behave in the male role. It is hoped that the male chosen is a worthy one.

If the school has a male counselor, he is very often the male selected. We have seen this work out very well in numerous instances. The counseling situation is best suited to this because a teacher does not have the time to spend privately with a youngster, whereas a counselor does. He can assume the father image gently but firmly. He must, however, be willing to do this and understand completely just what it is that he is doing. Lines of communication should be kept open constantly with the teacher, so that both are aware of the work being done, but the counselor must always keep the confidentiality of the youngster in mind.

## TAKE EARLY ACTION

Many teachers, particularly inexperienced ones, allow youngsters to develop into problems in their classes because they are reluctant to take action as soon as a problem becomes apparent. This is very unwise, for many reasons.

Girls and boys must learn that no wasting of time will be tolerated. They must learn that you, the teacher, are fair but firm. Once rules have been set up in your class, by both you and the youngsters, it is your task to see that they are followed. Here is a series of steps you might take with disruptive youngsters.

1. If children break the rules, you must speak with them immediately, pointing out that what they are doing is disruptive and is taking valuable time away from the work the class is doing. If you can do so, speak privately with the youngster to find out why he or she is being disruptive.

2. If the disruptive behavior continues, again reprimand the young-ster. If you have set up the monitorial system, point out to the child that he or she is in danger of losing his or her job.

3. The next step in your discipline procedure is to remove the child from the monitorial job but tell him or her that the job can be earned back by good behavior.

4. If the lack of cooperation continues, tell the child that unless he or she cooperates you will contact his or her parents.

5. Then, if necessary, do so. Write a note or telephone the parents, but be sure to get in touch with them. Tell them, without hostility, why you are contacting them and request their cooperation. Point out that you are calling because you are anxious to get their youngster to do the serious work of learning but that he or she is not willing to cooperate. Do not be nasty, do not be angry, but show concern, and ask for their help. "I don't want ——- to fall behind in his (or her) work," you say, "and he (or she) will, if he (or she) continues to avoid working in class."

6. After you have followed this procedure, you may decide to refer the youngster to the principal or the person in charge of discipline, or you may wish to contact the parents again, perhaps asking them to come in to see you. In either event, be sure you have anecdotal records to illustrate how the disruptive youngster has behaved and what you have done to correct the behavior.

We have heard parents say dozens of times when they are called into school for presuspension hearings, "But why wasn't I told there was a problem? Why did it get this far? No one from the school has let me know what my child has been doing." Their complaint is certainly justified, for they have a right to know.

It is true, too frequently, that it is difficult to reach a parent or someone in the family, but a registered letter or a phone call in the evening often succeeds. Working parents are particularly anxious for their children to do well in school. You are actually being considerate by notifying them, so that small problems do not become big ones.

We met one elected official, in a very responsible position, who showed us a letter he had just received from his son, written at his teacher's insistence and mailed by her. It stated that the boy had not been doing his work and was causing difficulty in the classroom. The gentleman was very upset by it. He took the matter very seriously and asked our advice—what should he do with his son?

We asked him if he had had time to talk with the youngster privately in the past few months, and he realized that he had not because he had been campaigning for reelection. We suggested this become the first matter of the day, and he agreed. "Do you think this is his way of getting my attention?" he asked? "You'll find out when you talk with him," we responded.

It is not only fathers but mothers, too, who are often too busy to have time for their children. Sometimes poor behavior in school is a plea for their attention. Early action on the part of the teacher can at least bring this matter to the fore.

## SEEK MEDICAL ATTENTION

There are times you wish to recommend to the parents that their child see the school nurse or physician, or their family doctor, because of some problem the child seems to be having. Children sometimes cannot sit still because of rashes, for instance (or tight underwear). They may be anemic, causing them to be lethargic in the classroom. Often the problem is due to poor vision, which is first discovered by the teacher, or by a hearing deficiency. When you sense something is wrong, here too it is better to take action than to ignore the situation. Parents are usually very grateful.

## CONCLUSION

After you have followed the series of steps of the discipline procedure, it may be necessary for you to contact the disruptive youngster's parents. It is extremely important that you make allies of the parents of this youngster. In many cases the disruptive child does not realize that you can communicate with his or her parents, or he or she thinks you will not bother to do so.

Once parents are informed of their child's disruptive behavior in school, they can persuade and encourage the boy or girl to cooperate with you and to learn self-control. The parents are in the position to do so and often are anxious to work with you to help their youngster get the most out of his or her education.

In your dealing with parents, you must be extremely careful to be fair and informative, for if you are hostile, you can do more harm than good. You must work with the parents to help the child, and in helping him or her, you help yourself. In speaking to the parents, do not dwell on misbehavior but try to show the child's good points and his or her potentialities. Never speak derogatorily.

Learn about the child from the parents, and try to establish a relationship with them so that should you need their help, it will be willingly forthcoming. It's important that you request the help from the parents, and not demand it. Our motto, which we hope will become yours, is, as we have already said, "What can we do, working together, to help your child?" Assure the parents, "Should you have problems, perhaps I can help you with them. At any rate, I'll be happy to try."

Years ago the Scottish poet Robert Burns wrote, "There is so much good in the worst of us, and so much bad in the best of us, that it scarcely behooves any of us to talk about the rest of us." Instead of enumerating the vices, let us emphasize and build on the child's good points.

If you use this approach, we can almost guarantee the cooperation of the parents.

# 5

# THE CHILD WITH LEARNING PROBLEMS

The paper airplane flew across the room with amazing accuracy. It landed right on target, and the little girl's hand went up.

"Bobbie threw a plane at me."

"Naw. I just threw it."

"You threw it at *me*."

"Can I help it if it hit you?"

"You threw it right at me."

"Naw."

"You did so. You didn't want to hit Mrs. Brown, so you aimed at me. I'm the farthest away from her desk.

"Oh, Bobbie," Mrs. Brown sighed. "You can't afford to miss this work. You need this lesson so badly!"

How true! And what a vicious cycle! The children who need the work, who have the learning problems, are the ones who are inattentive. It is almost as if they haven't learned before and they aren't going to learn now. What can we do about these youngsters who have learning problems that manifest themselves as behavior problems; who interfere with the teaching; who are disruptive—and who very often not only rock the boat but sink it too? For the disruption spreads from one child to another. A teacher who may have had one or two discipline problems suddenly discovers a whole class becoming very difficult to teach.

What can we do about this?

First, we must try to determine why the disrupters are disrupting. Wherein lie their problems? So often it is obvious that these children are the poor students—the ones who are behind in almost every subject area. They usually have difficulty with reading and arithmetic skills, and they have taken the attitude, consciously or subconsciously, "I can't learn—so why try?"

These are the children with true learning problems, who often become the disquieting element, the behavior problem in your classroom. And often the acts of misbehavior are the smokescreens behind which the child hides to cover his or her own inadequacies.

Of all the problems that face our children, learning problems are the ones we should be most concerned about for two reasons. The first is that we can often help solve them by careful diagnosis and painstaking work. This does not imply we can work miracles, but we can effect changes. We can teach methods of study, and we can help the child in the vast majority of cases to learn.

The second reason we should be concerned with these problems is because our system has helped create them. Many times this has been unwitting and most surely was unintentional, but nevertheless learning problems often stem from the fact that youngsters are passed from grade to grade without having mastered the skills required.

If we can overcome some of the deficiencies evident in the children's educational background, if we can help them achieve success, we can alter their entire lives. If we allow ourselves to be indifferent to their learning problems, the problems may be compounded while the children are in our classes, and the children may leave in worse shape than they came to us.

As educators, our prime purpose of course is to educate our youngsters, to communicate with them, to give them information, and most important, to equip them for their future lives. The child with learning problems is the real challenge to us. Bright and even average students are able to learn with far less effort on the part of the teacher than their slower brothers and sisters. The slow learner, the child who suffers from a mental block, the child who is unable to progress in school, these are the youngsters who require extra effort from the teacher.

It is essential to determine where the cause of the learning problems lies and in what ways we can help the children solve them. For what happens if youngsters are having such problems? As we have shown, they may become disruptive as a result of their frustration.

If the work is over a child's head, he or she may lose interest in record time, usually about ten seconds or even less, and turn to his or her neighbor for companionship. He or she may carry on an animated conversation or get into an argument. His or her entire attention is directed away from the work you are doing, for to pay attention, to try to follow the lesson, makes this child feel inadequate.

At times children with learning problems try to give the opposite impression. They may act like know-it-alls. We have had such children wave their hands violently, volunteering to answer every question, and when they are not called on, become furious. Sometimes, but not always, this child is hiding feelings of inadequacy. The techniques we suggest to help the child with learning problems are valuable because they get at the roots of the problem, the child's feelings of inadequacy, and how to overcome them—how to help him or her to learn.

All individuals are different, and their learning abilities and mental capacities reflect this. Not everyone of us is a genius, but nevertheless, one of the most interesting things about all human beings is the individual differences among them. When children start to go to school, not all are ready to learn. This factor has been recognized, and many programs have been established to help underprivileged children in this regard. Operation Headstart has been one of the most successful.

However, when children start to go to school, often the readiness is not considered and the child is taught, but does not learn. The class masters the first book they are given, but one or two individuals do not. The class progresses, but these individuals are left "at the post." It is here that very severe problems may be created. As the child moves upward through school, he or she often falls further and further behind his or her classmates, for learning is based on previous learning.

## LEARNING IS SEQUENTIAL

There are subjects in which a child may succeed if he or she is taught by a skilled teacher. Science, for example, in the elementary and even intermediate grades does not depend on previous learning as greatly as reading or arithmetic does. Neither does social studies—history, geography, and current events—if the teacher does not depend on the child reading the text to learn the material. But reading and the other language arts, and arithmetic and mathematics are based in great measure on previous learning. If a youngster had not mastered the basic, rudimentary skills, how can he or she proceed to other, more difficult ones?

We are firm believers in the teaching of reading through phonics. If youngsters cannot sound out a word and do not learn it "by sight," no amount of encouragement can get them to read it correctly. If children have not mastered the concept of addition, how can they go on to multiplication? Yet we know youngsters in the intermediate school grades who cannot subtract. These are the girls and boys who frequently become discipline problems.

All too often they may have had teachers who may have urged them to study, offered them all sorts of interesting tidbits, but did not actually *teach* them. Youngsters who have not learned word-attack skills (such as phonics), and who have been subjected only to "sight-reading" methods, attempt solutions, trying virtually anything. If they have been lucky, they have realized that certain letters often have the same sound and that they can take a chance on the word *into* sounding like the word *in.* But when confronted by the word *instant* they are absolutely bewildered.

Such children are all too often moved from grade to grade. They may even be held over once. But unless they learn fundamental skills, they continue to fall further and further behind the rest of the class and become more and more discouraged with the learning process.

They are also greatly handicapped because they cannot read textbooks, and get nothing but a headache from them. Yet how often does the teacher give an assignment that relies completely on reading? These unfortunate children and their slow-learning brothers or sisters who can read the textbook with a bit more skill but not comprehend it, how can they learn?

Probably the reading assignment is gone over in class, but often superficially at best. Then a test is given on the material, and the results for these youngsters have to be poor. It is almost guaranteed, for these boys and girls were not able to read the test. If the teacher reads the question aloud and gives an oral test, these youngsters will do little better, for usually they cannot write satisfactorily either. Their poor foundations are literally ruining them, and they become disruptive.

What can you do to help such children?

## ESTABLISH COMMUNICATION FIRST, THEN DIAGNOSE _____

**1. Try to establish communication** with the disruptive child. Arrange time to speak with him or her privately and quietly. This time should not be immediately after he or she has been disruptive, when you and he or she may be angry and upset. Rather, it should be after a good day. (You can structure this by giving the child special work he or she can handle, praising him or her for it, and you will have the "good day.")

Talk about the youngster's learning problems. Often the boy or girl will be ashamed to admit them or will be unaware of their severity. Explain, however, that you want to work on this to help him or her but that progress does not depend on you. It is essential that you get the child to realize you will help but that it is his or her responsibility.

"I really want to help you," you tell the child, "but you have to understand that I can't learn for you. You have to do that, but I'm here to show you how."

Use every bit of tact and affection you have toward the youngster. Win him or her over. You are needed by this child desperately. If you can convince him or her that you really care, that you "give a damn," you have half the battle won. We've seen our own enthusiasm become contagious.

However, be sure such children never feel you are sitting in judgment of them or blaming them for their inadequacies. Remember, no child (or, indeed, person) is ever perfect. The youngster will improve but will slip back as well. Learning is so often three steps forward, then two steps back. In time, the child will make progress.

Explain that first you must find out what his or her specific problems are and that you will use tests to determine them.

Write a note to the parents suggesting the child be given a complete physical examination, including hearing and vision tests. In the case of the latter, be sure that the doctor is an expert who can check for visual perception difficulties. Many children do not learn to read because their vision is impaired, but this is not picked up by an examination with the Snellen chart (the eye chart used in most schools).

An adequate vision examination requires a doctor who has studied this area extensively. There are situations where a person may see only the first three letters of a word, or the last. They may see the letters garbled. For example, one little girl read the word *left* as *felt.* This condition is not rare, but it is not common enough to be checked for routinely. Yet it has become a very serious problem in the lives of many people. Generally, such problems are referred to as "dyslexia," which originally was described as seeing letters backward (the letter "d" seen as "b", etc.).

When a youngster has a learning problem, we must try every avenue open to us to discover what it is. The physical aspect is the first to be checked out, because many times it is the easiest to remedy.

**2. Now do your diagnostic testing** to determine the needs of the individual children, especially those who are disruptive. You may choose the standardized tests used in many school districts, or you may create your own tools. The latter are good, or even better, than the former. But this testing must be done, even in the intermediate grades. You are not interested in the total test scores as much as in the items the child cannot answer correctly.

When grading the tests check the individual papers. It is very effective if you do this with the youngster sitting next to you. You are able to show the boy or girl the errors he or she made, but be sure you do not make the youngster feel he or she is inadequate. Then you can work out a program for him or her. You may find that not every child needs an individualized program, but many of those with learning problems certainly do.

To be more specific, even if you are teaching social studies or science in the intermediate school, if you discover a youngster whose reading is much below the grade level he or she is in, work with him or her on reading skills as part of social studies or science teaching. If possible, recommend help for this boy or girl in the form of special tutoring, if available, or special classes.

But be aware of the child's difficulty so that when you are teaching the class, you do not expect this youngster and others like him or her to learn material from a textbook. You must teach verbally. The work has to be made interesting and relevant to the child's life. You will find that if you teach in this manner, the youngster will often become less and less disruptive.

## Individualize Instruction

It is most important for you to work with the girl or boy directly, on a one-to-one basis. To find the time for this, give your class written assignments to do in class; by this we surely are not implying "busywork." But if you have them write two paragraphs, there is no reason why this work cannot be done while you are working with individual youngsters.

The same is true of reading. Library books can be read during class time. In fact, this procedure is very valid, for you can structure the quiet environment that is most productive to reading. You can supply books that the youngsters will enjoy, thereby showing them the pleasures of reading. During the assembly period or while your class is in the gym (with another teacher), you can do work with children singly or in small groups.

As you work with an individual child, such as the paper airplane designer mentioned at the beginning of this chapter, make sure you communicate with him or her. Let him or her know there are gaps in the foundation of his or her education that must be filled, or he or she will continue to have problems. We have found that when we "level" with youngsters, when we "tell it like it is," but without being critical, they react well. Even the most hostile youngster will realize you are really trying to help him or her.

"It seems to me, Josh," you say, "that you've never been taught how to pick out the ideas from a paragraph." By the way, ask the child what is meant by a paragraph. You may be surprised at the response. We have found that, often, children do not know words that are so much a part of our vocabulary that this seems incredible to us.

An example: An intermediate school typing teacher told us that for weeks she had been saying to her classes, "We are aiming for speed with accuracy, but speed without accuracy is useless." One day she suddenly asked the class, "Who knows what accuracy means? Raise your hands if you know." Only half the class knew. One wonders what the other half thought.

Returning to Josh, if he doesn't know what a paragraph is, it is a simple matter to teach it to him. Then show him how to select the main ideas. Give him work to do—you may even use social studies or science textbooks for this—and have him select the main ideas. Check his work to be sure he is doing it correctly. Then continue to see which other reading skills Josh needs to learn and work on those.

One motivational device we have found to give good results with youngsters with reading difficulties is making a tape recording of their oral reading. Explain you will hold this tape, and then you will have them make one at the end of the year so that they can compare the two and see the progress they have made.

You may wish to involve the parents or an older sibling in your remedial work with a youngster. It is worthwhile to invite the parent in to see you so that you can explain exactly what it is that you are doing—that you are trying to eliminate some of his or her child's learning difficulties. If you are able to, work out an instructional program in which a person at home can assist the child with specific assignments. These assignments will reinforce the material you are teaching him or her.

Just asking the parent to help, in the abstract, is never as effective as if you tell him or her you plan to send home definite instructions. For instance, a child may need to read aloud. Give him or her a note with a particular story indicated and several questions for the person tutoring him or her to ask. This system of sending a note with instructions home once or twice a week can prove very worthwhile. It will serve to bring the child and the adult tutor closer together, which is beneficial to both.

Emphasize to the parent, though, that if any progress is to be made, it will be accomplished only if the tutor has a positive attitude. If the child is berated or made to feel he or she is not achieving quickly enough, more harm than good will result.

While speaking with the parent, you may decide to mention the fact that the child has been disruptive. Go on to say that you believe this stems from his or her learning problems—and that you are very interested in helping him or her overcome both. Ask the parent to cooperate with you by discussing this with the child and by showing that everyone is interested in helping him or her. (It is a very rare parent who will refuse to do so.) Stress the idea that the youngster does not need punishment but requires assistance, both at home and in school.

## GROUPING WITHIN YOUR CLASS _____

You may find many children with similar learning problems or gaps in their education. If so, we have found the most effective means for coping with this situation is through grouping.

When you discover children who have the same needs, it is a simple matter to form a group and teach the skills to all of them. You may even, if you wish, find a bright student to teach them—but only if you can create a situation where they will subsequently teach the "bright student." Be sure the children realize the groups are temporary, set up to help them learn what skills they need to know.

"But," you say, "how can I do this? Not with my class. Hubert screams out and constantly fights with Darryl. There are several young ladies who are interested only in their own affairs. They aren't the least bit cooperative."

It is here that communication is so very important. You have to show this group of youngsters that they need to be able to read and comprehend what they are reading, and that this is what you are teaching them. Or they must be able to handle decimals, because our monetary system is based on the decimal system. Whatever you are teaching, you point out, you are teaching because they need this information.

If you can convince them of the truth of what you are saying, you may gain their cooperation. It is true, of course, that there may be other problems, and we will attempt to show you how to deal with those in subsequent chapters. However, we cannot stress too strongly the need for communication with the group and with the individual children, particularly with the ones who are disruptive.

It is important that you never label the group or the individual child. Take a positive approach, even with those who are usually disruptive. When a youngster has had a good day and has been cooperative, tell him or her that very same day, "Today it has been a pleasure to have you in this class. I know you can do this type of work every day." If this is true of every child in the group, be sure to make a statement of this type to each one.

## YOUNGSTERS WITH SHORT ATTENTION SPANS _____

Many children do not have severe learning problems but are immature and have very short attention spans. These youngsters need a great deal of physical activity, and if they are kept quiet for long periods of time may well become disruptive, though not seriously so. The key to handling this type of child is, when doing individual or group work, to vary the work. For example, you might have them work at the chalkboard for a few minutes, and then have them work at their seats.

Next, talk to them individually. Then structure a class situation with the entire class participating. The child with the short attention span needs a great deal of variety. Incidentally, this technique will benefit all of the youngsters, for it is an excellent way to prevent boredom and keep them participating actively. If many of your children have the problem of a short attention span (and you will find it far worse immediately before a holiday), look for these "changes of pace" and use them often.

You may read something to them aloud, having selected a story that is interest-packed. Choose material that will hold their attention. You may have them bring in paragraphs they would like to read aloud to the class. Choose subjects that hold the children's attention.

When a child has a short attention span and because of this is slightly disruptive, but is trustworthy, he or she can be the one you may send on errands. You may have him or her give out papers or do other tasks that will get rid of some of the energy that is often part of the cause of the short attention span. By considering this to be a learning problem, you can challenge yourself to find a solution for it.

## BOYS SEEM TO LEARN MORE SLOWLY THAN GIRLS

As teachers of intermediate youngsters know, boys seem to mature more slowly than girls. Boys have their growth spurt from fourteen to fifteen years of age, whereas girls have theirs from thirteen to fourteen in the intermediate school. It's amusing to see a couple walking along, with the boy a head shorter than the girl whose hand he is holding.

We feel that because of this difference in the rate of maturation, which is characteristic of their growth for many years, girls are usually the better students from the time they enter school until high school graduation. In college, the boys overtake them. But in any given class before then, it is usually the girls who outshine the boys.

Their work on concepts and comprehension may not differ, but in written work and often in reading, girls' achievements seem to be markedly better. Neatness, too, is a factor that may cause a teacher to consider work to be satisfactory although it may not be. This difference should be taken into consideration by the teacher. If your boys are more disruptive, they may have had trouble grasping the work you have been covering. They may need more help because they have real learning problems. You may have girls doing tutoring, but here too you can easily structure a situation in connection with physical education where the boys will teach the girls. This is relatively simple to set up and also supplies social situations for the two to interact.

## WE MUST TEACH EVERY CHILD TO READ _____

Because of its effect on the future of every child, it is incumbent on us to teach every child who cannot do so to read. This is a tall order, and we realize its implications, but it is impossible to overemphasize this need. Furthermore, far more often than not it is the child who cannot read who is disruptive. He or she is ashamed and frustrated. Moreover, often the problem has gone unnoticed for years and has not been solved.

If the problem is a severe one, we have suggested the boy or girl be recommended for special help. If *you* can remedy the situation and you make the effort, we are sure the youngster's disruptive behavior will change. We have seen dramatic changes as the child's feelings of adequacy increase. We have seen youngsters actually kiss their teachers when the youngsters found they were able to get their diplomas from intermediate school because they were able to meet the reading requirements.

Make no mistake—children do appreciate your efforts, your labors, and because they are getting special attention, they become your friends. Here is your chance to really accomplish something highly significant—to actually affect a change for the better in a person's life. For, more than anything else, if you teach a child to read, you make further education possible. Without this ability the child is stymied. He or she can rarely achieve academically, and he or she is the first to know it.

On the intermediate level, we've observed that "the bigger they are, the harder they fall." The big boys are so often the ones who, when approached confidentially, will admit, "I can't read so good." What a painful admission for any youngster!

If every teacher accepts the challenge, these children will learn to read, for where one fails, another may succeed. But if we duck it, if we hide behind our subject matter, if we do not accept this responsibility, it is the children who suffer. When they suffer, they become disruptive, and then we suffer. This vicious cycle has to be broken. We strongly suggest that you find out if, behind all of the calling out, all of the shouting, and even all of the fighting born of frustration and boredom, there isn't a youngster who is unable to read.

## MENTAL BLOCKS TO LEARNING _____

How often have you met a person who tells you, "I have a mental block," or words to that effect? One wonders if he or she really has such a block. It is entirely possible he or she may have, for, as our knowledge of psychology has increased, we have learned that certain procedures that were followed by many teachers in the past were the causes of these mental blocks.

To this day one of the authors has suffered the effects of being told, "You are a listener. When the other children sing, you listen." And this was when she was in the second grade! Other teachers have called children "stupid" or told them, "This is just too difficult for you." The subject may not have been too difficult, but merely hearing these words from a teacher can cause the child to form the type of mental block of which we are speaking.

You can prevent mental blocks from developing by being patient. If youngsters seem to be unable to master a topic that you are trying to teach them, it is best to change the subject and return to it on another day. Perhaps you yourself have thought of a different approach. Or perhaps you want to make another try with the previous one, because possibly what you were teaching has sunk in a little bit.

When you find youngsters who are not responding this time, it's important that you find another way to teach the topic. The more techniques you have at your disposal the better. Check your library for books of methods, ask your colleagues for suggestions, or ask your supervisor for assistance. Try not to allow the children to feel their inadequacy, for this may remain with them for the rest of their lives. This can, very often, affect their future learning ability.

We know of intelligent people who have never attempted to attend college because they "knew" they could not pass the intermediate algebra course required for entrance to many colleges. However, we also know of adults who have taken the algebra course and done well after having believed they had mental blocks in regard to arithmetic. They were able to conquer their feelings of inadequacy and give algebra a try.

If you encounter children who seem to close their minds and who actually adopt a mental block attitude, work with them, making sure they have some success in learning in the subject area, be it reading, science, mathematics, or whatever. Take the time to do this, for if they feel defeated in their formative years, their learning problems may become extremely severe.

## GEAR WORK TO THE CHILDREN'S LEVEL _____

Discipline problems are far more prevalent when youngsters are not being taught at their level of comprehension. This may be difficult for the new teacher to determine. If the work is too easy, the boys and girls lose interest, but more slowly than if it is over their heads.

One young teacher was having difficulty with a group of girls in one of her classes. She sought advice from an experienced colleague. He asked her if they ever did their work. "Yes," she replied, "but only when I give them really easy material. So easy it has to be almost babyish." His sage advice to her was to give them work that appeared to be simple but progressed, within the assignment, to more difficult concepts. She found that this technique worked well.

Another means of getting youngsters to participate is to begin with games, bringing in the material you are teaching. Every youngster, including those who are disruptive, seems to love games, and this device cajoles the slow learner. There are many worthwhile books of methods and games published by the Center for Applied Research in Education, West Nyack, New York. These will help you work with the disruptive child who has learning problems.

As suggested, begin with work that seems to be readily understood by every youngster, and go on from there. When starting a new topic, determine by questioning how much the children know about it.

For example, here is some work from the social studies curriculum. "Let's talk about our city," you say. "Who can tell me what services the city gives us? But first, what do we mean by the word *services*?" In this way you are teaching vocabulary as well as social studies, and clarifying for the youngsters exactly what it is you are asking of them. Many of them have learned in the first grade about the police and fire departments. This learning is then enlarged on. From the simple services you could then go on to the more complicated ones.

Remember that you must teach the disruptive child rather than rely on the printed page. Yet it is unfair to give him or her most of your attention. So often this is what happens. Recently a book was published titled *Let the Lady Teach*. The old saying "the squeaky wheel gets the oil" more than tells the story. Often within a class, certain youngsters, the disruptive ones, take up far more of your time than is their share. If you are aware of this, you can prevent this from happening.

Don't be afraid to introduce new vocabulary, but as you do, make sure each child understands the meaning of the words. Repeat them, put them on the board, have the class use them, and incorporate them into your lessons from time to time. If you do not, the new words will be lost to many of the children, especially those with learning problems. The teaching of vocabulary is tremendously important, for a knowledge of words and the ability to use them correctly is one measure of intelligence. Vocabulary is also a large part of standardized reading tests. When you teach it, you enable your youngsters to improve their scores, sometimes dramatically.

One error we've seen teachers make time and again is waiting for the class to quiet down, especially at the beginning of a period. It's then that the disruptive youngsters are in their element, for the rest of the class is not doing anything and can give them attention, and they do. Instead, if you have *written work* on the board, ready for the class to start working on, you will find that many will do it. You can then devote a little attention to getting the others, the disruptive ones, to begin. In this way the other youngsters' time is not wasted. If the work is geared to their level, we've found the majority of youngsters will start on their work if it is ready and waiting for them.

## BUILD THE DISRUPTIVE CHILD'S SELF-ESTEEM _____

Children with learning problems are often the potential dropouts, the ones whose opinion of themselves is so low that they must do something to compensate for what they feel they are lacking. We have seen such youngsters do many disruptive things that are only comprehensible once this factor is taken into consideration. They will find reasons to "cut" school, since the entire situation is a painful one for them. Many have actually forgotten why it was originally painful, but the distaste remains.

From the very first grade it is important that children be made to feel they can be successful in their schoolwork and that even if they are not doing perfect work, what they do is good and acceptable. Classes should be structured so there is an abundance of opportunity for success. How can you do this?

1. By giving simple assignments that every child can accomplish.

2. By gradually making the assignments more advanced and more difficult and helping those youngsters who need the help to complete them. Too often teachers give work and projects to the class and then do not help those who need assistance in finishing them. If you give an assignment, be sure each child has been able to complete it. If you do not, some of them never learn how to finish their work.

3. Even the slowest child can do certain things satisfactorily. Here are some examples of things every child can do:

a. Show-and-tell. This time-honored activity enables each child to show something. (It's a good practice to have on hand a few items so that if a child seems to be unable to bring something in, you can supply it.)

b. Supply a copy of the newspaper and have the children make charts using drawings, paintings, or pictures taken from it.

c. Make montages, using pictures cut from magazines. Select a topic and then have the children find pictures related to it. You may give each child or group a different topic so that there will not be a run on a particular type of picture. Foods that are good for us, sports, means of transportation, and types of buildings, are but a few topics.

d. Care for pets, plants, or fish tanks.

e. Keep the book or supply closets in order.

f. Bring in family pictures for an "Our Families" display, which you then put in a place of honor on a class bulletin board.

g. Find simple tasks that the child who has learning problems is able to accomplish.

It is almost undeniable that children who are unable to read well are also unable to write well—that their penmanship, their sentence structure, and their use of words are of questionable quality. By assisting them in becoming more skilled in these areas, you are aiding them in almost every subject area.

It has been found that there are relatively few teachers who actually teach a child how to write—how to physically hold the pencil or pen and use it, yet this skill is tremendously important. To achieve in school, a child must be able to express himself in written English. The use of a computer or typewriter does not negate this. (Nor does the use of a calculator negate the need for a person to have math skills.)

As youngsters move upward in school, they must be taught study skills. It is amazing just how many young adults entering college have never been taught these skills. These skills should be taught when the boys and girls are very young; taught at their own level, of course. The same is true of composition skills, for this too is extremely important throughout life. In the higher grades youngsters must answer essay questions, and many have no real idea of how to do so.

Skills, we have found, are far more an essential part of a child's background than facts. Without these skills, discipline problems are almost bound to arise.

If a youngster is overenergetic and is being disruptive, call him or her up to your desk and ask, "Can you write me a letter, telling me why you are behaving this way? I am really anxious to find out why. I want you to tell me in a letter." That letter will, very often, be extremely poorly written, and you can then tell the child, "I want to help you improve your writing. I think you can do much better than this. Do you want me to help you write?"

As you go over the letter with him or her, point out the errors and how to correct them. Do this quietly, warmly, but firmly. Get the youngster to see how important it is to improve his or her writing and show that you are confident he or she can do so. In this way you have taken the first step toward improving his or her behavior. By showing your interest in him or her, you start to break down his or her negative attitude.

# CONCLUSION

With children who are behavior problems, the first step you must take is to determine the cause of his or her behavior.

Open the lines of communication—talk to the children quietly and alone if possible, but find out what is troubling them. Very often you will discover the problem to be their lack of ability in reading or arithmetic. The children whose lack of skills causes them to become frustrated and feel inadequate are the ones who many times become the discipline problems in your class.

It's important that you determine specifically which skills these children are lacking and then teach the skills to them. The gaps in children's education cannot be ignored, for if they are, the problems become worse and worse.

These children cannot be taught by giving them reading assignments, for the chances of them learning in this way are very slight. Other factors too must be taken into consideration. For example, the child whose attention span is very short needs a great deal of variety in his or her educational life.

Every child needs to be able to read and write, and every teacher should be willing to assume the responsibility for the teaching of these fundamental skills. Your problem children are so often crying for just such teaching. Listen to them, try to help them, and you will find that they become far less troublesome in your classes.

The child with learning problems is the one we are bound by duty to help. We cannot ask it of the child's parents, or anyone else. It is in the area of skills that we must really help the child progress, for the boy or girl who cannot read or write, or does not have the basic, rudimentary arithmetic skills, may be doomed to failure all of his or her life.

# 6

## WORKING WITH THE FIGHTER OR THE QUARRELER

Big or small, fat or thin, boy or girl, bright or slow, any child can be a fighter or a quarreler. When you have a fighter or a quarreler in your class, you are bound to have problems. These youngsters cause incidents and provoke others to violent behavior. They are the fuse that smoulders but that may go off at any time. (Let us define our terms: usually a fight is a physical altercation, while a quarrel is a verbal one.)

Of course we have these young people in our schools. There is even the very unfortunate possibility of more and more of them in the future because the babies born of crack-cocaine-smoking mothers are reaching school age and have already shown they have many problems. Yet it is incumbent on us to learn to work with all children to the best of our ability and to try to change those with patterns of aggressive behavior.

When you have children in your class who are fighters, one of the first decisions you must make is whether or not this child is dangerous. If you believe he or she is, speak to his or her previous teachers to prepare yourself for untoward incidents. Should the youngster get into a fight, immediately refer him or her to the administration and to the school guidance staff.

Boys or girls who behave in this manner often need the services of professional counselors, and if the child gets into one fight in your class, discuss the case with the individuals mentioned as soon as possible. To ignore the incident may mean you are inviting another one. Of course, you will be working with the youngster as well, because it often requires a long time before you can obtain any sort of outside help for him or her, and time may be of the essence.

## DETERMINE WHY THE CHILD IS FIGHTING _____

There are myriad causes for why youngsters fight. Possibly the most serious is the fact that they have seen this as a way of life at home. They may witness disagreements constantly (and, too often, brutal ones), and since these usually go unresolved, the youngsters learn an antisocial pattern of behavior. If quarreling and fighting is a steady diet for them, one may expect them to regurgitate it in school.

Or the youngsters may have anger and hostility within themselves that has built up over a period of years and that they give vent to when they are no longer willing or able to control themselves. These emotions come to the surface all too easily.

Some girls and boys are psychologically ill, and the compensation and adaptation they have developed to cope with the illness may disappear temporarily, and they may suddenly break out in fighting. These disturbed youngsters usually present the severest problems.

There are scores of other, less serious reasons. We often live and go to school under crowded conditions. Pushing and shoving result, and it doesn't take much for a fight to develop. The population explosion, which is already taking place, makes this a constant problem, for which we should prepare our boys and girls. We can do so by teaching them how to get along with one another when an incident of this type occurs.

Attention seeking, very often from members of the opposite sex, is a strong catalyst. So are deeds such as throwing spitballs or pin-sticking. One of the major causes of fighting in the intermediate school we have found is talebearing.

This is but a small sampling of the precipitating causes of fighting. Our task, however, is not to list the causes but to remove them if at all possible. Quarreling is usually easier to control than fighting. Since we are most interested in avoiding an incident of either type, let us begin with that point.

## STOP INCIDENTS BEFORE THEY START _____

1. At the beginning of the second week after you return to school for the fall term, establish within your class rules in regard to behavior. Have the youngsters suggest a "Code of Behavior." Write this code on the board and have them copy it into their notebooks.

One of the items should deal with quarreling, another with fighting. Make sure all of the youngsters understand the seriousness of these situations. The time to discuss them is when there is no such action going on and when the consequences of these deeds can be brought out clearly and carefully. It's wise to give examples of causes, such as talebearing.

2. State your expectations clearly. "I know that every one of you will use self-control," you say to the class. Then ask, "What do I mean by *self-control*?" and discuss that concept. Teach the idea that every one of us, youngsters and teacher alike, must respect one another. Class discussions of this topic can prove to be very important and can be a great help to you in maintaining good discipline.

3. When problems between youngsters arise, encourage them to come to you so that you can act as an arbitrator or mediator. (The difference between the two is interesting. An arbitrator acts as a judge and gives a decision regarding the matter before him or her. A mediator acts as a intermediary, helping the two parties reconcile their differences themselves. You'll be called on to act in each of those capacities at different times.)

You will find the youngsters will come to you if they are convinced you are fair and unprejudiced. If you show no favoritism, they will feel comfortable approaching you. They should know by your attitude on previous occasions that you are interested in helping them solve their problems.

We've had youngsters come to us who were asked for money and then threatened by their own classmates. They did not go to their own teacher with their complaints because they had no confidence in the teacher, and in his or her ability to handle the situation. But we know of other teachers who under similar circumstances were able to solve the problem themselves.

You must assure the youngsters not once but often that you are willing and anxious to be of assistance, and that you really can help them when the need arises.

Encourage your children to come to you *before* a fight occurs so that you and they can prevent it from happening. "Michael is going to beat me up at three o'clock," Danielle tells you. You've heard this complaint a score of times. You find Michael and talk to him and Danielle at the same time. "What started this situation?" you ask. Then add, "It's more important that we settle it."

So often you will find talebearing, name-calling, or even innocent pushing in the halls to be the cause. Whatever the reason, the first order of business is to settle the argument to the satisfaction of both parties. Discussion, discussion, and more discussion! This is real teaching, for it is teaching one of the really important concepts of living, that we must talk out our difficulties and sometimes make compromises. What could be more important?

4. In addition to the "Code of Behavior" that you set up with your class, establish your own rules and inform the class of them. These cannot be ironclad. You must be flexible, for rules must at times be varied to fit the situation. However, this should occur only rarely.

You have to be fair and yet firm. Children need rules and are far more comfortable with them than without them. If they know that fighting is not tolerated, that will help prevent some incidents—not all, but some. Furthermore, your children will respect you for having established the rules and for having the strength to enforce them.

5. If the school has regulations in regard to fighting, make sure the youngsters are aware of them. In many schools, if a child is involved in an altercation, the parents are sent for immediately. If such a rule is not in force in your school, we suggest you establish it in your classroom. You need the parents' cooperation when disciplining a child involved in a fight, and you would certainly send for them anyway. If the boys and girls are aware of this, it usually proves to be somewhat of a deterrent.

In the event that a youngster is found to have a weapon of any kind—be it a knife, gun, or brass knuckles—the youngster must be sent to the principal immediately. He or she presents a distinct danger to the other youngsters, whom it is your duty to protect.

The same is true if you find a boy or girl with any sort of drug, or a bottle of alcohol or glue (which they use for sniffing). These are signs of big trouble and must be handled accordingly.

Often parents are not available for conferences, yet these can be of tremendous importance. One school district, the Newton-Conover School District in Catawba County, North Carolina, has solved this problem by sending counselors to the parents' workplace. Eight counselors visit workplaces one day of each month for 15-minute conferences.

This system results from the fact that North Carolina has the highest percentage of working mothers in the nation. The purpose of these visits is to get the parents more involved in their children's education. However, such visits might well be applied when it is necessary to see a parent because of fighting and other serious offenses.

Furthermore, letting the youngsters know that a school official is going to visit his or her parents' workplace if he or she gets into serious trouble can prove to be an excellent deterrent. This is something that no boy or girl wants to have happen. He or she must know beforehand, however, that this procedure will be followed if it is to prove effective in preventing problems.

6. While teaching every subject area, discuss the importance and the necessity for getting along with other people. You are teaching your children to be good human beings, compassionate and caring about others. This cannot be a by product but must be a basic concept, taught in many firm, strong lessons. Call it human relations, or brotherhood, or whatever, but teach your youngsters how to work together and how to understand each other. If youngsters begin to quarrel or if a fight breaks out, bring the issues out into the open by discussing them and by attempting to show motivation as well as immediate causes.

It is critical that you teach this kind of problem solving, that of talking out a problem with one's adversary. Help your children develop insights into the causes of quarreling and fighting. Give them some ideas about sensitivity and how easy it is to hurt the feelings of others. In short, assist them in growing into sensitive human beings and help them view a problem from both their side and that of their adversary. Try to get them to "put themselves in the other person's shoes."

7. Remember, nature abhors a vacuum, and idleness causes activity, which may well be of an unwholesome variety. Your youngsters should have a great deal of work to do. Keep them busy with ongoing projects of all kinds. Even first graders can work on picture dictionaries when they have completed their assigned tasks. Older children can keep library books in their desks, to be read whenever they have finished their work. As soon as a class enters your room, you should have work for them to start—work written on either a chart or on the chalkboard. (If you put this work on charts, you will be able to keep a file of them for use year after year.) This preventative measure is essential for good discipline.

8. Many problems arise just before holidays. Youngsters are excited, and anything can erupt, even in the best of classes. You can preclude this if you plan work that the youngsters will find exciting and especially interesting. The months after Easter until the summer recess fall into this same category. Trips at this time of year are very worthwhile and are excellent because they can be used to motivate the youngsters.

9. Never ignore a quarrel. If you haven't the time at the moment, make sure that you speak with the youngsters who were involved as soon as possible. This is important because the quarrel may smolder and break out again at another time.

The same is true if a boy or girl comes to you and tells you there is going to be a fight. If he or she is involved, keep the youngster with you until you can determine exactly what the situation is. But be sure you heed all warnings, for they may be very important.

10. Never leave a class unsupervised, for if you do you are looking for trouble. By doing so, you structure the situation for something negative to happen. The times we are living in are very chaotic, and we must guard against this chaos spreading to our classroom.

We know of one situation where the class was working quietly and the teacher stepped out into the hall to speak to a parent. In the course of less than a minute, a fight broke out, and a child was hit in the eye by a flying object and hurt seriously.

11. If your potential fighters are hyperactive, give them physical activity to use up as much of their energy as possible. We followed this principle with one boy who was a very serious discipline problem. An exhibition of the skills the children had learned in their physical education class was being given in the gymnasium. The boy moved a hundred chairs from the cafeteria to the gymnasium to supply seats for the audience. He then moved the chairs back after the program was completed. This proved to be an excellent means for constructive action, and his energy was channeled into useful activity. He did the job quickly, efficiently, and with much pride. Furthermore, his teacher was able to praise him, and he reacted beautifully. It was one of the few times he had been praised in school rather than chastised. (Of course, no child should be permitted to do such physical work unless his or her health card has been checked to be sure he or she has no medical problem.)

12. Reward good behavior. So often children are chastised when they are disruptive, but their good behavior goes unnoticed. Many teachers have found that rewards are a worthwhile technique.

Perhaps have a picnic. The youngsters can bring their lunches, and you can supply drinks or dessert of some kind. A trip to a local pizzeria at three o'clock is another great favorite. You might even show a suitable video on a Friday afternoon.

One highly successful teacher took her class for ice cream every Friday afternoon if there had been no discipline problems during the week. (This meant not a single incident.) Considering that her class was known as "the killers" by previous teachers, one can appreciate how good her method proved to be. The youngsters actually kept the disruptive boys and girls in line. The financial outlay was minimum, considering the entire picture, and the teacher earned a reputation far and wide for her ability to teach—because with good discipline one can actually teach, and she did.

However, do not reward any class when the reward has not been earned. If you are lax once and the youngsters learn that they can manipulate you, you'll have more trouble than if you never tried the technique in the first place.

## HANDLE PROBLEMS AS SOON AS THEY ARISE _____

1. "Without a bell, they came out swinging!" What do you do if a fight starts in your classroom?

**Use your voice as your weapon.** Shriek at those fighting, and shriek as loudly as you possibly can. Shriek in their ears, if possible. Often this will actually stop them from hitting each other. It is the least dangerous course of action you can take. Instruct every child nearby to move away, to keep anyone else from getting hurt or involved.

Send two youngsters for help. You should, from the very first day of school, know where to send for help in any kind of emergency situation. Send one child to the principal's office and one to the dean or another member of the administrative staff.

You will have learned, from the very first day of your teaching career, what the district or school policy is in regard to breaking up a fight. You may not be able to touch the youngsters, in which case you will have to continue shrieking as loudly as you can until help arrives.

If you are permitted to take further action and your shrieking has not helped, try the following procedure: If you feel you can be effective while being very careful of your own safety, try to pull the hair of both combatants. This is one strong emergency measure that I have used to separate battling youngsters on more than one occasion. I have done this with boys considerably taller and heavier than I am. The youngsters do not expect you to do this, and the element of surprise works in your favor. The fighting will usually stop.

However, it may require more than one adult to stop a fight. You must judge the situation, and you should be very cautious. A blow to the eye may permanently blind you, and blows to other parts of the body can be serious as well.

Separate the youngsters who are fighting. Then help them calm down and cool off. Sit them down, but far apart. Talk calmly and quietly with each one alternately. At this point, try to get them to see the problem they have presented—that this is a highly dangerous, most serious situation. Their parents *must* be sent for, although the fighters will probably beg you not to do so.

2. Determine why the youngsters were quarreling or fighting. If your handling of the incident is to prove effective, you must determine why it happened. Here are some of the questions for which you should try to learn answers:

a. Have these youngsters been involved in other incidents of this type?

b. Are these incidents frequent or rare?

c. Is either child prone to fighting? Does either one of them have a hot temper?

d. Does one or the other of the fighters have difficulty expressing him- or herself? (Often the inability to communicate causes many incidents.)

e. Is either of these youngsters mentally slow? Does either have difficulty understanding rules?

f. Is either having problems at home?

g. Does either child have difficulty relating to other youngsters or to adults?

h. Was a third party, an instigator, involved?

When you have the answers to these questions you have clues to the way in which you should handle the situation.

You must first discuss the fight with both parties as soon as each has cooled off. We have found that discussion is of little or no value when one or both of the participants is still fuming.

In your discussion bring out the fact that each human being is different, has his or her own personality, and that we have to learn to take this into consideration. There are people who have hot tempers, but, you point out to the youngsters, they have had to learn to control them. This control is very, very important.

If a third party was involved, what was his or her role? It has been our experience that the vast majority of quarrels and fights are instigated by third parties. They want to see "some action." They start it with remarks such as, "So-and-so said you called me such-and-such," or "X said you're gonna beat me up at three o'clock," or "I heard you said my mother (or father, sister, or brother, or even aunt, uncle, or cousin) is a _____."

When a third party instigates the difficulty, that person must immediately be brought into the discussion. (You may wish to make a rule in regard to this. We suggest, however, that you do this only if the situation has occurred—ex post facto, so to speak. If the youngsters have not been talebearing, why give them ideas?) Talk with the instigator and very strongly warn him or her not to continue this type of behavior. Should it continue, he or she will be treated as if he or she were in a fight.

If a youngster has been fighting because of a misunderstanding or because he or she has difficulty communicating a specific idea, it is a relatively simple matter to straighten the problem out. However, the task then becomes a greater one, for this child needs help communicating, and it becomes your job to assist him or her. Be sure the child comprehends why this incident took place so that there is a better chance it will not be repeated.

With children who are slow, it is important that the rules be spelled out for them. You must be careful and make sure they understand the rules, for they may interpret your words literally. We told one youngster he must not get into a fight because of special circumstances in his past history. He seemed to understand what he was told. However, he did have a difference with several boys, and instead of actually doing battle with them himself, he sent his sisters around. He obeyed my words. He wasn't going to get into any fights himself!

At times, especially on Monday mornings at 8:30, I have heard words such as "Mrs. Karlin, can I sit in your office this morning? I know I'm going to get into a fight with someone today." This request was heard once or twice a month, and I learned to honor it. When I did not, the youngster invariably got into difficulty—usually within an hour after I sent him or her to class. Problems arise at home over the weekend and they are often unresolved. On Monday these children come into school and are almost frantic. This situation will be discussed in a subsequent chapter.

Should you realize a child in your class is "uptight," or very upset, try to speak privately with him or her. If you don't seem to reach the youngster, which is possible, send him or her to the guidance counselor or assistant principal. If you can preclude a quarrel or a fight, you'll surely agree that it is important for you to do so. We know of one extreme case in which a boy actually punched a male teacher who was trying to stop him from running in the hall. It turned out that the child was furious with his own father.

Children who have trouble relating to other youngsters or to adults are more difficult to help. Here again your task is to bring such children out of their shells and teach them how to communicate with others. They may need professional help from the guidance staff, but you can assist them by having them work closely with other boys and girls in committees, for example. Choose outgoing youngsters who will draw the introverted youngsters out. Expressing your acceptance of them will also mean a great deal, for they may not know that you consider them worthwhile. They are easily hurt, so explain to them that you will happily give them as much attention as you can but that you are limited by time.

Check into your children's backgrounds during the very first days of the term. Learn which youngsters have had difficulty in school previously and speak with each one of them privately. Tell them you're aware of the problems they've had, usually because of volatile tempers, and that you would like to help them learn to control themselves. Make sure they understand that a short temper is an acceptable personality trait and that they can admit to having one. (Probably they are copying this behavior because they've seen it at home, and you would not want it to appear that you are in any way criticizing their parents.) However, outbursts cannot be permitted in school.

Show these children how important it is that they learn to control their tempers. Encourage them to tell you about times they have successfully controlled themselves, especially while they were in school. One youngster very proudly told me, "I almost got into a fight today, but I held my temper. Aren't you proud of me?" Indeed I was, for he was a boy who frequently had problems of this nature. Encourage your youngsters to take pride in this self-discipline.

You will find too that youngsters who have never fought before suddenly become "lions." This is often true when they suddenly begin to mature and "the hormones start working." Nevertheless, for whatever reason, once a boy or girl fights or quarrels, he or she needs your special attention.

Every human being needs love and affection. Never withdraw it, even when you are very angry. This is not to say that you shouldn't let a child know you are displeased. Of course you should. But get over it. Do not harbor a grudge. Once an incident is over, it must be considered over. Write a report of it for your files and then let the matter drop. Give the youngster a second chance, and even a third or fourth. By this type of treatment, firm but fair and loving, you teach the child to be a worthwhile human being. Realize that it is entirely possible that you are the only one in his or her life who is doing so.

It's interesting to note that often two youngsters who get into a fight are close friends. Once they've fought, don't allow them to sit together. When the fight or quarrel is over, they often become friends again, but allowing them to sit together may not be the best policy. You have to use your own judgment. If you feel the youngsters can get along together, allow them to do so, but discuss the incident with them first. Emphasize the point that the incident cannot be repeated.

## CONTROL THE CLASS WITH FIGHTERS OR QUARRELERS _____

1. Keep the class with disruptive children in it as busy as you possibly can. Find work that interests them and that is relevant to their lives. If acceptable to the administration, you might inject into the curriculum work on the immediate environment. For example, you might institute a clean-up campaign in the area of the school or plant trees and other plants. In class,

construction work or drawing seems to work well, as does making clay figures and dioramas.

Girls as well as boys get into fights. We have found that a class project, such as building and furnishing a dollhouse, can involve even obstreperous students. We told one particularly disruptive girl, "If you get into another fight, you won't be permitted to work on the dollhouse." It actually deterred her from fighting for several months, and she made several valuable contributions to the project.

2. Have as many periods of physical education as your administration will allow. During these periods, teach games that require skill and have the youngsters practice these skills. Use competitions to entice and hold the children's interest.

When you teach basketball to both boys and girls, you teach them very valuable skills, since basketball is often played in schoolyards and on the streets of cities and towns. As you know, many college scholarships are won by those who excel in basketball. (This is true for both young men and young women.)

3. Discuss the concept of fairness. Make the youngsters aware of the fact that it is unfair to have to spend an inordinate amount of time on the children who fight or quarrel. If the class understands that they will have to forgo some of the pleasant activities, such as basketball, because of the time being taken up by the disruptive youngsters, they will pressure their disruptive classmates to behave.

When dealing with any boy or girl, stress again the concept of fairness. Make sure no youngster feels you are picking on him or her. Assure this child, "Whatever I do for you, I would do for every child in this class. If I must be stern with you, I would be the same way with anyone else in similar circumstances."

4. When problems come up, discuss them with the class. Don't try to hide anything that happens, because the youngsters will learn about the incidents anyway. It is far better to have them hear about the incidents from you than to get whispered half-truths. This openness helps build their confidence in you as a person, and you will find as a result that they will come to you with their problems.

5. Use the concept of maturity as a basis for discussion and for your expectations of your children. You may tell them, "I know all of you are mature enough to discuss this problem." Discuss with them how certain behavior is characteristic of boys and girls at various ages. (Though we wouldn't tell them, for example, that first graders often pick their noses, even though they do.) Tie into this the idea that at their age (whatever that may be) they are mature enough to settle differences by talking about them

rather than by fighting. We've found that youngsters want to be told they are mature. They always consider that to be a compliment. Help them learn that sometimes the advice of other people will enable them to cope with a problem they are having.

6. You may wish to introduce the idea that people of whatever age may have serious problems, including their parents, and as a result be tense, anxious, or, to use the jargon of the day, "uptight." Teach the youngsters that this is the time to be understanding of them rather than ready to argue or fight with them.

We had one boy say to us after such a discussion that he could now understand why his mother and he fought so often. "There are nine kids in our family," he told me, "and my father works on a tanker. He's out to sea six months at a time. I never thought of how hard this is on my mother."

It is possible to do a real service if you can get through to the boys and girls that their parents have problems too, many of which the youngsters do not realize. These problems can make the adults very difficult to get along with. In this era of family problems of all kinds and of a very great generation gap, any teaching we can do to make youngsters understand the difficult situations that may exist is very worthwhile.

7. You may want to point out to the children that if any child is nasty to them, it may be because the offender is ill or tired, or has just had problems with someone else. In a word, he or she may have had a very bad day. Tell the child who was offended, "Because we all want to be worthwhile human beings, we will not get angry, but we'll try to understand the other person's unhappiness and not add to it."

The offender should have someone to whom he or she can talk. If you don't have the time, refer the child to the guidance counselor or to another adult who can listen and perhaps help the youngster.

8. You may wish to allow the youngsters to act out situations in which they express some of the emotions with which they are having difficulty coping. They can compose playlets or even act spontaneously. This type of activity is more easily done with older children, but you can try it with younger ones, giving them more direction. This will probably not work too well with every class, for you need verbal youngsters who are comfortable with words and are used to speaking. However, the attempt can prove useful, if not entirely successful.

## GAIN PARENTAL COOPERATION

It is an absolute must that you work with the parents of any child who you feel is a potential fighter, especially if that boy or girl has shown this type of behavior previously. Ask the parents quite frankly for their advice how to handle the youngster. You may gain information that will be of great help to you.

In the event that a quarrel or fight breaks out, it is usually a school rule that the parents be sent for immediately. Parents are often able to prevent further incidents, and they are, for the most part, very cooperative—providing they know that you are fair and that the parents of both youngsters who were fighting were called into school. Be sure to use the approach "What can we do, working together, to help your child?"

Many children never fight or quarrel in all of the years they are in school. Others will have only one or two incidents, mainly because they are deterred by parental disapproval or by their parents' annoyance at being called into school under these circumstances. Other boys and girls get into difficulty regularly because of foolish remarks or pranks.

To a great extent, youngsters reflect the attitude of their parents. If the parents are impressed with your interest and sincerity, it cannot help but rub off on the child. And if Adam is a fighter, or Eve carries tales, the parent may be able to stop this behavior—at least in school.

## THE EFFECTS OF PEER PRESSURE AND TELEVISION _____

It is impossible to ignore the effects of both peer pressure and television on youngsters. Boys and girls are extremely impressionable, and fighting and violence have become daily fare for many of them. The average youngster spends more time watching television than he or she does in school. Outside of the home, he or she will often look up to the older boys and girls, and if they are fighters, the younger ones may well emulate their behavior.

I recall one particular day when almost every young man, three hundred of them, in the intermediate school cafeteria was throwing punches at his fellows. There had been a World Heavyweight Championship fight the night before, and each boy had to do his imitation of the battle, which had ended very quickly with a knockout. We stopped the jabbing very quickly, before anyone was hurt. We learned that the scene had been repeated, on a smaller scale, in a nearby high school.

How do we deal with these stimuli? Again, discussion is the only answer. In the case of the intermediate school I discussed the incident with each class for a short time, immediately after the lunch hour ended. We spoke of the training necessary for boxing, and how boxing is not just throwing punches at one another. Then I reminded the youngsters that there was a school rule in regard to fighting and that what had happened in the cafeteria, should the behavior be repeated, would be considered fighting.

Peer pressure cannot be overestimated. It can also be used constructively. At times the help of an older brother or sister can be enlisted. Some teachers have found this to work well, particularly if they already had the older sibling in one of their classes.

There are times when other boys or girls will get involved in what was previously a fight between two youngsters. Obviously this is to be avoided, for the situation can become very difficult to control. It can be prevented by a lengthy discussion, with great emphasis on the need for everyone else to cooperate by staying out of the fighting. There must be rules in this regard—either school or class rules—and it is extremely important that there not be a general melee. From my experience, youngsters will show this type of cooperation if the need for it is explained fully and repeated from time to time.

## KEEP ANECDOTAL RECORDS

Because fighting may be, and often is, an indication that a youngster is seriously disturbed, an anecdotal record must be kept of each of his or her disruptive incidents. This record need not be long or involved, but it is a good idea to include the action you take in response to the child's action. Include the date and location of the incident too. Figure 6 shows an example.

### Figure 6

March 3

Danielle Doe in a quarrel with Jessica Smith. In Room 307. Danielle claims Jessica pushed her. We discussed the incident, and Danielle was shown the possibility that this was accidental, and that Jessica had not meant to push her.

March 31

Danielle Doe and Jessica Smith in a fight in the girls' locker room. Danielle claimed Jessica pulled her hair. Jessica denied it; said it was done by another girl. I saw Mrs. Doe and Mrs. Smith. Mrs. Doe said Danielle is quarrelsome at home as well. She said she would try to speak with Danielle.

April 16

Danielle Doe and Mike Jones fighting in school cafeteria. Mike said Danielle accused him of having taken her dessert from her tray. Mike denied taking it; said he was just teasing Danielle. We discussed teasing and the fact that every person reacts differently to it. Mike promised not to do it again. Danielle said she didn't believe him. I spoke with Mrs. Jones and again with Mrs. Doe. She said she was going to take away some of Danielle's privileges to stop her from fighting in school.

## CONCLUSION _____

There are many reasons why children quarrel or fight. Some incidents are caused by situations within the classroom; others stem from difficulties at home or among friends. However, our prime interest as teachers is to stop such incidents before they start. We can do this by setting rules and enforcing them and by making the youngsters aware of the fact that we expect them to exercise self-control and that we will act as mediators or arbitrators when necessary.

The youngsters should know too that should they engage in fighting, their parents will be called into school. This often acts as a strong deterrent. Above all, they must be taught how to settle their differences without fighting, and we must show them how to make compromises.

Because we feel many teachers do not know how to handle a fight in their classroom, we will summarize the steps to take. It is possible, indeed probable, that you will never need this information, but we believe it is far better to be forearmed. You cannot simply stand by watching. You must take immediate, firm action. *Steps one, two, four, five, and six are mandatory. Step three is not.*

1. Try to separate the youngsters. You can do this by shrieking, even directly into the children's ears. The sound of your voice may actually do the job.

2. At the same time, send monitors for help. Send for the supervisor and/or the principal.

3. If you feel strong enough, grasp each child by the hair. However, be very careful not to get hurt yourself. The pain inflicted by pulling the child's hair will disrupt the fight and prevent any injury from occurring. (If you feel this type of action may at some point be necessary, you may want to check with your principal to determine whether or not it is acceptable for you to do this.)

4. When you separate the youngsters, send one or both to different rooms or to the office to prevent a recurrence of the altercation.

5. Try to remain as calm as possible, for your own protection as well as the protection of the rest of the class.

6. Never allow a fight to be ignored. You must meet with the parents, and record the incident in the children's anecdotal record. Your supervisor must be informed and the dangers of the fight discussed with the youngsters who were involved, privately, and with the entire class.

We know of one teenage boy who suffered a brain hemorrhage and died as a result of a classroom fight over a girl. Knowing in advance what steps to take and then taking them may preclude such terrible, serious consequences.

However, you can almost certainly avoid this if you take steps to prevent it. By your attitude toward the youngsters, by your awareness of their mood, by your structuring of the classroom situation, by the confidence the youngsters have in you, you can do a great deal to avoid altercations. Even with a child or children with serious problems in your class, you can and must help them to cope with them. This can be done, if not 100 percent of the time, then close to it.

Your most potent method is teaching. By teaching your children to try to understand one another and to be aware of problems other youngsters may have, you may effect changes in their lives. (An excellent composition or guidance lesson is possible using the topic "The Problems Kids [use that word!] My Age Have to Face." Assure the boys and girls that they need not write their names on these papers and that the papers will remain anonymous. This is usually a learning experience for you, the teacher, and the results may amaze you. You might motivate the lesson by reading letters from one of the syndicated columns of the type that are so popular today. If your children open up, your eyes very well may too.)

Teach the skills of making compromises, of being tolerant, and teach your children by your personal example to respect and care for each other.

Parental assistance and involvement is tremendously helpful. Parents should be called in and informed if their child shows a tendency to fight or to quarrel. Most of the time this behavior is manifested at home as well as in school, but not necessarily.

If you have children with serious behavior problems in your class, be sure you refer them to the guidance counselor and to the administration. Often such children benefit from counseling and from the one-to-one relationship. If the counselor cannot help the child effect changes, he or she may refer the youngster to an outside agency.

Administration, too, should be made aware of those children who are causing serious difficulty in the classroom, and fighting is surely serious. It is necessary that the teacher, the parents, the guidance counselor, and the administrators act as a team to work with this particular type of problem, for then the solution is possible. If the fighting or quarreling is overlooked, the youngster usually becomes more and more belligerent, and the possibility of his or her functioning in the school situation becomes doubtful.

# 7

# THE ATTENTION SEEKER AND THE HYPERACTIVE CHILD

How many times have you looked at a child and thought, "That child really just can't sit still!" And you are more correct than you imagined! He or she almost literally cannot, and expecting him or her to do so is almost foolish, for that expectation is a carry-over from the days when children sat with their hands folded and had to listen—just listen—to the teacher. Unfortunately, children of this type may twitch and turn; jump around in their seats; doodle and draw; or fool around with others, talk, and become disruptive. They are hyperactive and have more energy than they require. If we do not take this into consideration, we will not meet their needs as individuals.

By the same token, how many times have you thought, "That child will do anything for attention!" That, too, is a truism, for in our classes are many children who will, almost literally, do anything for the limelight. Whether it is a positive or negative action, does not matter, so long as it is noticed.

Attention seeking and hyperactivity are not usually serious problems because neither, as a rule, is born of hostility. They are, however, serious in that they take up an inordinate amount of your time and of your class's time and often prevent the majority of your youngsters from working and learning. Attention-seeking and hyperactive youngsters can cause your nerves, as well as those of their classmates, to fray. Since these behavior patterns have many areas in common, we are considering them together. They are, of course, not the same, and we shall differentiate when necessary.

Attention seeking is usually the result of psychological causes, whereas hyperactivity is the result of physical ones. Both types of youngsters may run around a great deal, jump up and down, and leave their seats countless numbers of times, ostensibly to sharpen their pencils or to throw something into the wastebasket. Both types may wave their hands constantly in answer to your questions and may even call out to be noticed.

However, it is the attention seeker who tries to really dominate the class and who may resort to the use of unsuitable language. He or she may also dress in an outlandish manner. Neither type of child fits into a mold, not should we attempt to put him or her into one. The hyperactive child may doodle, tap, or whistle, and this may well carry over into adulthood. Sometimes the youngster bites his or her nails, or scratches various parts of his or her anatomy. Such youngsters may be unaware of their actions until you call their attention to them. Years ago they might have been called "nervous," a layman's term rarely heard today.

## CAUSES OF ATTENTION SEEKING _____

Attention-seeking children, we have often found, have many siblings and may come from homes where they receive little attention and often little love and affection. In such homes children are to be "seen but not heard" (a cliche of yesteryear). They may act out in class and become disruptive because they know the teacher will not beat them, although their parents might.

On the other hand, they may be only-children or come from a small family but still be starved for attention. They may come from a single-parent home, or both parents may be employed, and the youngster is a "latchkey child." Or the parents may be very occupied with their own interests. For whatever reason, the youngster has a strong psychological need for attention, a need that is not being fulfilled.

This is not to say that all youngsters do not need attention, for they surely do. We know of one gentle principal, Mr. Charles Finkensieper of Staten Island, who told a beautiful story of a pinch on the cheek and what it taught him.

One of the second-grade classes was being dismissed, and as the children walked by him, he reached out and very gently and lovingly pinched the cheek of a gorgeous little blond-haired girl, with baby blue eyes and rosy cheeks. She was truly a picture. As he did this, he saw out of the corner of his eye a little boy nearby who had witnessed this and was sticking his tongue out at him. "I understood immediately," Mr. Finkensieper said. "I went over and patted him on the head too. I realized the little beauty got all the attention and this boy was crying out for it."

Don't adults, too, sometimes fight for attention when we feel we aren't getting our share?

Many incidents involve children who become frustrated when they do not get the attention they are seeking, and who do more and more outlandish things. We have seen seventh and eighth graders come to school in clothing they know is unsuitable and for which they can be sure they will be reprimanded (one example being "see-through" blouses on young ladies who are quite mature). Indeed, this concept is very important—namely, that negative attention is preferable to none at all.

We recall an incident that occurred when the son of one of the authors was three years old. The family was entertaining some friends outdoors. The father was very involved in a heated discussion and was completely ignoring his little boy. When this became intolerable to the child, he picked up a broken branch that had been lying on the ground, dragged it over, and hit his daddy with it. The little one knew he would be punished, but any punishment would be preferable to being ignored. Very often young children constantly ask, "Why, Daddy, why?" or "Why, Mommy?" One reason is because in this way they can get and keep the parent's attention.

An attention seeker may be very bright, very slow, or any variation in between. He or she is usually, though not always, an extrovert. A high school friend of one of the authors became a movie star. In school she was most obnoxious, for she always sought the limelight in every class.

## CAUSES OF HYPERACTIVITY

It's been estimated that from one to five percent of youngsters of elementary school age are hyperactive. This may be the result of some type of brain dysfunction. There is also a theory that additives and colorings in foods can cause this type of behavior. NOTE: Although hyperactivity and attention deficit disorder (ADD) are frequently found in the same children, they are *not* the same disorder.

One of the major problems that face the teacher of a hyperactive youngster is that he or she is in constant motion. We observed one eighth grader literally do a dance while being spoken to by a teacher. When asked why he was moving around so much, the boy replied, quite indignantly, "I'm not." Then he added, "Can't a kid even stand still the way he wants to?"

One of the major problems one faces in teaching the hyperactive child is that the child can't concentrate for any long period of time. As a result, he or she doesn't complete the assignments you give and may fall behind. The excess energy hyperactive children have makes teaching them a real challenge.

## TECHNIQUES TO TRY WITH HYPERACTIVE CHILDREN AND ATTENTION SEEKERS

First and foremost, you must try to communicate with the attention seeker or the hyperactive child to establish rapport and to try to get through to him or her. Listen to the youngster and try to determine the cause of his or her behavior. Give the boy or girl some insight into the cause, but not too much. Do not burden a child beyond his or her years. (We recall one mother, a psychologist, explaining to her four-year-old son that he had to return his two-year-old sister's toys immediately because, she told him, "Your sister is a little girl, and she has a much lower frustration tolerance than you do." As the words came out of the lady's mouth, she decided to resume her career, which had been on hold, as soon as possible. "How could I possibly expect a four year old to understand what I was talking about?" she asked.)

If you can, determine the cause of the problem behavior. This will help you understand the child, but may or may not solve the problems presented in class.

When the attention seeker or the hyperactive child is disruptive, use the approach, "I'm sure you don't want to take the time from the rest of the class. It's not fair to do that. I can't spend a great deal of time on any one boy or girl. I'm sure you understand that."

If the behavior continues, you may want to repeat those words and then add "I think it may be necessary for me to ignore you if you can't learn to control yourself." Ignoring a youngster can be very effective, but it is also very cruel. While you may threaten to do this, we feel it should be done only as a last resort. For these types of children, it is really too strong. Emphasize instead the idea of being fair to all the other boys and girls.

Like every child, the attention seeker and the hyperactive youngster seek love and affection. You may find that sitting quietly with them for a few minutes, perhaps during lunch hour or after school (if permitted by your school district) and just talking can affect their behavior very positively. Invite them to do so with words such as, "Would you like to sit down and talk with me for a little while?" Rarely will a youngster say no.

In this way, you show a boy or girl you are not punishing him or her. You are just offering the chance to have a chat. If you make your meeting compulsory, it appears you are doing this as a means of reprimanding the child, and the entire slant of the interview changes. The youngster will clam up, and it will take time for you to thaw him or her out. This type of conversation is best done on an individual basis rather than with a group, and it is virtually impossible to do with an entire class. Although this technique is useful for working with the attention seeker or the hyperactive child, it is also really worthwhile for every child in your class. We realize this is difficult, but it is well worth your time and effort.

You may be able to sit with individual children while your class is working on compositions or reading. By doing this occasionally, you can develop rapport more easily. Do not, however, talk only to the attention seekers or hyperactive youngsters.

An extensive research project you can conduct with your class may help you cope with the problems of the attention seeker and possibly, but less likely, with the hyperactive child. When doing research, divide your class into groups. If the youngsters have not already done this type of activity, you must, of course, give them specific instructions, and you must choose topics that are of interest to them. After they have completed their work, have each group report to the class. The hyperactive youngster can be kept busy "looking up" various items.

Make this presentation a formal situation, and invite guests, such as the principal or other supervisors, to make the event even more outstanding. Stress quality, and also be sure that within each group every child participates. After such an activity, be sure to praise the work lavishly if it is praiseworthy. Every child benefits from this, and it is particularly valuable in teaching cooperative behavior.

Assembly programs are excellent for attention seekers and for hyperactive youngsters as well. One of the secrets of preparing and presenting such programs is to work with another class and another teacher. This prevents discipline problems from developing. Have the youngsters write their own plays and perform them. This adds greatly to the value and to the excitement of the activity.

You may wish to set up a "Little Theatre" and have groups perform so that all of the children get an opportunity to participate, but at different times. This may supply an outlet for some of the children, attention-seeking and stage-struck as well. Perhaps you can use an empty classroom, decorate it, put up curtains and scenery, and really convert it into a theater-in-the-round. The children will enjoy this and become very involved. You can then have ushers, stagehands, and a variety of actors and actresses. The venture is a stimulating and challenging one.

## SPECIFIC ACTIVITIES FOR ATTENTION SEEKERS _____

Class discussions are really enjoyed by the attention seeker. It is here, however, that you must be on guard that he or she does not take them over, which is what the youngster who behaves this way attempts, often successfully, to do.

Robert was a ten year old with this problem. His mother came into school asking that his class be changed. "I know Robert is very active in class," she reported. "He always volunteers, and his teacher always calls on him to answer her questions. He was quite happy, but he isn't anymore."

What had happened was that Robert's classmates had taken matters into their own hands. Since the teacher was doing nothing to remedy the situation but was aiding and abetting it, the youngsters decided to ostracize Robert. "My son has no friends," his mother commented. "I can't understand it. He's always talking about some of the kids in the class." Robert was not aware of the reason for the behavior of his classmates. His class could not be changed, so he had to endure the situation until the term ended. However, he was seen by the guidance counselor, who was able to show him how his attention seeking had caused the problem, and he was encouraged to change his behavior. He was able to do so, but only to a limited extent.

The following year, Robert was placed with a different group of youngsters. His new teacher was made aware of the situation and did not allow Robert to monopolize either class discussions or the question-and-answer periods. The boy was able to make and keep some friends and was much happier than he had been. Fortunately, Robert is a bright youngster, and the insights given him by the guidance counselor did make a marked difference in his life.

One technique to be used with attention seekers is the panel discussion. An activity such as this can give this type of youngster an outlet if you assign him or her to be the moderator. The same is true of a "town hall" discussion. You may want to tape-record these programs and replay them. The entire class usually enjoys this. ("I can't believe I sound like that," is the most common comment, for our voices sound different on tape than they do to us.)

Another device you can use is to have the attention seeker actually teach the class. Of course, be aware that this can be resented, so offer the opportunity to other youngsters as well. Prepare the "teacher" in advance by showing him or her just how you plan a lesson and some suggestions of how he or she could proceed. This may be a valuable experience for any child. We know of several teachers who chose their profession because they were given this opportunity when they were in grade school. Here too, choice of topic is one of the major factors, for if a child is working on an area in which he or she is interested, he or she becomes intellectually involved with it. Allow the child to select his or her own subject and then make sure he or she researches it thoroughly. Your objective is to make this lesson successful, and any help you can give the youngster to accomplish this should be given.

Some attention seekers will resort to the use of foul language to gain the attention they so desperately need. Should this be the case, it is essential that you immediately speak with the child and make him or her understand that this behavior will not be tolerated by you because *you have very high standards for every boy and girl in your class.* From experience we know that most children seek to be elevated and do not wish to be considered in any way to be inferior. Show such children that, while they may not be bad or unintelligent, they make a very bad impression when they curse. (Children consider the use of any unsuitable language to be cursing. We have been told not once but a number of times, "My teacher curses." When asked what the teacher actually said, the reply has been, "He said 'Damn it.'")

There is no need for us to write of the preponderance of foul language virtually surrounding all of us, young and old alike. "Four-letter words" abound and are used on television and in films. It is no wonder that boys and girls will repeat them, and repeat them they do, sometimes incessantly. However, insisting that only fine language be used in your classroom and emphasizing high standards, you will find, will work. Everyone wants his or her school, or home, or work to be the best. By using this psychology, you can help the youngsters develop pride in themselves, which every human being needs. "Not every person can do everything well," you can tell your youngsters, "but you can choose your words carefully, so that they reflect the fine person you are." If you try this approach, the favorable results may surprise you.

You may find that it's necessary for you to teach many new words to some of your youngsters, for they may not have them at their command. Obviously, self-expression depends largely on one's vocabulary. One language arts teacher told of being thrilled when one of her boys said to another, "What's buggin' you, man? Why are you so belligerent?"

What about the attention seeker who plays the big shot? If we were to analyze him or her, we would probably find a very insecure person, but we are teachers, not analysts. Here too, you must talk with this child and try to get across to him or her that this type of behavior will turn people away. It is a basic need to be liked and respected, and youngsters can understand that if they act in a self-aggrandizing way, they will very possibly be shunned by their peers. Developing insights of this type may take a long time, but it is time that is very well spent. The youngster who plays big shot is often a disruptive one, needing attention and private discussion if you are to reach him or her at all.

## SPECIFIC ACTIVITIES FOR HYPERACTIVE CHILDREN _____

First and foremost, hyperactive children need much physical activity. They will thrive on physical education classes. If it is possible, you may arrange to have them attend extra classes, provided, of course, that you obtain the permission of the teacher in charge. Explain to the children beforehand why they are being put in special programs and how they will benefit. Emphasize the fact that they must be the best-behaved youngsters in the entire class.

You will find running races, relays, jogging, and even the establishment of a track team to be excellent for your hyperactive children. Your entire class can participate in this type of activity and benefit from it, for many youngsters today do not get enough exercise. We were told by a kindergarten teacher, "I can't believe it. I'm an old lady and overweight, but I can outrun the five year olds in my kindergarten." She teaches in an area where the parents are afraid to allow their children to go outdoors after school because of crime in the neighborhood. However, many youngsters who live in relatively safe neighborhoods don't exercise enough outdoors because of the lure of television or video games.

Should you form a track team, the actual performance of the youngsters is not as important as its motivational value and the fact that you can have your children practicing by running almost daily. Training children to "keep in shape" and arranging contests will benefit the hyperactive children and the others as well.

Many tasks around a school can be given to the hyperactive child and will prove beneficial to both the youngster and the administration. For example, he or she is a natural for putting up the chairs in the cafeteria after lunch hour is over. Bulletin boards need to be decorated, another gainful activity for this type of youngster. Even the counting of notices or other materials and their distribution seem to satisfy the needs of the hyperactive child. However, it is important that the job never be given immediately after the youngster has been disruptive. It goes without saying that the child's doctor's consent must be obtained before the youngster is asked to do any strenuous activity.

You may wish to give the hyperactive child a special series of assignments such as drawing posters, coloring, taking care of pets, "policing" the classroom (a word that is preferable to saying "cleaning" the room), passing the wastebasket around. If you assign these tasks indefinitely and train the child to do them unobtrusively, not only do you help fulfill his or her needs but accomplish worthwhile tasks as well.

As teachers, one of our primary tasks in regard to hyperactive children is to teach them how to use their energy in an acceptable manner. One young woman, now in college, doodles constantly. She claims it enables her to listen more attentively, and she is an excellent student. In our teaching we should take this factor into consideration when working with hyperactive children.

If hyperactive children lack self-control, approach the subject by showing them that they are fortunate, for they have a great gift—lots of energy—but that if they misuse it they are actually cheating themselves and others as well. Suggest ways to take advantage of this physical condition. One might be by playing the drums or another musical instrument. This would use the energy constructively, and the idea usually appeals to youngsters. Be sure to stress the need for self-control, for this is the key to the youngsters' lives.

## THE GUIDANCE APPROACH WITH BOTH THE ATTENTION SEEKER AND THE HYPERACTIVE CHILD

Of course, you will want to see the parents of either of these types of children. When you do, take the approach that the reason you are requesting the interview is to learn more about the child. You may wish to make the point with the parents that the problem presented is serious in that the child is interrupting instruction and wasting the time of the class.

Has he or she always behaved in this manner? Does he or she demand attention at home? If he or she needs more of the parents' attention, are they able to give it? Can the mother or father, for example, play ball with the child, or tennis, or golf? If this is not possible, can the parent get the youngster involved in a club situation, where he or she can get attention but be part of a group? Discuss with the parents the steps you have taken and seek their cooperation. Do not, however, give the impression that you are throwing the whole problem in their laps. As always, your attitude is tremendously important, and you must convey the idea that you are constantly looking for and trying new approaches to solve the problem the child's behavior presents.

Very often it is a good idea to suggest a physical examination, particularly in the case of the hyperactive youngster. If you believe this is necessary, you may prefer to have the school nurse sit in on your interview, and then he or she can make the suggestion. Physicians can prescribe medication that makes it far simpler for the child to adjust to the classroom situation.

Be careful not to alarm the parents. A good way to begin the discussion is with words such as these: "Does Billy run around a lot at home? He is full of energy in class, and unfortunately, sometimes he seems unable to control himself. He does waste much of his time, and I hate to see him doing that." Use all the tact and diplomacy you can in conducting this interview.

In recent years research has been done that strongly suggests hyperactivity may be caused by food additives. Dr. Ben Feingold's book *Why Your Child Is Hyperactive* details the full story. One Long Island elementary school teacher tells of the dramatic change in a boy in her class whose mother read the book and followed the diet outlined in it for her son. "The child, a second grader, had actually climbed on the radiators," the teacher reported, "and he had done many very outlandish things. After his mother put him on the Feingold diet, he changed completely. I actually forgot the problem he had been."

"Then came the Christmas holidays, and the boy's disruptive behavior returned. I telephoned his mother and asked if he had gone off the diet. 'Yes,' she said, and apologized. 'It was hard to keep him on during the holidays.' As soon as he stopped eating foods that had additives, he once again behaved normally." Will this diet work for every hyperactive child? Probably not, but in this case it did, and in scores of other cases as well.

When working with either the attention seeker or the hyperactive youngster, be sure to convey the message that sooner or later he or she will lose friends as a result of his or her behavior. Potential loss of approval of his or her peers may provide a powerful incentive to affect change in his or her behavior, since this is one of the strongest of social pressures. Very often the child is totally unaware of this. "Like bad breath or body odor, no one tells you, but you may find people shying away from you," you may say to an older child.

After you have established rapport with the child, these insights can actually come from him or her if you ask, "Do you have many friends?" If the reply is yes, then you may say, "But you don't want to lose them." If it is no, you can proceed from there. In any event, it is important that the child realize exactly how he or she behaves and how that "turns off" people. If you can teach him or her this concept, you've accomplished a great deal.

Because we all know of some teachers who still give writing assignments to hyperactive youngsters, assignments such as "Write 300 times 'I will not talk in class,'" we must mention this practice here. Please, please don't! It is an anachronism, a relic of the past, and it teaches the child absolutely nothing. An assignment of this nature requires no mental effort and will never result in any insight on the part of the child. If you are really exasperated, you may have the youngster write you a letter, telling you why he or she is behaving in the manner in which he or she is, and whether or not he or she considers it suitable.

You may assign class topics such as "Working Together in This Modern World" and have the youngsters discuss how this can be done, and why it is so necessary. If you feel the need to keep any child occupied because you are about to lose your cool, why not have the boy or girl do a poster suggesting ways to cooperate with one another in class.

Through each of these activities, which incidentally may be used under other circumstances, you are teaching something. When you give such an assignment, it is a good idea to give the youngsters some ideas so that they have a means of getting started. Very often children cannot begin writing, but they can continue once started, for their thoughts will flow. Or you may have to give them a whole series of ideas. This is better than having them disrupt your entire class, and, again, you are teaching a valuable lesson. Citizenship, cooperation, a feeling for one's fellow human beings, all are so important that we can spend a good deal of time on them without feeling we are wasting a minute.

We must teach all of our youngsters, but especially the attention seeker and the hyperactive child, that they have responsibilities to their classmates and to their teacher, and that disrupting class causes loss of valuable time, time they cannot afford to lose.

This concept cannot possibly be repeated too often. We must teach the reasons why we have rules and regulations, and that these were made, as are our laws, for the good of everyone. Far too often the disruptive child feels the rules are for everyone else. He or she must be shown this is not true, that the rules and regulations are good for everyone, including him or her.

Above all in dealing with children with problems, approach them without hostility. This may mean that after they have been disruptive you give them something to do and say, "I will talk to you later, when I am not so upset. Right now, I am extremely so." Then, after you have cooled off, you can be far more effective than you could have been at the moment. If you are able to keep your sense of humor, if you can maintain your mental equilibrium, you are far better able to handle any type of situation that arises. There are very few teachers in this world who can be calm and collected all of the time they are dealing with children, but if you can avoid dealing with the youngsters when you are angry, if you can laugh when you feel like crying, you will come out far ahead.

We watched one young lady dismissing her class. They were healthy, outgoing seventh graders, and it was obvious this was a "Thank God It's Friday" day. As she managed to escort them out of the building, her face grim but determined, one of the most hyperactive but really innocent-appearing boys came up to her. He was one of her disrupters, known to us as a "buster." He approached her after the class had left, and we moved closer to hear what he wanted to say to her. These were his exact words: "Good-bye, Mrs. Beautiful. See you on Monday." This is typical of the hyperactive youngster, who although he causes his teachers much distress and anguish does not feel the slightest bit of animosity towards them. Needless to say, "Mrs. Beautiful" walked out of the building with a big smile on her face. (And when she smiled, she was, indeed, beautiful.)

## CONCLUSION

While not usually really serious problems, the attention seeker and the hyperactive child can take up much valuable class time. The causes of their behavior are different, but for the most part the manifestations are the same. It is essential that you try to develop rapport with these youngsters to enable you to work with them. You must also refuse to permit them to waste class time. Foremost in your treatment of these boys and girls must be your effort to get them involved, truly involved, in the work the class is doing.

The user of obscene language usually falls into the category of the attention seeker. By trying to raise his or her standards, it is possible to effect changes in his or her behavior.

Physical activities are an absolute necessity for the hyperactive child—and your ingenuity in creating these activities can prove most worthwhile. With both of these types of youngsters, parental involvement will help you reach and teach these boys and girls. Medical assistance may prove to be helpful with hyperactive children. Remember, these young people are rarely hostile and will react badly to hostility (as most human beings do). They will frequently respond beautifully to a teacher who treats them with firmness but also with affection and understanding.

# 8

# THE UNDERACHIEVER
# AND THE
# NONMOTIVATED CHILD

If you are having disciplinary problems with youngsters in your class who are underachievers or who are not motivated, we believe you must try to solve these problems by considering them to be learning difficulties and treating them as such. These children, in the early years, are rarely seriously disruptive, but they may well develop into disciplinary problems. More often they are nuisances. Since they are not involved in the work the class is doing much of the time, their minds wander; they seek and find other distractions. We shall outline some techniques for working with these youngsters, aiming toward helping them improve their learning and turn away from mischief.

The underachiever and the nonmotivated child have many characteristics in common. Both do relatively poorly in their schoolwork. Both exhibit little interest in the material you are teaching and participate as little as they possibly can.

Yet there is a very great basic difference: Nonmotivated children usually have less academic ability than underachievers. The latter have shown, by standardized tests in reading and arithmetic, that they are capable of doing better work than they are producing. They do not live up to their academic potential. They often have an erratic record: When you look at their permanent record cards, you see a pattern that may include high grades on standardized tests (showing their capabilities) and either high or low grades in their subject areas.

One of the reasons for this is the variation in demands that teachers have made on them. If a teacher requires a lot of work and considers classwork and homework in addition to tests, the underachiever usually will not do as well as if the teacher gives grades on the basis of tests alone. The reason for this is simple. Underachievers often do well on tests—particularly in their early school years. Their other work reflects the attitude we are concentrating on in this chapter. As the youngster advances and gets older, however, his or her achievement lessens—his or her marks become poorer—and all too frequently his or her behavior becomes a problem as well.

This type of youngster is often the spitball thrower, the conversationalist. He or she is the one who, when accused of wrongdoing, looks at you innocently and says, "Who, me?" These youngsters do not consider themselves to have problems, but as far as the teacher is concerned, they surely do. They can usually be prevented from being a nuisance by a firm teacher, but remedying their pattern of underachievement requires a great deal of work.

The nonmotivated girls or boys are those whose performance records on standardized tests indicate a low-to-middling series of scores. This is accompanied by an equally unimpressive series of grades. These youngsters are simply coasting along. They grasp what they can, but they do not actively participate in the learning process. They may or may not do their homework, and, far too often, do not. They are generally followers rather than leaders. If a friend, usually a bright underachiever, says, "Let's go to the park today," they agree with alacrity. They will engage in mischief because they are bored. They attend school because attendance is mandatory, but they are not being educated.

The sad part is that such youngsters are not stupid. They do not have serious learning difficulties, but they have no concept of the value of education. Their mothers have often told us that their children aren't interested in anything special, but they love to watch television. In class they may be annoying because of their lack of interest, but mostly they are the youngsters who are not outstanding in any way, who are part of the group.

Much of what will follow will be relevant to both underachievers and nonmotivated youngsters. Differences will be pointed out and taken into consideration in the techniques we suggest.

Underachievement and lack of motivation have come to the fore because they are two of the major problems facing college educators today. These young people often decide that they want to attend college when they graduate from high school. Very often they are not prepared, and even if they are accepted, their days of higher learning are short-lived. They account for the sad statistic that almost 50 percent of freshmen flunk out of college and cannot return for a second year. They are unprepared, not only educationally but psychologically as well.

The patterns of behavior exhibited by these underachievers and by nonmotivated youngsters are often evident as early as the primary grades. If these attitudes are not corrected at that time, the problems become far more pronounced. It is really necessary that we as teachers find ways and means to solve them as soon as we become aware of their existence. The youngsters' entire futures may be at stake. They are constantly being affected. Let us first look at the possible reasons for these behavior patterns.

## WHY CHILDREN BECOME UNDERACHIEVERS OR NONMOTIVATED STUDENTS

1. Basically, both of these problems develop as a result of a combination of factors. Being exposed to teachers who permit the children to do little or no work is an extremely important one. If youngsters have teachers who give them a sense of responsibility, who check their work, who establish standards and refuse to allow even one boy or girl to fall below those standards, the youngsters develop work habits that go far toward preventing them from becoming underachievers or nonmotivated students.

2. If on the other hand we encounter a child who has problems because of his or her parents' attitudes, it is necessary that we try to change these attitudes. In other words, we must try to work through the parents to get to the child. There are so few fields of endeavor in the world today that do not require education that any parent who disregards this needs educating himself or herself. By carefully discussing this, by attempting to show parents the effect their attitude has on the child, by bringing out the need for the training that almost every job requires, perhaps we can affect change in the parents, which will then filter down to the child. In addition to this, it is important that we show the pupils themselves what education can do for them.

3. This brings us to a very important third reason. A great many children waste a great deal of time because they, themselves, have no concept of how important education is in their later lives. They are unaware of the importance of training, the requirements for skilled and even for unskilled jobs, and of the position they put themselves in when they do not have the education they need and cannot compete on the job market. It is our task to teach them the economic facts of life. Yet this material is found in very few curricula.

Career education is a subject area that has been introduced but that has not been picked up in many school districts. It is ironic that we can spend hours as teachers discussing relatively inconsequential subjects. How much more valuable it would be to teach our children how to find their way in the world of work.

When you show your youngsters that their education is really preparing them for their future work and that this is one of the most important things their education can do for them, it is possible to convert the underachiever and perhaps motivate all your students.

However, the boys and girls should also be helped to see the immediate value of their schooling. It is very difficult for a third grader to look nine years (or more) into the future. How can you show them that what they are learning today is important? The answer is to find areas that touch their lives.

Can very young children engage in the battle against litter? Of course. You would be hard-pressed to find any more willing participants in a neighborhood clean-up campaign. This does not mean you announce, "Children, today we are going to clean up our neighborhood" and expect them to rush out and do it. But with a well-motivated lesson preceding it, they will. A film showing rats and the connection the number of rats in an area has with the number of uncovered garbage cans and dirt in the streets can really motivate the youngsters. The same is true of raccoons, which have proved to be terrible pests in many places.

A dynamic speaker (possibly the teacher), a series of newspaper articles, a filmstrip, a video—all regularly used motivational devices—can give the needed impetus to a neighborhood clean-up campaign.

Check your area for soot. Place clean, dampened white cloths on your window sills. Then investigate—where does this soot come from? Or take a walk through your area, looking for litter. One class discovered that in a large park there were only two litter baskets. They brought this to the attention of the city's park department and asked for permission to construct refuse containers. Of course the request was granted with alacrity.

Relevant education! It's important to all youngsters, and especially so for boys and girls with problems.

4. Check your underachievers and nonmotivated children to determine whether they have specific learning problems. It is possible that they have never learned study skills. We have found this is an area far too many teachers ignore. You will find a brief guide at the end of this chapter.

Have your pupils developed good work habits? Very often youngsters will enter your class with no concept of how to proceed with an assignment. They need you to teach them the way to do so.

We recall one boy in intermediate school who said to a counselor, "I don't know what that teacher wants."

"But Ronald, you've been in Mrs. X.'s class for three months," the counselor replied.

"I still don't know and I ain't gonna do it," the boy answered defiantly.

"I'm not going to do it," the counselor automatically corrected him.

"I'm not going to do it," Ronald replied dutifully.

"Can I help you with it?" the counselor asked.

The child looked at him quizzically. "You mean it?"

"Sure," the adult answered. "What did Mrs. X say?"

"She said, 'Write a theme on the Louisiana Purchase.'"

"Why is that so difficult?" the counselor queried.

"I don't know what a theme is, or how to write one," the boy responded.

"Why didn't you ask Mrs. X?"

"I didn't want to show all the kids in the class how dumb I am," the youngster muttered sheepishly.

It is entirely possible that half of the youngsters in the class did not know what the word *theme* means. Had the teacher gone over the entire concept and how to handle the assignment, her results would surely have been better.

## GETTING THE UNDERACHIEVER TO ACHIEVE AND THE NONMOTIVATED YOUNGSTER TO WORK _____

1. Help these youngsters gain self-confidence. Both of these types of boys and girls may become discipline problems if allowed to go their own ways, uncorrected by the teacher. The problems develop from the very first grade, and, as is the case with so many problems, the old adage, "An ounce of prevention is worth a pound of cure" applies.

You can build up the self-esteem and self-confidence of these young people by finding assignments they can do—and do well. Show them that they can succeed and contribute to the work the class is doing. Every youngster can, for example, inspect the streets in his or her neighborhood and then have his or her parent call the sanitation department when an accumulation of garbage or rubbish has been discovered.

This is just one of the many ways in which a youngster can do something positive for his or her community and so gain in self-esteem.

Try to bring the youngsters with poor self-image into this type of activity. In the early years, their problems may not manifest themselves as discipline problems, but in time they very well may.

2.  Show the underachiever and the nonmotivated youngster his or her academic strengths and try to help him or her develop interests in such academic areas as literature or science. For example, there's Eric, who was a discipline problem in elementary school. His teachers called in his mother frequently to discuss his behavior. As he told it, her "presence was requested, once or twice every term." One astute teacher realized this boy was not being adequately challenged and in the eighth grade assigned a paper on the topic "parthenogenesis." This was the first really fascinating scientific subject Eric had ever encountered, and it fostered an interest in science, which became his lifetime vocation and avocation as well. His behavior improved as if by magic, and in high school he became an honor student.

Many youngsters have talents and interests that are never discovered, never revealed to them. We as a nation lose a great deal of brainpower as a result.

You can elevate your children by introducing them to subjects that may seem at first to be far above their heads. We recall one teacher, Mrs. Roberta Schoenbrun of the Oceanside, New York, school system, who did a fascinating project year after year with second graders.

Using an incubator that had been constructed by one of the parents and fertilized duck eggs that she obtained from a special farm, Mrs. Schoenbrun and her class set out to raise ducks. From the time the eggs were incubated until the ducklings pecked their way out of their shells, the children observed their development and kept notes on it. The youngsters then wrote books with pictures detailing the experience; they had learned the word *embryology*, which was the title of their books. Mrs. Schoenbrun was well known in the school district as a result of this work, and the little ones who had been in her classes never forgot this project.

Look for the unusual, the out-of-the-ordinary, for in these days of television, teachers are called on to be more creative than ever before. Many nonmotivated youngsters can be captivated by work on prehistoric man and of course, the current rage among the very young, dinosaurs. In language arts science fiction, the possibility of life on other planets and mysteries of all kinds seem to capture the imagination of most boys and girls.

Even five year olds today are very interested in the extremely popular Ninja Turtles™. It is surprising to learn that virtually none of the girls and boys, and this is true of older youngsters as well, know after whom the turtles are named. (Leonardo is, of course, Leonardo da Vinci, the famous painter and inventor; and Donatello was a famed Italian sculptor.)

3. If you have many underachievers or nonmotivated youngsters in your class, you will find you need extra special motivation for each lesson. That is a tall order, but your introduction, your "gimmicks" are very important in this regard, for you must entice attention from the children who are inattentive and create interest among the disinterested. At times the motivation will come from the youngsters. We recall hearing about a fifth-grade class that snapped to attention when a child brought a dying squirrel into school. The teacher used the situation to great advantage immediately.

"What shall we do?" she asked. "What can we do to keep this little creature alive?" Every child eagerly came up to the desk to see it and some made suggestions. IMPORTANT: It's unwise to handle sick wild animals. The squirrel could have been rabid, for example.

"What happened to the poor little thing?" the teacher asked the little girl who had brought the squirrel in.

"I found it drowning in the brook," the child replied.

The lesson that followed was a wonderful one because every child was involved, every child cared, and everyone wanted to help. Not just a few, but everyone. The story doesn't have a happy ending, because while the squirrel was taken to a veterinarian, he could not save its life. However, the classwork went from animals to drowning to the value of all life. It was memorable—obviously—because the story was told to me by a young adult years later.

4. Give your underachievers, your nonmotivated youngsters, and perhaps your entire class some guidelines on how to study. You may wish to use the short guide in Figure 7, which is addressed directly to the youngsters.

## Figure 7

---

To study you must have some printed material. That material may be the notes your teacher has given to you. If so:

A. Go over these notes, asking yourself questions about each point. For instance:

What is the importance of this?

Whom does it affect? Why?

What connection does this work have with what I already know?

What is there about this point that will help me remember it?

Figure 7 *(cont.)*

B. It may also be material from a textbook. To study this:

1. Read the material, and as you read it, make a list of every important or key word or phrase. Also list important dates.

2. After you finish reading, consult your list of key words, phrases, and dates.

3. For each one, try to explain its definition or meaning in terms of the chapter.

4. Then ask yourself to explain how each key word, phrase, or date is used to make an important point in the chapter.

5. If you cannot answer the question above, reread the part of the chapter that discusses it.

6. Reread the entire chapter once more.

C. To study arithmetic:

1. Select five examples or problems of each type being studied from your textbook.

2. Work each of these out.

3. Have someone check your work. This may be someone at home, or your teacher.

4. If you made an error in one, figure out why you made that mistake and do the example or problem again until you get it right.

5. Do five more examples of the type in which you had difficulty, making sure you are correct this time.

6. When you find a type of problem or question you cannot answer correctly, get help from your teacher.

D. If you are assigned to write a composition:

1. Jot down a list of your ideas before you start to actually write the composition.

2. List every idea that comes into your head. You may not choose to use all of them, but you will have them if you need them.

3. You may discover that one idea leads to another.

4. Discuss the assignment with another person or persons. You will find that their ideas will help you and also stimulate you to come up with more ideas of your own.

E. Try to find a *quiet* place in which to study. You will use your time to the best advantage if no one disturbs you (This includes the telephone).

F. Use the above suggestions, following them exactly. Shortcuts don't work. Make sure you do your studying by writing rather than merely reading and repeating.

Figure 7 *(cont.)*

G.  Talk about your studies with your parents or other adults. In this way your mind and your speech work together to help you retain what you are learning.

H.  If a classmate needs help and you teach the work to him or her, you both will benefit. However, it's necessary that you attend to your work and do not socialize.

## SETTING STANDARDS

Many underachievers and nonmotivated youngsters, as we have said, need to be prodded and encouraged and need to have standards set for them. We suggest you do the following:

1.  Define and structure your assignments very clearly. For example, if you give an assignment that involves questions, have the youngsters copy the questions into a notebook, leaving space for the responses.

2.  Collect written homework, grade it, and return it. You need not grade every word, but if you do so at the beginning of the year, you will find it will not be necessary later to grade each paper, because the youngsters will have started to develop good work habits.

3.  If an unsatisfactory assignment is turned in to you, return it to be redone. This is very important for the underachiever. Do not accept any inferior work. If youngsters find they are required to do satisfactory work, many of them will.

4.  Discuss the youngsters' work with them. Make sure they are aware of the requirements and that they are capable of completing them. If they are having difficulty, work with them, and ask for help from older siblings or from parents.

5.  Reward the youngsters with good grades, but only for work well done. If underachievers are given decent grades for little or poor work, why should they try to do better? If they do work hard, however, their grades should reflect this. Be fair, and show the youngsters the base on which you are grading. We feel there are boys and girls who do not care about getting good grades, but they are a small minority. Of these, many feel defeated and have developed the "I don't care" attitude as a defense mechanism. By showing youngsters how they can succeed, we can help them change this attitude.

6.  Have all of the youngsters keep notebooks and be sure you grade them on them. We have found it is the underachievers and the nonmotivated

boys and girls who do not do this. They therefore have no notes from which to study and no tangible example of their work in school.

Parents will often say, "Doesn't he get any work in school? He never carries books or takes a notebook to school." They are right. If you, the teacher, require, demand, and emphasize this, your pupils will comply. If you are undemanding, you encourage laxity—and the youngsters suffer.

## BRIGHT CHILDREN WHO BECOME DISCIPLINE PROBLEMS

Let us consider the bright children who are in danger of becoming discipline problems. Perhaps they do not even fall into the category of underachiever. Perhaps they are doing enough work to get by. But they are becoming a bit of a nuisance, or worse. Is it because their ability is unchallenged and their imagination not touched? Are they just plain bored?

What can you do about such a situation?

1. Find work that is commensurate with their ability and that will start them working. Assign topics for them to research and have them share these assignments with the rest of the class. Even in the first grade, the bright child can, for example, tell stories to the other boys and girls, stories he or she has heard or seen on television. (However, limit the time that each child can speak. Some can go on and on, for what seems like hours.)

The young child can get information from the library—if someone reads it to him or her. Older youngsters can be given problems to solve that require obtaining data. They can show films, filmstrips, or even videos to the class and then lead a discussion of them. The child who is scientifically gifted can perform simple experiments for the class or do demonstrations (either carefully supervised, of course).

2. You may wish to establish a tutoring relationship in your class between the very bright children and the children who need help. Fostering friendships of this sort is beneficial to both. The gifted child has an outlet, and the slow child benefits from the help he or she receives. The teacher must guard against any show of arrogance or superiority, however. The point to be emphasized is *service*.

3. The bright underachiever can be given a topic to prepare and then teach to the class. This can prove to be a technique that is very effective with other bright children as well.

4. Have the bright, but obstreperous, child learn to operate equipment such as film projectors, tape recorders, and the like.

These are clues for you to consider as you think of your underachievers and nonmotivated youngsters. By studying them and individualizing instruction procedures you can meet their needs, challenge them, and motivate them.

## CONCLUSION

Should you have underachievers and nonmotivated youngsters in your class, it is most important that you try to change their behavior patterns. If these youngsters are not working, they are looking for other ways to use their energy. Often they do not cause significant problems, initially, except in that they distract and waste the class's time. However, they can become full-fledged discipline problems. These youngsters can be helped, cajoled, prodded, and required to work. If you, the teacher, are willing to make the effort, and it takes a great deal of effort on your part, you can get these youngsters to achieve.

A youngster of this type will take the path of least resistance, but if you can make him or her want to achieve, his or her pattern of behavior will change to suit you. We do not mean to imply that you should be cruel or unpleasant, but that you be firm and businesslike. The permissive teacher may teach youngsters many things, and his or her philosophy is not, by any means, entirely at odds with ours, but we believe there must be a stress on achievement and on pride in workmanship if youngsters are to benefit fully from their education.

A girl or boy who never takes notes, never reads a book, or never completes a task or assignment will have a very difficult time throughout his or her lifetime, for what employer, and what husband or wife, could constantly tolerate this? Underachievement and lack of motivation, too, remove from society the contribution of those individuals. Can we as a nation afford this?

# 9

# THE SCHOOL PHOBIC, THE TRUANT, AND THE LONER

Perhaps the most bewildering situation a teacher can encounter is that of a youngster who is a school phobic. This is literally a child with a phobia about attending school. Despite the efforts of the teacher, this child resists coming to school. Like the truant, the phobic is deeply troubled, but for different reasons. The loner is a child with a completely different problem.

## WHAT CAUSES A CHILD TO BECOME A SCHOOL PHOBIC OR A TRUANT?

The phobic often develops this phobia as a result of having an overprotective mother. For reasons of her own, the mother's interests are served by having her child with her. We have seen mothers who encouraged their children to stay home, who wrote excuse notes for imaginary illnesses, and who went as far as to hide the children when the attendance officer visited the home.

An interesting aspect of this problem is that often when such girls and boys reach the age of twelve or thirteen they find they have missed so much schoolwork that they refuse to go to school. Because of being prodded by the authorities, their mothers now try very hard to get these youngsters to attend, but they refuse. Terrible scenes may ensue or quiet ones—we have witnessed both—when the youngster will not enter a classroom.

There are many other reasons why children develop school phobia, of course. One is that some youngsters have been conditioned—because of unhappy experiences—with teachers, or with other children to dislike school. One woman of our acquaintance was considered by many to be a superior teacher, and indeed for many of the children who were in her class she was, for she prodded them to achieve a great deal. However, she would choose one youngster, almost always a boy, and make that youngster a scapegoat. That child's life for the year she was his teacher was miserable. A close friend of ours still gets red-faced and upset when he talks about her, and he was a student of hers in the sixth grade, some forty years ago!

Children may be traumatized for life by being called "stupid" or by any unthinking, insensitive remark from a teacher, from another adult, or even from another youngster. Incidentally, the person saying these things might be totally unaware of the damage he or she is doing.

Truants are youngsters who for reasons other than having a school phobia just don't attend school regularly. Here too, the reasons for their behavior vary. Often they feel tremendously inadequate and consequently inferior to the other youngsters. Billy was such a boy. He was polite and handsome and could verbally express himself without difficulty. However, in the sixth grade he became a truant. He had never learned to read, and in the sixth grade he was slightly older than the others in his class, for he had been held over once. His self-respect was at stake. He found two boys willing to avoid attending school, and all three rarely walked through its doors.

This brings to mind the influence of other youngsters. The opinions of peers are very important to most girls and boys, and when a child finds friends who are willing to "play hookey," he or she is really tempted. If he or she has had negative experiences as a result of truancy, he or she may not become a truant; but if his or her parents ignore the fact that the child is not attending school, or aren't around to show their disfavor strongly, the child may well develop into a perpetual truant.

School holds little or no interest for these youngsters, and they are unwilling to accept the reality that they need an education to succeed later in life. This is a hard point to get across if their role models drive very expensive foreign cars purchased through the fruits of involvement in illegal activities.

We set up a program through which we had speakers from the local police department discuss with the youngsters such illegal activities and the penalties usually associated with them. Many seemed to be duly impressed, but while we had tried to cajole the truants to come in to school for this program, not one of them came on the scheduled day, although they were very well aware that the program was directed toward them.

## UNDERSTANDING THE LONER _____

The loner is really quite different from the school phobic and the truant. Loners are youngsters who have difficulty establishing relationships with others—be the others adults or youngsters. They have not learned how to talk to others or to feel comfortable with them and as a result stay by themselves. They will often bury themselves in books, or actually try to hide in corners. This is not necessarily because they don't like people (although they may not) but because they are shy to the point of it affecting their functioning.

Because a boy or girl is alone and lonely, he or she may develop into a school phobic or a truant. It is for this reason that we consider the loner in this chapter. Perhaps the outstanding case that we can recall of a school phobic who had started out being a loner, was Leslie.

Leslie was a very bright girl who had joined her class in the fifth grade. Although she was new to the group, the other girls seemed willing to befriend her, but she would have none of it. They seemed to embarrass her, and she began to miss days of school. These absences became more and more frequent, although she always came in when the teacher announced a test. She did very, very well on any test she took, in spite of the fact that she missed so much of the classwork.

By the middle of the year Leslie simply stopped coming in at all. "I can't come to school," she told the counselor, who had telephoned her mother and asked her to bring the child to school. "I get sick every morning, and I can't come in because I have to go to the bathroom constantly."

Her parents had been aware of the problem, but nothing was done about it until the school guidance counselor discussed it with them. "It will pass," Leslie's mother said. "She knows all of the work, and she can miss a few days." However, the counselor was able to persuade her mother that professional help was needed. Leslie was given home instruction with the provision that she have psychological testing. This revealed the need for therapy. It took several years of that therapy before Leslie was able to return to school on a full-time basis.

Unfortunately, the prognosis for loners, phobics, and truants is poor. Certainly you will work with them to the extent that you can, given that they don't come to school very often, if at all. Such youngsters need professional help, in and out of the classroom, for their problems are serious ones. Before you send in a referral to the guidance counselor or, if your school doesn't have one, to the administration, be sure you have some anecdotal records. These are vitally important and should include the work you have done with the particular child and the effects, or lack thereof, they have had.

Attendance personnel are skilled in working with youngsters who are truants or school phobics. They communicate directly with them and with the parents when possible. In many cases attendance personnel are able to offer concrete assistance. We have seen attendance teachers work what seemed to be wonders. They may spend hours and hours talking with individual children and their mothers or fathers. They make a decided effort to seek out the parents, often visiting the child's home to do so. Needless to say, this does not work all of the time, but when it does, it can make a great difference in the child's life.

## COMMUNICATE WITH THESE YOUNGSTERS _____

If it is possible for you to develop rapport with the school phobic, the truant, or the loner in your class, you can really help him or her. If you don't, he or she will come and go, scarcely touched by his or her encounter with you. Developing rapport takes time and effort, but it is a must if you are to succeed with youngsters with these problems. If you are able to get the child to discuss his or her lifestyle with you, you may be able to determine the reasons for his or her behavior.

It is difficult for a child to admit to having no friends or being unable to keep up with the work the class is doing. The other youngsters may tease him or her and make life miserable. If on the other hand you become the child's advocate, the situation may change dramatically. Of course, you cannot favor this child over the others, but you can treat him or her with respect and with kindness and hope this attitude will rub off on the rest of the youngsters.

One develops rapport by talking and listening. Try to find out from the child why he or she doesn't come to school. It may be possible for you to help directly—as, for example, when another child in the class is annoying him or her. See if you can get the youngster to answer very specifically, saying, "I'd like to help you. Please tell me how I can."

## SPECIAL WAYS TO WORK WITH THESE CHILDREN _____

There are other things a teacher can do to make attending school more attractive. Here are some suggestions:

1. Create a pleasant atmosphere in your classroom. Some youngsters will seek to avoid a teacher who speaks in a very loud voice or screams at them. Little ones develop fears and fantasies as a result of being "yelled at." It is easy to forget that some young children are very sensitive to noise.

2. Let the phobic, the truant, or the loner know that you accept him or her and that he or she is an important member of the class. Showing acceptance, that you really care about him or her in spite of the problems he or she presents, can go a long way toward changing the youngster's behavior.

"I come to school because Mrs. X. told me she is very unhappy when she doesn't say 'Good morning' just to me," little Sheila told the attendance teacher. The latter had been working with the girl for months and had finally gotten her to the point where she was willing to try to go to school. She was placed in Mrs. X.'s class because of the warmth and caring for which the teacher was known. The kids loved her, and she loved them. It worked. Sheila came to school regularly.

However, the next year she was placed with another teacher, entirely different in temperament and attitude. Sheila reverted to her old behavior pattern, and the entire process of rehabilitation had to be begun again.

3. When one of these youngsters is absent, you can have a talk with the rest of the class, saying to them, "I really need your help. It's very important to me that So-and-so come to school. If you can help me accomplish that, I would be very grateful."

Many youngsters are anxious to help you, and that's the basis for this technique. "What can we do to get him to come to school? What do you suggest?" you ask the class.

The girls and boys themselves will give you some ideas, and because the ideas come from them, they will be more prone to follow through. You can't say, "I want you to be friends with So-and-so," because that doesn't work. If the child is unpopular with his or her peers, you might be able to find out why this is so. We recall one seven year old saying, "I don't want to sit near XYZ. He needs to take a bath. He smells bad." This situation was referred to the school nurse, who took care of it by contacting the parents.

4. Ask the class officers if they can help you make the youngster more comfortable. They may be able to do so.

5. Seat the loner, the school phobic, or the truant near warm, outgoing youngsters, those with whom it is easy to make friends. Just this simple action may help the situation.

6. Discuss the youngster's problems and obtain the cooperation of other members of the staff. In that way the principal, the assistant principal, and the other teachers will have a kind word and a smile for the child. This helps make school a pleasant place to which the child possibly will want to come. By sending him or her on an occasional errand, he or she feels important and has the opportunity to speak to other members of the staff. What child does not like to run errands?

7. Have the class do committee work, creating an interaction among all of the students. Find out what talents the problem youngster has and structure the situation so that you can use those talents—be they drawing, painting, musical, athletic, or literary.

8. Praise the work the youngster, as well as other members of the class, does whenever you can. Display it to call attention to his or her talents and abilities—even if it is so simple a thing as a handspring. Sincere interest, a pat on the back, a smile, a kind word—these may help bring the youngster into school permanently. Warmth and affection are the penicillin we can use, and they can be used lavishly and effectively.

9. In any manner you can think of, nurture the youngster's self-esteem, and do anything you can to make him or her less unsure. It has been said that each of us makes our own price tag, and if we can enrich a girl or boy's belief in himself or herself, that can make a big difference in his or her entire life.

10. Problem children may be given specific sets of chores for which they are responsible and which they should be made to realize are important to classroom management. This nourishes their self-importance, and, in a pleasurable way, develops their sense of responsibility. There are many jobs to which they may be assigned. (See Chapter One for suggestions.) These make the child feel needed.

When you do this, inform the youngster's mother, so the mother can say, "Your teacher is depending on you to (and she names the task). How can you not go to school and disappoint her (or him)?" Discuss this with the parent beforehand and recommend this approach.

## PARENTS AND THEIR REACTION TO THESE PROBLEMS _____

When dealing with the school phobic, the truant, and the loner, parental cooperation cannot be overemphasized. You must be extremely careful not to antagonize the mother or father, or possibly the grandparent, with whom you might have to deal. The adults may feel threatened by you, so your first task is to eliminate their fears by your attitude and understanding. It is best that you invite them to come in to see you rather than summon them.

When a parent is invited to see you, she (and it is usually the mother who comes in) or he is often worried, anxious, and upset. If you sense this, make every effort to put the parent at ease. Say at the very onset of the interview that the problem is not monumental and that, with his or her cooperation, it can probably be solved.

Try to begin with an affirmative statement. Find something praiseworthy to say about the child and say it immediately. Even if a child is truant, one can say, for example, "Bobby shows he is independent." Never mind, right now, that independence is causing the boy to act in a way that doesn't benefit him. By speaking this way you are able to ease the tension the parent is probably feeling.

Then state the problem succinctly—neither over- nor underemphasizing it. Next ask the parent for suggestions. How can the situation be remedied? In the case of the loner and the phobic as well as the truant, the parent should be made to realize just how important his or her role is. Even if you are aware of the fact that the parent tolerates, or may even support, the child's absences from school, do not let on that you believe this to be true.

We recall the case of Lucille, whose mother kept her home. When we spoke to the woman she said, "I need her at home more than she needs to go to school. She's smart enough now."

The fact was Lucille *was* needed at home because her mother was ill. The teacher, learning this, made a referral to the guidance counselor, who in turn contacted a social service agency, and help was obtained for Lucille's mother. The girl returned to school, and although she was unable to do much homework for lack of time, she nevertheless was able to keep up with the work the class was doing.

You may encounter a situation like this, but most of the time absences are not for this type of reason. Press the parent to be firm and insistent that the youngster attend school. The habits a boy or girl develops in early life become part of his or her character. A sense of responsibility must be developed as early as possible in the young person's life if he or she is to ultimately become a happy, useful citizen. Furthermore, to compete in today's world, every person must be literate and have a basic education, which begins in elementary school and continues through high school.

In the case of truants, phobics, and loners, special counseling is often needed, and the parent should be encouraged to accept it. The seriousness of nonattendance should be brought out—lest the child form unwholesome and undesirable associations. Truants often become involved in robberies and other serious misdemeanors and are ready victims for drug pushers.

Many parents are extremely reluctant to accept the fact that their child has a very serious problem. It is our duty as teachers and supervisors to help the parents really understand the severity of this problem. Then and only then can it possibly be solved, and almost always professional help is needed.

It is extremely dangerous in this day and age to stick our heads into the proverbial sand. Better a little action now than tragedy later. The basic concept that must be emphasized to the parent is that youngsters who are not in school often get into serious difficulties. An example of the very seriousness of the situation is the case of little Mikey (short for Michael).

Mikey was a bright, mischievous sixth-grade youngster whose behavior was extremely erratic. He was capable of doing good work in school but often did not bother to do so. He loved to "fool around." One day the boy was sent for by the principal, who had received complaints that a child fitting Mikey's description had been seen overturning garbage pails in the neighborhood. A furious homeowner had threatened to let his dog go after the boy if it happened again. His dog happened to be a pit bull.

Mikey was not in school when he was sent for, but the principal telephoned his mother and asked her to come in to talk with him about the boy. She was very resistant. "I know he's full of the devil," were her exact words. "Why do you have to see me?"

The principal insisted. "Please come in on Monday, anyway. I feel I must talk to you," he said emphatically.

The conference was never held. The mother called to say she had guests from out of town and would be "too busy." Another appointment was set up, and that one was broken too.

One month later the principal attended Mikey's funeral. Mikey had engaged in overturning garbage pails, and the homeowner had done what he had threatened to do, turned his dog loose. To escape from the animal, Mikey ran away—right in front of a truck.

The principal had tried to convince the parent that there was a serious problem, but the mother had totally resisted his suggestions and even his admonitions that something had to be done, which he had stressed in his conversations with her.

When a youngster is absent from school, his or her parents should be notified. Far too often this procedure is ignored, yet it is vital that it be followed. Telephone calls are the best way to reach a parent, especially if the absences seem to form a pattern. Postcards or letters are also used, but often they are intercepted by the youngster and never reach the person for whom they are intended.

It might be wise to enlist the aid of the father. However, in a great many cases he is absent from the home, and the mother or grandmother is unable to cope with the child's behavior. It is this factor that has caused the problem to arise. If at all possible, notify the youngster's father and ask for his cooperation. In the event that he is absent from the child's life, perhaps a counselor or a male teacher, or even an older brother or cousin, can substitute and help get the boy or girl to go to school.

We have suggested parents set up a reward system for good attendance. This may serve to establish a different behavior pattern from the previous one. The teacher may offer to notify the parents when such a reward is in order. Accentuating the positive rather than the negative is an effective way of building desirable habits.

Try to have the parent leave any interview in a good frame of mind. If you are sincere, she (and it usually is she) or he will feel you are trying to help her and her child, and her cooperation is insured—to the best of her ability. However, in dealing with a school phobic, a truant, or a loner, the parent is often unable to do very much with the child. Do not expect miracles—and do the best you can. Be sympathetic as well as firm. It is to be hoped that both you and the parent can help this boy or girl.

## CHECK THE RECORDS FOR RELEVANT INFORMATION _____

If in your class you have children who you feel are having attendance problems, check those children's records. Very often a study of these records will reveal a great deal of pertinent information and enable you to see a behavior pattern beginning.

A youngster has been on record as having attended school regularly. Suddenly he or she changes. Why? Often this change will coincide with family problems. Has the parents' marriage broken up? Has the mother gone to work? Is there now inadequate supervision of the child? Does either parent drink to excess? Is there enough money to meet the needs of the family? Is the father living in the home? Who is now in charge of the child? Are there problems with other siblings?

The death of a parent can cause tremendous psychological effects. Even the passing of a grandparent can have strong emotional repercussions. When you discover the cause of a child's problem, you are far better able to understand and work with him or her. However, be very careful of the manner in which you approach the boy or girl, for he or she may be very sensitive about his or her personal life. Youngsters very often are.

There may be a physical problem. Is the child a stutterer? Are his or her eyes crossed? Is his or her sight normal? Has his or her hearing been tested? Is the boy or girl small for his or her age? Is he or she possibly a victim of malnutrition? Or to the contrary, a condition that is more common today, is he or she overweight and possibly a compulsive eater? A check of the records might disclose also a serious psychological or emotional problem. Children with these problems often act out in school and very often play the role of the fool. They will shout out or take pride in causing others to laugh. They do this because they are hurting badly inside.

Very often, psychological problems manifest themselves as physical ailments. Ulcers are classic in this type of situation. The aforementioned compulsive eating is another type of problem. While these youngsters certainly should have medical attention, the teacher is in a position to help in other ways.

One such way is by unearthing some talent the youngster has and structuring the opportunity for it to be displayed. When the pursuit of a talent such as painting, for example, can be encouraged, it is possible the boy or girl will spend much time at it and the overeating will be curtailed.

As teachers we should be knowledgeable of each child's idiosyncrasies, which are sometimes indicated on the records. Percy was such a child. He could not be spoken to in a loud voice, or shouted at. If he was, he would become violent, shriek back, flail his arms, and often a free-for-all would result in the classroom.

His regular teacher was aware of this and never put the boy into that situation, but on several occasions substitute teachers did. The results were almost disastrous. The problem was solved by placing Percy in another class, with a teacher aware of his behavior pattern, whenever his regular teacher was absent. Everyone who had any contact with this youngster was advised to virtually whisper when speaking to him.

Percy returned to school to visit several years later, to tell us it had been discovered he had very sensitive hearing, and that he still had pain when he heard loud noises. This accounted, in part, for his behavior. "When my mother shouted at me at home, I became furious," he said, and that behavior carried over into school.

There are youngsters who are frequently ill and who catch every ailment that is "going around." They are classed as constitutional inadequates. Their absences are usually legitimate, and they should be given every consideration insofar as making up their schoolwork is concerned. It is hoped that they will outgrow this condition.

## HELPING THE PHOBIC, THE TRUANT, AND THE LONER _____

1. When a child's attendance is erratic, he or she particularly needs to be made to feel part of the group and at ease with the other youngsters. This will not happen if the teacher makes comments such as we heard one gentleman say, in a very sarcastic manner, "It's nice of you to come to school today, Eddie." Youngsters take their cues from the teacher, and Eddie would not feel welcome in this classroom because of comments such as this.

2. Find out the reason the boy or girl doesn't come to school. If you can make the youngster comfortable, perhaps he or she will confide in you. A case in point. One little second grader was absent for days at a time, having told his mother he was having stomachaches. He was examined by his physician, but no physical reason was found. Speaking privately with the boy, the teacher was able to extract the information from him. He was being blackmailed by an older boy who attended a nearby high school, but who would wait for the smaller child in the morning and accost him. The

problem was solved when the principal of the elementary school called the situation to the attention of the principal of the high school.

The older boy denied being serious when he asked the child for money. However, he never did it again after the child revealed what had been happening. Another route was worked out for the younger child, and there was no further contact between the two.

3. Can the youngster read? Has he or she fallen behind in reading or in any other academic subject? Does he or she need help to "catch up"? Is there a need for tutoring, or can this help be given during class time? Many times absentee youngsters miss a great deal of work and fall further and further behind as each term progresses. Should you have such a child in your class, perhaps this situation can be remedied. You may even have to ask for help from the parent, but in this situation they are usually only too eager to help.

4. Give the absent child an ongoing project of some sort, one that he or she likes and that will give him or her a reason to come to school. Can you use music, for example? Teaching the child to play the recorder or the guitar might do it.

This worked wonders with Felicia, a seventh grader. It was arranged that the school music teacher would work with her once a week, teaching her the guitar (by far the most popular instrument with young people). However, if Felicia was absent even once from school, there would be no lesson that week. I recall her turning up one day with a very sore throat, saying in a hoarse voice, "I can't miss my lesson. I love it."

Science or art projects are other possibilities. In one social studies class a huge diorama was being made, and attendance was excellent as a result. The problem youngsters were so interested they came in just to work on it.

5. If you have a boy who needs a male model, perhaps the school can supply one. A male gym teacher, for example, can work with the child on a one-to-one basis. This can help even if it is only once a week.

6. Have something exciting going on. The aforementioned project of Roberta Schoenbrun, which involved the incubation and development of ducklings, brought even sick children into school. All were enthralled and excited. Contests, games, and class trips work, encouraging all of the youngsters to appear.

We recall vividly a language arts teacher, Mr. Charles Glassman, who did a unit on the supernatural. Boys and girls came in who had been absent for the entire term because their friends had told them about the unit and they didn't want to miss it. (A number of youngsters would wait for Mr. Glassman an hour before they were supposed to come to school, hoping he would arrive early so they could discuss things such as the Ouija Board and

(ESP) extra sensory perception.) Stories of supernatural phenomena abound, and these were an integral part of the unit.

7. Start fresh. At the beginning of each term, make sure each youngster feels he or she begins with a clean slate. Past misdemeanors should be forgotten—and everyone has the opportunity to begin anew. No teacher should ever come to a classroom with preexisting ideas. If a child has been an attendance problem or a problem in any other way, make no mention of it.

However, once the problem manifests itself in your classroom, it is well to point out to the child, privately, that in the light of his or her previous record this is a specific weakness of his or hers that you, as the teacher, would like to help eradicate. Tell him or her, "I know you've had this problem, but this is your opportunity to start all over again, and I want to work with you. How about it? Will you let me help you?"

## CONCLUSION

The school phobic, the truant, and the loner are classified together in this chapter because for various reasons they do not attend school regularly. Theirs is, indeed, a very serious problem. Getting them to come to school regularly is usually the task of the school administration and special staff, but it is the teacher who must work to keep them coming.

What can you, the teacher, do? You can attempt to communicate with the youngster, to establish rapport with him or her, and to learn what the problem actually is. Why would this particular youngster stay away? If you can learn this, you can go far toward solving the problem.

You can try to structure the situation so that the child feels comfortable and welcome. If possible, the cooperation of the other youngsters in the class should be requested. Activities should be created that will give the child with problems some measure of success. The troubled youngster should be given responsibilities within the classroom, so that he or she sees the need for attending.

The parents' aid must be enlisted, and, if need be, the parent should be educated to insist the girl or boy come to school. The child's previous records should be studied for clues. How can you best reach this type of youngster? By speaking to him or her in a kind fashion, you may be able to determine whether his or her difficulty comes from a situation within the school. If so, how can it be remedied?

By behaving in a positive fashion toward these girls and boys when they do come to school, you help them overcome the problems they are having. They need sympathy and compassion. It is easy for a teacher to become annoyed when rebuffed by a youngster with whom he or she has been working who still stays out again and again, but one must treat this philosophically.

Try to be a diagnostician, to determine exactly what it is that is keeping this youngster away. What powerful drives, and they are powerful, are causing his or her absence? What entices him or her elsewhere? If such youngsters believe you are really trying to help them, that your sympathy is genuine, they may disclose their secrets. Does the child feel "out of it"? Is his or her personality recognized in the classroom? Are his or her good works on display? Does he or she feel inferior because he or she can't read or function academically?

A word, a smile, a touch on the arm every day when the child does come in, a little private discussion, and help with academic areas when help is needed—these may be the magic that will bring the truant, the phobic, or the loner into school, possibly even regularly.

# 10

## THE PHYSICALLY HANDICAPPED CHILD AND THE CHILD OF POVERTY

We consider the physically handicapped child and the child of poverty in the same chapter because their situations have many similarities, and many methods will apply to both types of children. Physically handicapped children are those who are in some manner restricted because of their physical condition—be it poor eyesight or hearing, or the loss of a limb, malformations or malfunctions of any part of the body—or those whose size produces feelings of inferiority.

Children so handicapped may have psychological problems resulting in an inability to perform at the same level as their peers. If they feel "different," this may cause them to become frustrated and angry, and this in turn may result in their being problems in the classroom. Let us report just one such case.

We were called into a classroom where a first grader had thrown himself down and was banging his head against the floor in sheer fury. His mother had truthfully told his teacher that "Billy has temper tantrums," and complained, "He doesn't ever listen to me." The child was removed from the class and sent home.

The next day the teacher spoke quietly with Billy. He watched her intently, gazing at her with beautiful brown eyes wide open. She sent him back to his seat, then called to him because she thought of something else she wanted to say to him. He ignored her. She called again. He still paid no attention. When she tapped him on the shoulder, Billy whirled around. The young woman suddenly realized the problem. "My God," she thought, "he doesn't hear me."

And that, of course, was the problem. Billy had lost 75 percent of his hearing, yet no one had spotted this loss until she did. This story has a happy ending, for with a hearing aid, the youngster's hearing improved and his frustration disappeared. It would be wonderful if we could work such magic all of the time, but unfortunately we cannot.

Children of poverty may feel as frustrated as this child did because of his hearing loss. They may live in a slum or in a slightly better community, but if they are poor, the results of this poverty on their psychological development may cause them to have many problems that show up in our classrooms. **One out of every five children living in America today lives in poverty.**

Then too, there are the youngsters who are homeless and live from day to day on the streets or in shelters. **In the major cities, one out of four homeless people is a child.** Those children are in our classes, too. How badly all of these boys and girls need to be educated, for without education they have little chance of improving their circumstances!

Most teachers do not have the personal experience of having been poor. Ours has often been called the "affluent society," and for many people it undoubtedly is. However, living in the midst of plenty and not sharing in the riches makes people angry, and the boys and girls in your class may well display this anger. This anger leads to disruptive behavior.

As of 1989, 98 percent of American households owned at least one television set, and 63 percent owned two or more sets. This statistic shows us that even those living below the poverty level are able to view the lives of the rich and famous. Is there any wonder that they become acutely aware of the differences between their lifestyles and those of other people? What one sees on television can cause hurts that warp the personality almost beyond belief. In this land of plenty, the statistics are staggering.

Of the 20 percent of children living below the poverty level, the breakdown is very important. While the majority of children living in poverty are white, 39 percent of Hispanic children and 45 percent of black children are poor. It has been estimated that one in five youngsters entering school is learning impaired as a result of the poverty of the mother. This causes babies to be born with low birth weight. The mother may have taken drugs or alcohol during her pregnancy or simply not had enough prenatal care or good food.

If a pregnant woman eats a diet deficient in vitamins, particularly vitamin B, one scientific theory concludes that the intelligence of her unborn child will be diminished. In 1973 the number of families with children receiving Aid to Families with Dependent Children (AFDC) was 83.6 percent. By 1987, that number had decreased to 59.8 percent. The need had not lessened; the rules were changed. (These statistics were furnished by the Children's Defense Fund, Washington, D.C.)

As teachers we cannot possibly ignore such factors and close our eyes to the problems facing youngsters living in poverty. At times, even those of us who feel we are sensitive don't behave that way. We just don't realize exactly what it means to be poor. A case in point: Denise came to school one day in shorts. A seventh grader, she was reprimanded severely by a supervisor, for this was against school rules. The girl said she knew it was wrong and took the man's words without attempting a reply. Suddenly she burst into tears. "My sister took my dress, and I tore my skirt," Denise whispered. "This was the only thing I had to wear," she added. The supervisor was really upset because the girl's story was, without doubt, the truth. This man is a compassionate person but unthinkingly he had wounded this little girl, whose psyche could not withstand such onslaughts.

In working with troubled children, we always seek to determine the problem. In the cases mentioned, we must try to determine whether the physical handicap or the poverty has done psychological damage. Of course, try to learn something of their backgrounds by speaking with the youngsters quietly, being very careful not to make them feel you are prying into their lives.

Another method is to have the entire class write a paragraph on the topic, "If I could do anything I wanted to I would . . ." Careful reading of these papers may give you insight into the troubled children's minds.

You may teach a class with many youngsters who are either physically handicapped or handicapped by poverty. You will find that some have been far more badly scarred psychologically than others. It is often the case that the deeper the scar, the more disruption these children will cause, and the more difficulty you will have in teaching them self-control. There is no question that the conditions in the entire world today reflect, in part, these deep psychological wounds.

## RAISING SELF-ESTEEM

The school situation, we feel, is the great equalizer. The teacher is often unaware of the conditions under which his or her students live, or their economic situation, or anything else about them. Parents will often spend money for clothing for their children long before they buy anything for themselves. Nevertheless, we often, but not always, have an idea of who is poor, who is physically handicapped, and who needs our special help.

We believe, and much research bears this out, that children can be encouraged to achieve and their self-esteem raised when they are made to feel they are capable human beings. You may wish to try this method: Tell your children, "I have asked for all of you to be in my class." They may very well be skeptical. Some may be disruptive youngsters with real problems. Indicate your awareness of this by saying, "I know all of you aren't perfect, but who is? This is a heterogeneous class. Of course you don't know the meaning of that word, but *hetero* means 'different' and *geneous* means 'grouping.' It is a way of saying that each of you is on a different level of learning. I plan to experiment with you, to make this the best class on this grade."

This technique does work. The youngsters may well still be skeptical, and so add, "Is there anyone who is *not* willing to take part in this experiment?" Ask for a show of hands. Usually youngsters want to partic- ipate in experiments. Explain then that you will keep records and also inform them of exactly how the experiment is progressing. Build on this by using diagnostic or pretesting and following lessons with achievement tests of your own (not the standardized variety). Construct the tests so that your boys and girls do well—every one of them.

When youngsters are handicapped, it is essential that they do well. You may have to spend more time with them as they may require special attention. You may also have other youngsters work with them. Build on the idea of an esprit de corps, of the achievement of the entire class. With everyone working together you teach one of the truly important lessons of life—cooperating with others.

You may have to omit the discussion of heterogeneity with younger children. But boys and girls, when told they are the best class and con- vinced of it, will behave that way. However, don't tell them they are if it is unbelievable. They don't have to be the best in all areas, but if they cooperate, you can tell them that makes them "the best" in your eyes.

## EVERY CHILD MUST LEARN TO READ _____

IF YOU ARE TEACHING IN A DISADVANTAGED AREA AND YOU HAVE A CLASS IN THE LOWER GRADES, MAKE IT YOUR MOST IMPORTANT GOAL THAT EVERY CHILD IN YOUR CLASS BE ABLE TO READ. BY SO DOING, YOU FURNISH THE KEY TO ALL KNOWLEDGE TO EVERY CHILD—FOR READING IS, INDEED, THAT PRECIOUS KEY. IF THIS BECOMES YOUR PERSONAL GOAL, YOU WILL BE AMAZED AT THE PERMANENT EFFECTS YOU CAN HAVE ON THE LIVES OF YOUR CHILDREN.

IN THE UPPER GRADES, SHOULD YOU DISCOVER A CHILD WHO HAS NOT MASTERED THE MECHANICS OF READING, IT MAY BE NECESSARY FOR YOU TO START AT THE VERY BEGINNING, WITH PHONICS, IF THIS CHILD IS TO CONTINUE AND ACQUIRE ANYTHING RESEMBLING AN EDUCATION.

One highly successful teacher, who retired after more than forty years of teaching, was asked, "Did you ever have, in your entire career, any children you couldn't teach to read?" She thought for a few minutes, then replied, rather shamefacedly, "Yes, I confess I did. There were two." Yet she had taught in a very poor area—which still is very poor, but which now has many children who cannot read. "My goal had always been", she said, "'Every child must be able to read when he or she leaves my class.'"

## WHAT IT MEANS TO GO TO WORK

It may be difficult for some readers to realize, but one of the facts of life in some areas is quite foreign to many people. There are boys and girls who have never been in actual contact with anyone who gets up and goes to work each morning. They have not had a role model of this type. Where, then, if not in school, will they be exposed to this concept?

It may be brought out when one teaches social studies and compares different occupations. In the lower grades there are units on the police, the fire department, the sanitation department, and on other public service occupations. In the upper grades many other careers are discussed. However, because there are very few teachers who have ever experienced the lack of a work-structured situation, this is a point not very often brought out.

Another manner in which this point may be taught is by showing that when a child goes to school, it is as if he or she is going to work and has responsibilities. He or she must get to school, must get there on time, must be prepared to do work, and must behave in such a way that he or she will be able to do that work. These responsibilities should be stressed again and again.

Starting at the beginning of the school year, these responsibilities must be outlined and discussed. Then, when a youngster doesn't behave in an appropriate manner, he or she can be reminded, "You have responsibilities. I know you won't forget them. I know you are mature enough to handle them." By treating a girl or boy as a mature person, you can achieve far more than by chastising them.

## MAKE THE CHILDREN FEEL IMPORTANT

Youngsters with problems caused by physical handicaps or by poverty are often conditioned to defeat. It seems to be all they expect of life. Their experiences in school often seem to emphasize this, and their feelings of unimportance grow and grow. With that comes disruptive behavior and the accompanying discipline problems.

How can this be changed? How can we make these youngsters feel as important as anyone else? One of the best tools you have at your disposal to work toward remedying this situation is the establishment of positions as monitors, as outlined in the first chapter.

Try to make your youngsters who need to be made to feel important monitors of the highest order. They may, for example, greet guests or serve as guides during occasions when parents visit the school. Prepare sashes of the school colors for them to wear. If your school has a color guard, try to arrange for them to be part of it.

You may choose children to write on the board, serving as your "right hand" (or your left, if you happen to be a "lefty"). However, do this only if the child's writing is easily legible. To allow the child to serve in this capacity if his or her handwriting cannot be understood is surely not doing the youngster a favor.

Seat the girl or boy with problems close to you. The proximity to the teacher, with a few confidences from you, will do wonders to making any youngster feel "like a big shot."

When children are physically handicapped, try to help them do every activity the other youngsters can do (providing you have their physicians' permission). Allow them to play any games they are able to play. This can do a great deal for these youngsters toward making them feel equal to the other boys and girls.

## FIND ALL POSSIBLE ASSISTANCE

As is the case most of the time when dealing with a disruptive child, communication with him or her is the key if he or she is to be helped.

We shall always remember the first grader who came to school after having been absent the day before. When his teacher asked him, softly, why he hadn't come to school, he replied, "My mom and me sat up all night because we were afraid the rats might bite the baby." This incident occurred many years ago, but, unfortunately, it could still happen today. While we have seen improvement in housing conditions, there is still a very long way to go.

If a child is disruptive and his or her behavior may be caused by either a physical handicap or poverty, it is vitally important that that child speak with either the teacher or with someone else in the school who may be able to be of help to him or to her. The teacher is in the front lines in this regard, and by his or her working with this youngster, doing guidance in a quiet manner, the child's behavior may change.

Often the guidance counselor should work with the youngster. In addition to actually counseling the boy or girl, the counselor is able to apply for help from one or more appropriate social service agencies. Outside counseling or financial help may be obtained in this way. Most counselors are knowledgeable and able to arrange for this type of assistance. When such a referral is made, the youngster must be helped to understand that this measure is not a disciplinary one but one taken to help him or her.

It is entirely possible that youngsters may become disruptive because they are hungry and irritable. Many schools serve lunch, and some serve breakfast as well. Your boys and girls should be encouraged to eat the meals provided by the school. Malnutrition may seriously affect a child's development, both physically and mentally. If at all possible, the school lunchroom should be made attractive so that the youngsters are happy to have their meals there.

There are times when children don't come to school because they don't have the clothing or shoes they need. Sometimes the Parent Association "pitches in" and supplies what is necessary. This can be very important for parents who are receiving public assistance. They often have great difficulty purchasing clothing for their children. Even in schools where one would not expect this problem to exist, it arises from time to time. The astute teacher frequently becomes aware of such situations and can do much, quietly and without fanfare, to help the youngsters in his or her class.

Assistance for the physically handicapped boy or girl depends, first of all, on the discovery of the existing defect. Certain defects are very obvious—a shortened arm or lameness, for example. Others, such as heart conditions, poor eyesight, or poor hearing, should be disclosed by a review of the health record cards. Even then, there may be surprises.

One such case was a little girl, Katie, who was in the first class I taught. Unbeknown to me, although I had checked the health cards, Katie had to take medication daily. There were times she conveniently "forgot." This would cause her to pass out. When this happened the other children became very upset and disruptive. Katie finally had to be excluded from this class, a regular class, and placed in a special group for handicapped children.

If you have physically handicapped youngsters in your class, the wisest procedure for you to follow is to discuss them with the school nurse, and, as soon as possible, with their parents. Confer with the guidance counselor as well. Speak to the children's previous teachers and when these youngsters are promoted, be sure their conditions are noted on their record cards. It is also worthwhile to talk with their new teachers about their illnesses so that the teachers are forewarned that unexpected situations might arise.

When handicapped children take part in any physical activity, be sure they do so with the written consent of their physicians. This is necessary, for example, because a child may have a heart condition that precludes exercise.

## HELP THE YOUNGSTER FUNCTION IN THE CLASSROOM _____

1. As early in the term as you can, try to communicate with the youngster, showing that you understand his or her problems, be they physical or economic, and that you will be of as much help as possible. Of course, be tactful.

2. If the youngster seems to be frustrated, help him or her get rid of some of that frustration. If possible, give the child some physical activities that will get rid of pent-up emotions. Time spent in physical activity can be very worthwhile, for it is better for a child to hit a baseball than to hit another youngster.

3. When a youngster is in an angry mood, if he or she realizes that a friendly adult is there to talk to, be it teacher, counselor, or supervisor, disciplinary problems can sometimes be avoided. "I'm going to have a fight with Jackie," a youngster once told his teacher. His face was red with fury. "Why?" she said softly. "What did he do to get you so angry?"

"He laughed at my pants," the boy responded.

Indeed, the pants were torn in an embarrassing spot. The teacher said to the child, "No, don't do that. Go into the gym and hit the punching bag as much as you like. Then come back and we'll talk about it." This may seem to be unorthodox, but with a child who is so pent up as this one was, the best way to handle the situation is by first giving him a physical outlet, and then when he has calmed down discussing the problem. (Of course it includes talking with Jackie, too.)

4. Youngsters have, at times, been quite cruel, and laughing at a physically handicapped or poorly dressed child is far from unheard of. Staring at him or her is more insidious. It takes a great deal of work with a group of youngsters to get them to understand the pain the boy or girl may experience as a result of the unthinking behavior of others. This is a very important aspect of our teaching—to help all of our youngsters become sensitive to the feelings of others. You can, of course, see how necessary this may be—if you have a child in your class who has been the object of such behavior.

5. If a child is not achieving academically because of his or her frustration with life or with physical handicaps, this adds to his or her problems. By helping the youngster keep up with the class, we at least eliminate an extra source of frustration. If the youngster is learning, at least some satisfaction results from this, and he or she is more comfortable in his or her mind

as well as in the classroom. Academic failure often results in rejection of the teacher and of the material being taught, and discipline problems frequently ensue.

6. The child with sight or hearing deficiencies must receive special consideration. Consider Lloyd, a boy who wore thick glasses and who made a constant nuisance of himself in the back of the room. His teacher was an inexperienced young man who did not perceive any problem—other than the fact that Lloyd was disruptive. It was the librarian who suggested to the teacher that perhaps the boy could not see from where he was seated. "Don't ask him," she said. "Let's ask the school nurse."

On investigation it was found that Lloyd could not possibly have seen the chalkboard from his assigned seat in the classroom. As a general rule, **any child who has either a visual or a hearing problem should be seated at the front of the room.** It is worthwhile to check to see too that no girl or boy is seated behind a youngster who is taller than he or she is, so that his or her view is blocked. This simple measure may prevent discipline problems from developing.

## FULFILL PHYSICAL NEEDS THROUGH SOCIAL SERVICE AGENCIES

The liaison person dealing with social service agencies in most schools is the guidance counselor. If a school does not have a counselor, that responsibility would probably fall to an assistant principal or even the principal of the school. In either event, one of these persons has, as part of his or her professional duties, developing contacts with the local agencies and knowing to which agency a youngster or his or her family should be referred.

Confer with the counselor when you know one of your pupils is in need of help. The assistance may be financial or it may be that which is offered to handicapped persons.

When youngsters misbehave a great deal, it is worthwhile to try to win them over by talking with them and showing that you are sincerely interested.What is a better manifestation of this interest than helping find solutions facing them and their families? We overheard one girl verbalize this, as she said to her friends, "Let's be good for Mrs. X," as they entered her classroom. And the child was absolutely right, for this teacher really "gave a damn" about her students and went out of her way to help them.

Teachers are often the first English-speaking people with whom immigrants who can't speak the language come into contact. If we can help them with their problems, we influence their entire thinking about our country.

## TAKE TRIPS TO BROADEN HORIZONS _____

Children handicapped physically or by poverty need to have their horizons broadened, for far too often their parents have been unable to travel with them. When we use the word "travel," we mean going anywhere, for we have met youngsters who have never been more than one mile from their homes. This is true for many reasons—the two most common being lack of funds and lack of initiative. It is as much a part of our professional work to introduce this aspect of learning as to introduce any other.

To facilitate taking trips, divide your class into small groups. We found six youngsters per group worked well. Place any children who present discipline problems in different groups. Choose, or have the youngsters choose, a group leader for each group for the day, and have that boy or girl become responsible for the others in the group.

Before taking any trip, prepare the youngsters for it by discussing why you are taking the trip and what you expect the class to get from it. Give an assignment to be handed in afterward. Also discuss, privately, with each child who might be disruptive specifically what you expect from him or her in the way of self-control. Singled out, in a one-to-one relationship, the child should respond to your sense of urgency that the trip be a good one and that he or she show the maturity to behave well.

We strongly believe that no youngster in a class should be prohibited from taking a trip. The boys and girls who present discipline problems are often the ones who need the experience the most. However, be sure the youngsters understand their responsibilities. They should be spoken to and informed that if they misbehave, they will not go on future trips.

Lack of funds should not prevent children from participating. You may either have each child contribute a bit more than his or her share to cover the expenses of the others (without saying so), or you may seek aid from the Parent Association or from school funds. Many schools encourage the youngsters to earn money for class trips through projects such as washing cars, or cake sales.

Trips are an excellent opportunity to meet parents. Use them when you have a child who is presenting problems. Invite his or her parents to accompany you on the trip, and spend some time talking with them. Learn about the family and about the youngster's earlier childhood. Discuss, very carefully, the problems you are having with the boy or girl. By always using the concept, "What can we do, working together, to help with your child?" you are often able to obtain the aid of the parent—which very often makes a tremendous difference in the behavior of the child.

## SETTING UP PROJECTS

Much can be done by project work to raise the children's self-esteem. Troubled children, we have found, react very well to a large project situation. Decide with the class what type of project they would like. It might be a travel fair, with children working in groups of twos or threes for each country or for each state. (You might wish to work with sections of the United States.) If your class is multinational and children represent their own backgrounds, the results can be spectacular. We've seen this combined with a food fair that was educational as well as fattening, but so satisfying.

Perhaps your project might involve money. Banking, various currencies, wholesale and retail marketing might all be involved. For science classes, a project encompassing the various branches of science—biology, chemistry, physics, geology, anthropology, psychology, and such specialties as botany, zoology, and physiology make an excellent project. Others include occupations (with guest speakers included), methods of transportation, or means of communication. You might try a dissection of a newspaper, with each committee showing how articles are actually constructed.

While the youngsters are working, they must be actively supervised, and any disruption that occurs must be handled immediately. You might say, "I know you would like to take part in this project, wouldn't you? Do I have your word you will cooperate and do your share of the work? Is there any help I can give you?" Place your disruptive children with youngsters who will continue to work. We have found that the threat of removal from a project was often enough to keep disruptive boys and girls in line. Of course, help any group that needs your assistance.

To use a completed project most effectively, display it, and have the pupils write invitations, inviting the parents, the principal, and other important people to see it. If the project is completed by Open School Week, it is worthwhile to show it then. Be sure to label all work with the children's names so that the youngsters themselves see their accomplishments—and so that visitors, too, see them.

## CONCLUSION

The physically handicapped child and the child of poverty have many problems in common. Both may often feel frustrated and become disruptive as a result. The problem is more common with the poor, for one child out of five lives in poverty. In the major cities one of every four homeless persons is a child.

Even among the poor, television sets abound, and there the youngsters see on a daily basis the different lives of people who have sufficient money to live on. This contributes to their frustration. Poor women are likely to give birth to children who later have learning disabilities as a result of low birth weight. School has been called the "great equalizer" in terms of finances, and, indeed, there is more equality in the classroom than in the outside world.

What can we do to help both the physically handicapped and the child of poverty? We should work to raise these children's self-esteem by making them feel capable of doing the work we give to them. We must make sure that no child leaves our class who cannot read. This will make a tremendous difference in the life of every child.

Because there are children who have never had the experience of seeing a person get up and go to work every day, we must be sure to bring this out in social studies class, while teaching occupations or at other times.

Physically handicapped children and children of poverty need to be made to feel important, as all youngsters do. Class trips and projects can help in this regard. Both types of handicapped youngsters often need assistance, which the teacher and the guidance counselor can provide. Perhaps the help of outside agencies is necessary, and some school personnel should help the children's families obtain it.

Above all, we should try to understand these children. They may well live in a world that is very different from ours, and the bridges are few. The frustrations and the consequent times of disruptive behavior are often many. But only if we can enter in some way into these children's worlds can we help them to the fullest. Try to draw them close to you, for only then will you be able to teach them and to change disruptive behavior into self-control.

# 11

## YOUNGSTERS WHO ABUSE ALCOHOL, DRUGS, OR INHALANTS

One of the most serious and most tragic problems involving the youth of the entire world of today is substance abuse. This is a threat not only to adolescents but to younger children as well. Substance abusers are found in all age groups, in all areas of the world, and in all strata of society.

While public awareness seems to be concentrated on narcotic abuse, the substance that is abused the most is actually alcohol. Certainly the use of marijuana, heroine, cocaine, and crack cocaine, are all too frequent. We must also consider pills, the amphetamines and barbiturates, called "uppers" and "downers." Chemicals that are "sniffed," the inhalants, are yet another type of substance abuse, and have been abused for years.

The youngster who abuses any of these substances may be talkative, boisterous, and rambunctious. But he or she may instead be withdrawn and "out of it," confined to his or her private world.

*In the event that you suspect any youngster is abusing any substance, you should immediately contact the guidance counselor or the principal. (In some schools, there are special guidance counselors who work specifically with youngsters whose problems are drug related.) If the authorities agree with your observations, they should immediately get in touch with the parents of the youngsters involved, for, in cases of this type, time is of the essence.*

## TYPE OF ABUSE _____

### Alcohol Abuse

Youngsters usually drink beer or wine but on occasion may consume hard liquor. Any of these, but most often the latter, are taken from their parents' supply. Alcohol acts like a sedative, with a tranquilizing effect on many of the youngsters, but it may stimulate others. It first acts on the part of the brain that is involved in self-control. This may cause the boy or girl to quarrel with or even attack and fight with other youngsters.

When any drug, including alcohol, is consumed, the amount that can cause serious problems is determined by the body weight of the consumer. Therefore, youngsters can suffer liver or heart damage after having drunk much less than adults.

The prevalence of alcohol abuse among America's high school students can be seen by these statistics. In 1988, more than 92 percent of the students had consumed alcohol in the past year, and according to the Children's Defense Fund, four out of ten high school seniors have been drunk in the past two weeks. The two leading causes of death among teens are alcohol related accidents and suicide.

Youngsters too often see their parents using alcoholic beverages and, sadly, emulate them. Beer drinking is very popular among the young.

A youngster who has been drinking any form of alcohol may appear "tipsy." His or her breath may smell of alcohol, his or her face may be red, and his or her speech slurred. It is very possible that he or she may become disruptive and shout or fight. If a child appears to be drunk, he or she should be removed from the classroom situation immediately, before serious problems result.

### Crack Cocaine or "Crack"

Cocaine is a stimulant that comes from the leaves of the coca plant. A white powder, it is commonly "snorted," or drawn in a small amount into the nose, where it is absorbed quickly by the nasal membranes. Other users inject it into their veins. In either case, the person feels a surge of pleasure, called a "high." Like other drugs such as heroine, it is very addictive, and possession of it is illegal.

For years, cocaine was expensive, but within recent years a pellet form, called "crack cocaine" or simply "crack" has become much more readily available. It is this form that is sold to the youngsters, often within a short distance of the schoolyard. Children of parents who use this drug are well aware of their parents' activities, just as they are that the parents abuse alcohol.

Cocaine and crack cause a sudden increase in the heart rate and in the blood pressure. Youngsters feel they can accomplish anything, physically or mentally. One sure sign of the crack user is that the pupils of his or her eyes are dilated, and he or she appears euphoric. Since hunger is diminished, he or she may not eat.

In the classroom, the crack user may well steal other youngsters' belongings, or even the teacher's, to buy the drug, which causes a strong psychological and physical dependence. He or she may get into arguments or fights. Again, if a child appears to be under the influence of the drug, he or she should be removed from the classroom.

## Marijuana

Marijuana, often called "pot" or "grass," has been the drug of choice for young people for many years. It is the dried leaves of the hemp plant, and its use is illegal in the United States. In 1988, 47 percent of high school seniors reported using it on a regular basis. The dried leaves are rolled into a cigarette, which is then smoked. It produces a "high" that usually lasts from three to five hours.

It is believed that most youngsters begin at the age of twelve to smoke pot. Generally it is introduced to them by friends, and it is much cheaper than crack. The most frequent reaction is a dreamy or relaxed state, the eyes become reddened, and the mouth dry. The person seems to feel more aware of his or her senses and surroundings. Another, although far less frequent, reaction is one of panic and anxiety.

Edward was in the eighth grade when it was discovered by one of his teachers that he was selling pot to some of his classmates, and to some younger boys and girls. This came as a shock, for this young man was a good student and was never disruptive. If he did have red eyes, no one noticed them. He never seemed high, for a very good reason. "I only smoked after school," he told the guidance counselor. "My parents weren't home, and I smoked in the back yard so they couldn't smell anything."

When marijuana is smoked, it gives off a very distinctive sweet smell, a fact of which Edward was well aware. In spite of using the drug, this boy was able to keep his grades up, and his appearance as well.

One of the problems associated with marijuana use is that it often leads to the use of drugs such as cocaine or heroine. This is particularly true when the habit begins when the marijuana user is a child.

## Inhalants

The use of inhalants has been increasing in recent years. It's simple to understand why this is so. Many are household products and so readily available that teenagers are easily seduced. Here too, they are introduced to this procedure by their peers. Years ago the glue used for making model airplanes was sniffed, and today such products as whipped cream, butane lighter fluid, and many different household sprays such as paints and Scotchguard™ are abused by youngsters.

In the Starting Place, a Hollywood, Florida, drug-treatment center, the staff reported in January 1991 seeing more teenagers seeking help for using inhalants than for crack cocaine use.

The Chemical Specialties Manufacturers Association is so well aware of the problem that they are producing posters and videotapes to be shown to youngsters in the sixth grade and above. The organization is concerned with the brain damage that can easily result from inhalant abuse.

You may possibly recognize the young person who is using inhalants because he or she may complain of nausea or double vision, or have a nosebleed.

## RECOGNIZING THE VARIOUS TYPES OF SUBSTANCE ABUSE

Janine was a perfectly behaved sixth grader who confided to her teacher that she had been sniffing cleaning fluid. When she was questioned, the girl replied, "I broke up with my boyfriend. I just couldn't face the day without sniffing."

It was learned, however, that she was not alone. Three of her friends had joined her—and they said they had been doing this every school day for a month because, they said, it made them feel good.

This brings up the need for education—of even very young children, in regard to the dangers inherent in the use of any chemical or drug when it is not prescribed by a physician. These young ladies were shocked to learn of the potential for brain damage that can result from sniffing. Many drugs found in the home can be abused, from cough medicine to diet pills. Some of them are extremely deadly.

Should you have a child in your class who is behaving peculiarly, observe him or her carefully. Very often drug or chemical abusers lose interest in their schoolwork and show other behavioral changes. Apathy sets in. Their clothing and appearance may deteriorate. (Do not confuse this with current styles, however.) There are many signs of abuse—drunken appearance, stupor, drowsiness, or dazed appearance. Other possible indicators are a lack of coordination, aggressive behavior, giggling, or excessive talking, and disruptive behavior.

If you believe a youngster has taken any drug, have the boy or girl write a paragraph. It is a good idea to have the entire class do this, to avoid singling out the youngster. If the boy or girl is under the influence of some drug, often he or she cannot write and will produce "chicken tracks." If you get these scrawls, you have almost positive proof. If the child can write, he or she may still have taken something, but you have no proof in either direction, so you have to keep observing him or her carefully.

"Inhalants are among the most deadly of drugs, more likely to kill than other drugs," says Jim Hall, head of the Miami-based Up Front, a national drug information group. "They're toxic substances, and the dose level is not controlled or regulated."

While you probably will never see these effects, they may include nausea, double vision, or nosebleeds. Others are abnormal heart rhythms, organ and brain damage, and, ultimately, death.

## THE UNDERLYING INADEQUATE PERSONALITY OF THE EXPERIMENTER

Children who drink alcohol or take drugs may often be those who cannot cope with the problems presented by the world around them—be they in school or at home. Because they are unhappy, because they cannot face the trials and tribulations the day brings, because they may be bored or unhappy and seek a "lift," they need some external stimulation, and they find it in pills or booze, a pellet or a sniff.

However, there are other boys and girls who take drugs or use alcohol for a much more superficial reason. They are talked into experimentation or they try drugs because, they say, all their friends are doing it. It takes a very strong person to be able to reject an activity that his or her peers are pushing. Years ago some youngsters would try to reject cigarette smoking; today it's probably alcohol. The need to be "one of the boys" (or girls) is uppermost in many young people's minds. It supersedes any misgivings they may have about trying drugs. What is worse to a youngster than being called "chicken"? How many youngsters can, as former first lady Nancy Reagan proposed, "Just say no."? Perhaps there are some but surely not all.

## THE OPEN DISCUSSION OF THE EFFECTS OF DRUG ABUSE

Because of the spread of this epidemic, drug education should begin with children in kindergarten. Of course, all teaching must be geared to the level of the children's understanding and must be handled very carefully and deftly. The following simple poem illustrates this point. We suggest you read it aloud, dramatically and with sincerity. We are sure it will entice and really hold the youngsters' attention. After reading it, ask your class how they felt about Kate. Ask too, how they think she could have been helped.

You may wish to expand on the poem by having the class draw posters describing it and hanging these around your room. You may decide to have the youngsters dramatize the poem. You want to keep the message alive and in the minds of the girls and boys.

### "Kate"

### by Regina Berger

She died, not in a hospital,
With doctors and nurses on call,
And Mom at her side, giving her all,
To spare her child suffering and pain,
And pray to heaven that she be well again.

No, this is not how she died.
She died alone, at the top of a cold staircase
    in the dark,
Alone, and in agony, she died,
Shedding hot tears that could not
    be dried.

And she cried, "Oh, Mommy, Mommy!
Forgive me! I trusted a stranger
    more than I trusted you.
Mommy, Mommy, please help me!
The pain! I can't stand the pain!"
But Mom heard her not and found her not,
Though she searched everywhere.

"My little Kate didn't come home
    last night,"
Said the frantic mother to the
    policeman,
And a sob tore her words apart
As she stood there with a
    breaking heart.

And the kind cop wiped away a tear,
As he saw her tremble,
    tremble with fear.
"We have found your little girl,
    my dear."
And the policeman turned his head
    away.

For he could not bear to see the
  mother's face twisted in pain.

While he tried to comfort her,
  saying
That her baby would never suffer,
  suffer again.
As he spoke the sad words
The mother fell to the ground
When she heard how her poor little
  Kate had been found.

And that mother knelt and prayed
  for her child
Who had died that day,
And would be buried
  in the churchyard,
  not far away.
And she added, "Sweet Heaven,
  save us all
  from such a fate,
As that which befell
  My darling,
  My darling,
My own little Kate!"

Dark and soft and beautiful
Had been the little girl's eyes.
In school she had won
  many a prize.
For often a sweet song
  she would write and sing.

What pleasure to Mother and
  teacher and friends
  she could bring!
But sing and write she
  would do no more
Words that flowed
  from her heart's tender
  core,
For those gentle eyes
  were closed forevermore.
Asleep in the churchyard
  near the countryside

Of the drugs she had taken
Our little Kate died.

Many teachers have had their classes write poems about spring or fall, sunshine or flowers. Perhaps you might change the topic and have the youngsters give their impressions of drug or substance abuse. Unfortunately, many children are very familiar with this and can draw ideas from their own experiences.

A class poem, with all of the youngsters participating in its writing, is a very effective technique. You will probably find that one idea fosters another. Of course, you will be called on to supply a word or phrase, and your enthusiasm will help carry the project through.

## BECOMING A FRIEND IS THE FIRST STEP

No teacher should stand in judgment of any girl or boy, no matter what the situation is. On the contrary, the adult must try to be the shield, protecting the youngster from pernicious influences. By your manner, by your actions and words, you must convey to your pupils that you are their friend, that you really care about them, and that your one and only intention is to help them. As we have said, the substance abuser is generally an unhappy child or one who is easily led by others.

Sometimes a teacher does offer friendship, and the offer is not accepted. This often comes as a distinct shock to the adult. Should this happen to you, you must continue to convince the youngster that you really do want to help. The French have a saying that applies here: "Tout comprende c'est tout pardonner" or, "To understand all is to forgive all."

However, should a youngster confide in you, you must call the situation to the attention of the administration so that help can be obtained. This presents a difficulty, for the child may feel he or she is being betrayed. This requires you be very deft in your handling of the problem.

"Bobby," you might say, "we have to get some help for you right now. You realize, don't you, that your life may be in danger? But if we can help you right now, immediately, you can be spared misery, suffering, or even death." This type of conversation is extremely difficult and requires you to show how sincere you are. "You know what I'm saying is true," you would say to the boy or girl. "You know that I am not exaggerating. I don't want to see anything happen to you, and it could." Point out, too, that we read in the newspapers or see on television news programs all the time that a person has died because of an overdose of a drug or because of an automobile accident caused by driving while under the influence of alcohol.

## REFERRING THE CHILD WHILE WORKING WITH THE PARENTS _____

As soon as parents have been informed, you may be able to do a great deal to help them as well as the child. Do all you can to encourage the parent to work with the guidance counselor in contacting the appropriate social service agencies, where assistance can be obtained. Remember to stress the importance of the time element and that action be taken immediately so that tragedy can be averted.

You are in a position to befriend the boy or girl by telling the parents of the youngster's good qualities—which will help the child to overcome bad habits and even addiction. There are those parents who will throw up their hands and disown their children. Unfortunately, this is all too common. It is with this type of parents that the teacher must do everything he or she can to convince them that assistance is obtainable, that the youngster can be helped, and that they are not to feel helpless in this situation. Substance abuse has been and can be conquered in a great number of cases—depending in large measure on the amount of support offered by the parents and the help they can obtain for the boy or girl. It is possible there may not be an agency in the immediate community, but by consulting the guidance counselor or the school administrator, one can be located. But again, time is of the essence.

## PLEAD FOR UNDERSTANDING _____

You, the teacher, may have to plead very strongly with the parents on behalf of the child. Often this youngster has already been in difficulty and the parents are angry.

Let us consider Randy. At the tender age of fifteen she has been taking various types of pills for two years. She is lethargic, and her appearance shows a total lack of interest. Her schoolwork is virtually nil. She does, however, always carry an armload of books.

An interview with her mother disclosed the total lack of communication between the two. Frequently, the mother has used even so harsh a phrase as "Don't bother me" when the child sought to talk to her.

The family receives public assistance, and there are five children. The mother is quick to tell the teacher that Randy has always caused her trouble. "My other four are so good," she repeats often, "but I don't know what's the matter with this one. What can I do?" When that last question is answered, Randy's mother does not follow through. Even when informed the child is a drug abuser, she is not willing to face up to the situation. "I'll speak to her," she says, and that is all she does. Her tendency is to sweep it under the rug.

If neither the teacher nor the counselor is willing to pressure this mother and make her understand the great need Randy has for her understanding and help at this crucial time, the girl has little chance of recovery. She does wish to gain her mother's approval. The large number of books she carries to school is indicative of this wish. She needs much help—of a professional nature.

However, if this mother can be made to see how vitally important her role is, she can be the main instrument in saving the child from becoming an addict. The teacher or guidance counselor's forcefulness in speaking to the parent is all-important. If you are placed in such a situation, you must realize your potential for good by really communicating with and changing this mother's attitude.

## BRIDGING THE GENERATION GAP

All human beings need to be respected. There is no child, regardless of age, who does not long for recognition. Youngsters want their opinions to be heard, and their voice, their presence, their ideas to carry some weight. In the classroom, we must make them feel they are important people, lest they seek other companionship and other "teachers" who will make them feel "like big shots" and possibly ensnare them with flattery. Should these be pernicious persons, they might seriously damage the child's personality and character, for it is in just these situations that drug addicts come into being. We must preclude our children from becoming involved, or if they already are involved we must try to wean them away. This is particularly true when their "teachers" are their peers.

The situation is a very delicate one, for young children are, for the most part, "with us." They trust us—and it is usually not too difficult to gain their confidence. However, they do grow up, and by the time they reach the early teens, the tendency is to band together. They exchange confidences with their peers rather than with teachers or parents.

Never ask a youngster to be an informer. If you have created the atmosphere in which girls and boys feel comfortable coming to you, perhaps they will bring you information that may save them or their friends, or both, from possible disaster. Here again, it is the rapport you have developed that will enable youngsters to speak to you confidentially.

Of course, you would never belittle a child. Whatever problem he or she has, belittling will make worse. During the teenage years this may be exceedingly difficult, but if they are treated with affection and respect, even these boys and girls can be won over. This is what we mean by bridging the generation gap, and we promise you from our experience that it can be done.

## MAKE EVERY CHILD UNDERSTAND THE DANGER OF SUBSTANCE ABUSE

No educator can possibly ignore the deep importance of preventing substance abuse. Even seven year olds have been approached by drug pushers, and boys and girls of that age have been found drinking alcoholic beverages. Every teacher should have a program of some sort dealing with these problems. Education is the only way to arrest the epidemic among the young, and it has to be done in the classroom on a day-to-day basis.

How can you do this intensive teaching? One way is through the use of the arts: pictures, stories, anecdotes, films, plays. We've already mentioned the use of poetry.

One of the most gripping books you may have your youngsters read is called *Go Ask Alice.* There is no author mentioned and the story is told by an addicted child. It is an education for the teacher as well as for the youngsters.

We have found that while much in regard to drug abuse is available, less is available on alcohol abuse, which is far more prevalent and will continue to be so as the youngsters advance in age and schooling.

Most boys and girls are well aware of these problems, and they are extremely involved in them. We have seen a noisy group come to order instantly when the topic was brought to their attention. We had an assembly of five hundred seventh graders waiting for a film on this topic to begin. The teacher in charge tried to quiet them down. "Don't bother," the speaker said. "As soon as we begin showing the film, you'll be able to hear a pin drop." It was uncanny how quickly that auditorium became silent.

Most older youngsters are getting some education in this field, but younger children need it too, in larger measures, if we believe that "an ounce of prevention is worth a pound of cure." They need lessons of this type very frequently.

If you have any youngsters in your class whom you know are taking drugs or drinking alcoholic beverages (beer surely is included in that category) gear your lessons toward them, but of course without this being apparent to the others in the class. Try to show the serious consequences of their acts. Don't sit in judgment of the youngsters, lest you alienate them. Rather, try to make them feel that you are a friend, for only in this way can you possibly reach them and obtain the assistance they need.

If young children have never been told, how are they to learn about overdosing? This is particularly important if they are small in size and light in weight, because the amount of a drug or alcohol a person can tolerate safely is determined by his or her body weight. How are the children to learn of the danger of buying drugs and taking them—that they may have had rat poison or strychnine added to them? How can the boys and girls get this information if we don't teach it to them? How can they learn that pills their parents have in the medicine chest may poison them, or that household products when sniffed can be deadly? Forewarned is fore-armed!

Every teacher should be knowledgeable in these matters but should not exaggerate or make overstatements. The teaching must be factual, for there is nothing so convincing or potent as the truth. Teenagers, in partic-ular, feel they know it all, and if you tell them something they believe is untrue, you have to be able to back up your statements, or they will pay no attention whatsoever to anything else you say.

For example, adults will list all of the "dangers" of marijuana, yet at the time of this writing the research is almost inconclusive. There is, however, one fact that is undeniable, that smoking pot is against the law. This is the type of information we must give them if we are to avoid a credibility gap. We must use objective material—facts—which the young-sters will respect, and we must always listen carefully and patiently to every statement every boy or girl has to make on the subject. If we are to win their confidence, we must make them feel we respect their opinions or they will shut their minds to our teachings.

A word of caution: When showing a film on the subject of substance abuse, preview the material first. We recall one filmstrip on heroin addic-tion that could have served as a training film in how to shoot up. The pictures were so explicit that one could really follow the instructions. Another filmstrip gave an idea of what a person experienced when he or she was high. Done in full color, it made the experience seem very attrac-tive. Fortunately, the teacher had previewed these materials, and while he showed them at a faculty meeting, they were never shown to the young-sters, which had been the original intent.

## DRAMATIC EDUCATION

When children in your class are substance abusers, you might wish to consider taking them to places such as the morgue or to psychiatric wards of hospitals. There they will see lessons that are never to be forgotten. However, before you do this take the trip yourself, to be sure the desired effect will be produced. We once, for example, saw a young person dead of an overdose—really tragic to behold.

But we have also visited rehabilitation centers where the surround-ings are so pleasant (and this is not an exaggeration) that children coming from undesirable circumstances could want to be placed in such a center. You must use judgment and discretion. A similar warning should be in effect in regard to inviting ex-addicts to speak to the youngsters. We know of instances where they have become heroes for the children, glamorous figures, "with a fascinating past." This may prove to be risky business. Caution must be taken to be sure the speakers invited produce the desired effect. Sad to say, many "reformed" addicts return to their addiction, and an ex-user today may be a user again tomorrow. Giving him or her the opportunity to become friendly with the children in the school can set up a potentially dangerous situation, particularly if you feel the youngsters have been experimenting on their own.

It is far safer to show films, have panel discussions, and involve your local police department in your program. Many police departments have speakers who can discuss substance abuse and who have learned to communicate on the children's level of understanding.

## KEEPING THE MEANS OF COMMUNICATION OPEN _____

Many times the substance abusers are children who are seeking approval and who want friends. If they will allow you to be their ally, you can work with them. Talk to them privately, on a one-to-one basis, and try to develop good relationships with them. You may find yourself rebuked or virtually ignored. Never take this personally. Instead, reassure the boy or girl, saying "I am your friend, and I am honestly interested in you. I shall try to help you whenever I can." We have seen young adults return to see teachers years later as a result of such conversations. (Of course, you would never make such statements if you did not mean them.)

Some youngsters too often get the feeling that no one "gives a damn." It is terribly hard to reach them, but these are the ones who desperately need you. Their lack of self-esteem may be reflected in their dependence on drugs or alcohol or in other patterns of behavior, but if you can show them you care, there is always a chance you can be of real help to them at some time. The words we have suggested are simple, almost obvious, but it's tragic how rarely they are said, especially to the child who needs to hear them. He or she may be disruptive or hostile, physically dirty, or unattractive, and because he or she has so many problems is probably uncommunicative. Even if you feel your words aren't being heard or accepted, say them anyway. Keep the lines of communication open—on your end at least.

## KNOW YOUR NEIGHBORHOOD _____

There is no question as to which substance is easiest to obtain—inhalants head the list because they are in the home. The same is true of pills in all varieties, for the household medicine chest may be a veritable treasure.

When it comes to drugs and liquor, accessibility is a bit more compli-cated, but surprisingly not much. We know of one shop where a fourteen year old could easily purchase wine. Hard liquor was a bit more difficult. Most of the young people who drink alcohol start with wines because they are relatively inexpensive.

A case in point: Stanley, a tall, handsome boy, had a good word for everyone. He would smile pleasantly as he greeted people in the halls of the school. He was constantly wandering, even when he should have been in class, but he chose not to attend whenever the desire to "cut" came over him. He was a joker who had a good time and helped those around him to do so too.

By the end of the first marking period he was failing every subject. A meeting with Stan and his mother was arranged. As we sat around the table, the boy's expression was completely different. He was not smiling. The conference was eminently successful. Stanley stopped missing classes and his work improved. But he no longer smiled. Although behaving civilly, he was certainly not pleasant. One day in the hall, one of Stan's friends was heard to comment, "How he has changed—since he stopped having a bottle of wine for breakfast"! It was later learned he purchased his wine at a local store.

It is important for us to teach our youngsters that alcohol is as much an addictive substance as drugs, and possibly even more so. If they become alcoholics, this will have an effect on their entire lives. They may, for example, drive while intoxicated and cause accidents, for one half of all traffic fatalities are caused by drunk drivers.

Should we hear of shops where alcohol is sold to minors, this infor-mation should be turned over to the principal immediately. The same is true of drug dealers, of course.

In any class discussion, be extremely careful you do not pass judgment on the adult user of alcohol. It is necessary to discourage children from its use, but one must be careful not to condemn the adult—particularly the social drinker. We know of one case where an alert seven year old told her class, "My father drinks." "Oh, no," said the teacher. "I know your father, and he certainly doesn't drink to excess." "Yes, he does," insisted the child. "On the holidays he drinks part of a cup of wine. I saw him."

Surely many children have seen the results of alcohol abusers on the streets and in public places, but should there happen to be a member of the family so afflicted, it is important that the child not be embarrassed. Nevertheless, the problem drinker should be discussed, in the hope of discouraging the children from experimenting with alcoholic beverages as well as inhalants, pills, and drugs.

## CONCLUSION

The variety of substances being abused by youngsters today is an indication of the seriousness of the problems being faced all over the world. Alcohol leads the list, followed by drugs, inhalants, and pills. Any of these may cause disruptive behavior in your classroom, or may cause lethargy and sleepiness.

If a youngster seems to be behaving as if he or she is abusing any substance, careful observation is necessary before you report the situation to the principal. He or she in turn will contact the parents.

After this is done, you will still have the youngster in your class. The child may use a substance because he or she feels his or her personality is inadequate, or because he or she is experimenting. It is extremely important that you educate the youngsters, not only the abuser but the entire class, regarding the very dangerous nature of substance abuse. You may use stories, anecdotes, poetry, and art to do this. Films may be used for this purpose, as well as speakers from your local and state police departments.

Try to keep the lines of communication open between you and the child who is a substance abuser. By working with youngsters who are abusers on a one-to-one basis and assuring them of your interest and desire to help them, you may be able to do so. Assure them of the confidentiality of your conversations with them and never ask them to be informers.

Remember that the information regarding substance abuse that you give to your children, particularly when they are young, can have a strong positive effect on them.

# 12

## ABUSED CHILDREN, CHILDREN OF SUBSTANCE ABUSERS, AND CRACK KIDS

In this chapter we consider abused children and the children of alcohol- or substance-dependent parents. We also consider crack babies. These are the children of mothers who were addicted to crack cocaine and took the drug during their pregnancies. In this way it might be said they abused their unborn children.

It is sad to say, but children have been abused since time immemorial in different ways. However, it is only in comparatively recent times that this evil has come to the fore. In 1986, the name Lisa Steinberg became almost a household word. This little girl was abused so badly by a man who considered her his daughter but had not adopted her legally that she died of her wounds. People including teachers had been aware of her tragic life, but no one had stopped the sadistic individual who inflicted so much pain on an innocent child.

This case brought attention to the entire area of child abuse. Teachers today are asked to identify the signs of abuse and neglect and report them to the principal immediately. It is hoped that no signs will be unreported.

## RECOGNIZING THE ABUSED CHILD

### Physical Abuse

Many times a child will come into school with bruises and welts. It is a very unusual child who will tell you that they were inflicted by someone in his or her family. By speaking with the child you may be able to determine if the bruises were the result of abuse, but you must be very deft in your questioning, for the abused child is often wary of contact with any adult.

Other signs of abuse include unexplained fractures, or abrasions or lacerations. There are just so many times that a child can say "I fell" or "The cat scratched me" before a trend is noticeable and suspicious. If the youngster is withdrawn or is repeatedly absent, that too is worth checking into. An abused child may well be struck with terror if you tell him or her that you want to see his or her parents.

It takes a very wise child to realize how much his or her behavior at school is influenced by events taking place at home. It is impossible for the teacher to be aware of these events unless the child discusses them, and the chances of this happening are few. However, we are all familiar with the stories of adults "kicking the dog" when they need something on which to take out their frustrations. How tragically often though the "dog" the parent kicks is a child.

This child then comes to school and may react in different ways. He or she may withdraw into a corner, retreat into "another world," and by so doing attempt to find shelter from the horrors of his or her life. In this situation, he or she is often ignored. "Michael is sleepy today," his teacher may reason. "I wonder how I can wake him up?"

But if Michael is angry and if he shows this anger by aggressive behavior, he is much more surely noticed. It is our hope that through the discussion in this chapter and throughout this book you, the teacher, will become aware of the varied problems facing many of our youngsters and that you will take them into consideration when you deal with all children. Abused boys and girls often become abusive in the school situation.

A case in point: In my capacity as assistant principal, I was in charge of the eighth grade. Discipline cases were brought to me for "handling." A tall boy, whom we shall call Joey, was escorted into my office by two male teachers. It was necessary for each of them to hold one of his arms. "He beat up a little kid in his class," one of them informed me. "We thought he'd kill him. He hit this kid so unmercifully it was like a nightmare." They removed their restraining hands, but Joey was still actually shaking with anger.

"That kid laughed at me," he said, "and I had to hit him." Joey was still so furious it was almost impossible to quiet him down. I telephoned his parents, and spoke with his father, who immediately said, "I really can't understand that boy. I just beat him yesterday. He's so stubborn I had to use a cat-o'-nine-tails on him."

On investigation, the father's story was indeed true, and Joey had the marks to prove it. Is it any wonder that this boy had a great deal of rage and that the first person who crossed him and whom he could master because of his size he physically attacked? If a child is treated with violence, is there any wonder he becomes violent himself? If he is treated with brutality, how can he help but brutalize?

Joey subsequently responded favorably, as we hoped he would, to people caring about him. The guidance counselor befriended him and tried to work with the parents as well. However, Joey was not removed from the home by the social workers assigned to the case. The story does not have a happy ending, though, for the father is still suspected of beating one of his nine children with the dreaded cat-o'-nine-tails "because they're stubborn." Joey, though, seems to have learned to avoid doing things that get his father angry at him and so has been able to escape many beatings. While one of his brothers has run away from home, Joey has not, saying, "I have to stay around to help the little kids," referring to his younger brothers and sisters.

Joey's teachers had been made aware of the situation, and by understanding and loving kindness helped him to adjust to the school situation. He became aware of his need to take out his anger on his classmates, and he learned some self-control. They, too, learned not to cross him. He still got into some fights, but they were of less serious nature than previously and were less frequent.

## Sexual Abuse

A type of abuse that in previous years was kept a deep dark secret and is only now coming into the light of day is sexual abuse. In many homes there are stepfathers, "uncles," or other males who abuse either boys or girls. Fathers do, too.

In one case we had, a lovely, red-headed, freckle-faced young lady, thirteen years old, went to her guidance counselor and asked straight out, "Can you help me? I want my father to leave me alone. He keeps bothering me." It turned out that the father was not only molesting this girl but her two sisters, aged nine and sixteen, as well. The mother's work took her away from home much of the time. As a result, she claimed she knew nothing of what was happening. After much investigation the case finally became a police matter. The mother, siding with the father, moved the family to a nearby state.

Incredible as it may sound, there was word that the father was also molesting their son, aged twelve. The mother came into school, highly irate. "Do you think my husband is queer?" she shouted.

Because of the move to their new home, little could be done to help the girls. However, they learned they could refuse to accede to their father's demands, and they threatened to turn him over to the police in the state to which they had moved. The mother, too, did not leave the girl home when the father was there.

What had motivated the thirteen year old to talk about her problem? "My boyfriend told me this had to stop, and he said I could talk to my guidance counselor," she said. "My boyfriend said it would be confidential." It was.

In many schools children as young as kindergartners or first graders are taught lessons that relate to sexual abuse. The intent is not to frighten them, but to alert them to the possibility that something of this nature may happen to them and that if it does, help is available through you, their teacher. Sexual abuse is not limited to any particular group and may be found in the homes of the affluent as well as in those of the poor. As has been shown in newspapers throughout the nation, the making of films involving child pornography seems to be a growth industry. There would be no markets for these films if no one were purchasing them.

It will depend on the policy of the school district as to whether teachers will include lessons on sex education in their curriculum, but every teacher should be aware of a child who gives indications of being abused.

Children often cover up or deny abuse, usually for fear of reprisal by their parents or other adults. We recall several instances where youngsters spoke to their teachers about their friends being sexually abused. These girls were referred to the guidance counselor, who followed up. In every one of the three cases, the child involved denied any abuse and said that she was unhappy for other reasons. One felt she was Cinderella, because she was forced to do much of the housework.

Youngsters watch television, and since so many women have "come out" on TV and told of their fathers abusing them, our young girls and boys are well aware that these things do happen. By assuring them, without mentioning specifically why, that help is available from you or from the guidance counselors, you can give them a possible source of aid. Speak to the youngsters privately or to the entire class, but in either event make very sure that no one child is ever identified.

## Parents Who Are Alcoholics or Substance Abusers

We recall seeing a poster that showed a little girl about five years old saying, "I have an alcohol problem. My daddy." How true that can be! Very often alcoholic parents or substance abusers are abusive to their mates and to their children. A father may frequently become violent, a mother completely out of touch with reality.

These parents have their addiction as their priority. Their commitment is to drugs or alcohol rather than to their families. The youngsters often are not fed properly and may be physically dirty and unkempt. Their homes are in a state of chaos. It is not uncommon for a substance abuser to teach his or her children how to steal to obtain money for drugs, or for the youngsters to be introduced to drugs or alcohol by the parents.

## Crack Kids

Within the last several years, children are coming into our schools who, because their mothers used drugs, particularly crack cocaine, are called "crack kids." While in the most serious cases, crack babies are born deaf and blind, many appear to be normal but have had damage to their nervous systems. As a result, they seem to be unable to sit still or to focus, and their attention span is very short. A good description is found in an article which appeared in the May 13, 1991 issue of *Time* magazine:

> "At a special kindergarten class in the Los Angeles area, a five year old named Billie seems the picture of perfect health and disposition. As a tape recorder plays soothing music in the background, he and the teacher read alphabet cards. Suddenly, for no apparent reason, he throws the cards down on the floor and shuts off the tape recorder. He sits in the chair, stony faced. "Was the music going too fast?" the teacher asks. Billie starts to say something, but then looks away, frowning. The teacher tries to get the lesson back on track, but Billie is quickly distracted by another child's antics. Within seconds, he is off his chair and running around."

We know the present generation of children entering our schools will contain many more crack kids. How we will deal with them is in the process of being worked out. As is pointed out in the same article, "According to the National Association for Perinatal Addiction Research and Education, about one out of every ten newborns in the U.S.—375,000 per year— may be affected by substance abuse each year."

## Children of Alcoholics

In a 1982 report by Joseph S. Califano, Jr., the special counselor to Governor Hugh Carey, as part of the New York State Heroin and Alcohol Abuse Study, the following facts were stated:

- In one city, New York, at least 10 percent of the children under age twenty are living with an alcoholic parent.
- Over 500,000 children of alcoholics (COAs) are in our schools and often are the disruptive children in our classes. Their problems tend to increase greatly as they mature.

- COAs run four times the risk of becoming alcoholics. They tend to grow up and marry alcoholics.

- COAs frequently display serious psychological and emotional disorders from an early age.

- They are more prone than others to fail in school, abuse drugs, become pregnant at an early age, and become truant or delinquents.

- They experience severe difficulties in school, work, and with family and social relationships.

- COAs are subject to physical, sexual, and emotional abuse. Fifty percent of all incest cases hospitalized were COAs. Sixty percent of all reported family violence cases were from alcohol or substance abusing families.

- COAs of either alcoholic or substance abusing parents suffer neglect of both the drinking/drugging parent and the non-abusing parent, and the neglect continues even after sobriety is achieved.

These findings are based on a variety of studies.

We have noticed that COAs often believe that it is because they are "bad" their parents drink or abuse drugs.

Listening to the child who you suspect has alcohol or drug-abusing parents and sympathizing with him or her can make a really tremendous difference. Unfortunately, there are some difficulties with which you can help only by making referrals. Guidance personnel or the administration may be able to take some action that will aid the youngster. Of course, never refer the case until the child gives you permission to do so, for outside intervention can add to the problem.

## MAKING THE YOUNGSTERS COMFORTABLE SO THEY WILL CONFIDE IN YOU

Possibly one of the most important aspects of working with children is assuring them that their stories will go not further than your ears. It is surprising just how sensitive boys and girls are in discussing their home situations. They need the assurance that no one will know of their troubles, or that if someone else must be consulted that person will be completely trustworthy. The child should be told of any transfer of information and asked for his or her permission before it is released. *If the child refuses, his or her decision must be respected unless it is a matter of child abuse. In that case, the abuse must be reported to the principal or his or her staff.*

When I was teaching, and later a counselor and assistant principal, I always told the young people they could consult me it they had problems, and I never failed to stress the confidentiality aspect. One easily sees how embarrassed a child may be if, for example, he or she cannot pay his or her class dues. (These are the expenses the family is asked to pay for when the child graduates.)

Other problems, such as those of a sexual nature, are even more delicate and need extra-special care. Often one must read between the lines and try to draw the child out. Many times really serious, complex problems such as drug or alcohol addiction are involved.

Confidentiality is surely important when a father is molesting his daughter, or a brother molesting his sister, or when any other family member is involved in child molestation. However, confidentiality is equally important to the youngster, although it may not seem so when a seventh-grade young woman asks, "How can I keep my boyfriend from going too far? I really love him, and I don't want to lose him, but I don't want to get pregnant either."

## CONFIDENTIALITY CANNOT BE STRESSED TOO MUCH _____

When you keep "confidential records," they should be just that, for a record open for everyone to read can prove to be an embarrassment for both you and the youngster.

If a boy or girl must be referred to another person, do so, but explain fully to the child why you must make the referral. Be sure he or she understands that you are not breaking faith with him or her.

Confidentiality does not mean, however, that you do not encourage the child to seek help from his or her parents. I have often asked youngsters, "Who do you think, in this whole world, cares more about you than anyone else? Who is really your very best friend?" In all my years of asking this question, I had only one youngster tell me he hated his mother. This turned out to be a very tragic situation, for the mother had given the little boy up for adoption, and he did not consider his adopted parent to be his mother.

When you feel you must communicate with a child's parents, make sure the boy or girl understands the exact reason you must take this action. It may seem surprising, but frequently it proves to be a relief to the youngster, who is often seeking to tell his parent something but has been afraid to do so. Also, the child can be sure the family will react better to you—an adult and an outsider—than they would if informed of a problem by their own boy or girl.

At the same time that you are assuring the child of confidentiality, you should discuss the relative universality of the problem.

## PROBLEMS, PROBLEMS EVERYWHERE _____

Is there a person alive who honestly feels he or she has no problems? Yet to youngsters, problems are a constant source of embarrassment, something to be locked out of their consciousness, if at all possible. But even if they lock them out, their behavior may be affected, and they may easily become disruptive.

Very often I have told youngsters, "No matter what your problem is, I have heard worse. Not only that, but almost every child I know has problems of one sort or another. Your parents drink? They use drugs? So do parents in many other families. You fight with your brothers and sisters? So do the kids in almost every family I know. Don't worry. I won't be shocked or surprised by anything you tell me, and perhaps I can help you."

This type of talk really helped, and most of the girls and some of the boys "opened up." When this happens, it is possible for you to help them and by so doing improve the classroom situation.

## TECHNIQUES YOU MAY USE IN THE CLASSROOM _____

1. Because many children of alcoholics or substance abusers live in chaos, you should use routines and structure your class so that the children know what to anticipate every day. (The monitorial system outlined in the first chapter of this book is an example of structuring.) By using this technique, you can give the youngster a feeling of safety and security, that is missing from his or her home life.

2. A child from this type of home has many things on his or her mind. Did his or her father come home drunk the night before and hit the youngster? What else might have happened? Taking this into consideration, you realize that you need to motivate the child if you are to gain and keep his or her attention.

3. After you have taught a lesson, give the class notes to copy, so that every child has to do some writing each day. This has a calming influence, and if a child is disruptive, you have the opportunity to speak to him or her while the rest of the class is busy.

4. Set goals for this youngster that he or she can fulfill. Help the child feel he or she has achieved something and then praise him or her. The chances are great that this boy or girl has never received any kind words at home. Like every human being, he or she needs to be made to feel worthwhile.

5. Plan your school day so that the youngster from this type of home may do his or her homework while in school. Many times I have heard a

child say, "I can't do my work at home because there is always someone shouting or a radio or television playing very loud." Or it may be, "Because my parents fight."

6. Plan each day so that there is something fun for the children to do, something that will cause the child to forget his or her problems and just have a good time. One teacher had an ice cream party every Friday afternoon, if all the classwork had been completed. She recalled that at the end of the term, one of the girls in her class said to her, "I'm sorry I can't be in your class next year." The teacher asked why, and the child responded, "That's the only time I ever have ice cream."

7. Don't be reluctant to teach lessons on drug or alcohol abuse. If there is a special drug coordinator or guidance counselor who is on the staff to do this, invite that person to your class. The child from a substance-abusive home needs to have these lessons so that he or she understands the problems and the dangers that are ever-present in his or her home.

## WORKING WITH CRACK KIDS

1. Crack kids need special attention and special teaching. The amount of research that has been done is small, and so teachers are determining what works and what doesn't as they go. These children are believed to have a potential for violent behavior, which, it is hoped, they will outgrow. However, many require placement in special education classes, with fewer youngsters and more teacher aides.

In a three-year pilot program in the Salvin Special Education School in Los Angeles, the results have been good. Of the fifty children involved, from three to four years of age, more than half have been able to transfer to regular school classes, with special tutoring and counseling. The reasons for these results, according to the staff of the center, include the following:

- Small classes (eight to ten children per class). This permits the children to make attachments with the teachers.

- Fixed seat assignments and a rigid routine. These provide continuity and reliability, enabling the children to predict what will happen to them and help them master the environment.

- A set of rules that the children understand and can follow.

- Protection from loud noises and other disturbing stimuli.

- Activities rather than pencil-and-paper exercises.

2. Crack kids have difficulty focusing and sitting still. In one kindergarten class a little boy is called the "Philadelphia Flash." The city is the one from which he came and the "flash" is for the way he moves around, no matter what the teacher is doing with the class. She has devised many activities for him, but she is worn out at the end of the day.

3. Crack kids have both positive and negative feelings, and their teachers must learn to accept these and work with the children sensitively. It is difficult to predict their behavior, for each child may react to an internal or external stress differently.

4. Since these children are easily distracted, they need to be placed in a room where noise is at a minimum.

5. Much must be learned about dealing with crack kids, so it is advisable for those teaching them to attend workshops and conferences and also to read as much professional literature on the topic as possible.

6. Remember, you are faced with youngsters whose prenatal development was influenced by factors to which other children have not been subjected. There may be many differences, but they, like other children with problems, need teachers who are willing to give them special attention and who will form attachments with them that can make a tremendous difference in their further development and in their lives in later years.

## LEARNING ABOUT YOUR STUDENTS THROUGH LANGUAGE ARTS

When children suffer from problems about which they can do little, they become frustrated. If we are to help our children, we must find means for them to express themselves, to vent their emotions. We can do this by talking with them, and most assuredly, we should. But at times we are totally unaware of their problems and see the disruptive youngster as being uncooperative and even "just plain mean."

We've found, as have many other teachers, that we can use language arts to learn much about our pupils. For example, a teacher assigned to her sixth graders the following topic for a composition: "If I Were Able to Do Anything I Wanted to, I Would . . ." Most of the boys' thoughts were centered on sports. "I would play baseball with the Mets," one very small boy fantasized. However, one very disruptive boy wrote in an entirely different vein: "I would kill my father before he kills my mother or me. He only comes home when he wants money for drugs." The teacher was shocked by the revelations in the paper, but she suddenly understood the boy. She spoke to him and then sent him to the guidance counselor. The child cried for an hour after he understood he was in the safe hands of the guidance counselor.

You may have your youngsters write on such subjects as any of the following:

How Do I Get Along With My Family?

The Most Exciting Thing That Ever Happened to Me.

The Nicest Person I Know and Why I Think So.

How I Can Bring More Happiness to My Family.

What *Love* Means to Me.

## HELP CHILDREN OVERCOME FAMILY NOTORIETY _____

What effect does a "skeleton in the closet" have on a child? So often the youngsters are extremely sensitive about problems within their families, problems over which they have no control. If it is possible for you to assure the boys or girls that they are responsible only for their own behavior, you can help them immeasurably.

Areas of sensitivity are many and varied. How does a child feel when he knows the local newspaper carried a story, "John Doe arrested for armed robbery"? Particularly when other kids ask, "That's your brother, isn't it?" Is it surprising to learn that John's brother punched the boy who asked the question, knocking him to the floor?

Surely the teacher would never mention the newspaper article, but invariably other children have seen it. However, at some time in the future, a class discussion centering on the topic, "Each person should be judged by his or her own behavior" is particularly necessary.

Often children are sorely in need of something that improves their self-esteem. Participating in team sports can be very effective in giving a child a positive self-image and can change a youngster's behavior pattern—in some cases almost as if by magic. This is what happened in the case of one thirteen-year-old young man, whom we shall call Lester.

Lester was the fifth oldest in a family of eight boys. He showed some signs of following in his family's footsteps, but at a rate which seemed almost unbelievable for one so young. Two of his brothers had already been convicted of armed robbery. Lester was tall for his age, and pleasant looking. He said very little. In films he would have been labeled as the "strong, silent type." It was difficult to get to know this boy.

Lester was absent from school the day of the basketball team tryouts. His homeroom teacher discussed the boy with the coach, and it was agreed Lester would be given a chance anyway. He did beautifully and seemed to be a "natural." Before he was accepted for the team, however, he was told the rules, and the point was made to him that if he were involved in any activity that was even suspicious, like any other player, he would be dropped from the team. Lester gave his word and kept it.

From his first day as a player, he was a different boy. His is a real success story, for he went on to play high school and then college basketball. His interest in and love of the sport enabled him to overcome his home environment. His brothers never did.

Just as excellence in sports can help a child overcome his home life, so can an interest in music. Many famous musicians have overcome handicaps through this interest, some of these handicaps having been environmental, others physical or psychological. The point, of course, is that a child needs to feel that he or she is a worthwhile human being, no matter what problems his or her family has.

## CONCLUSION

The disruptive child in your classroom may well be the victim of child abuse. It is essential that you, and every teacher, learn to recognize the symptoms of this vicious behavior. These include visible bruises, "black eyes," welts, and broken bones. However, when abuse is even suspected, be it physical, mental, or sexual, you must be very deft in handling the situation but you must surely refer it to the appropriate authorities.

Parents who are alcoholics or drug abusers most often place their addiction far ahead of their responsibilities toward their children. Pregnant women addicted to crack cocaine often cause their children to be born with behavioral and learning problems due to suspected damage to the infants' nervous systems. These children are now entering our schools. Children of alcoholics (COAs) have long manifested difficulties in our classrooms.

Probably the most important thing you can do as a teacher of children whose parents are alcoholics or drug abusers is gain the confidence of the girls and boys whose family lives are so affected. If they are able to confide in you, it is possible for you to get help for them.

You may find parts of your language arts program will help you learn about your students. It is extremely rare for any child to be totally without problems, and the disruptive ones even more so. By showing the universality of this, it is possible for you to change his or her behavior.

There are a number of ways in which you can help the COAs and the children of drug abusers. Working with them on a one-to-one basis, being firm but friendly, and having structure in your classroom are very important. Using strong motivational devices, setting goals, and careful lesson planning will help in dealing with disruptive youngsters.

By assuring your students that they are judged by their behavior and not that of their parents or siblings, you can ease their minds and perhaps improve their behavior.

Crack kids are in need of special help, for they have very short attention spans and cannot tolerate distractions. It is advisable that you learn as much as possible about them. To date, research on crack kids is being done that will be published in the future.

# 13

## CHILDREN DISRUPTED BY SEPARATION, DIVORCE, DEATH, OR HOMELESSNESS

In the last thirty years there have been four major upheavals in the mores of this nation. They have been called "revolutions," and they are the women's revolution, the black revolution, the sexual revolution, and the technological revolution. Each has played a role in family life, and, as a result, children have been affected.

Many youngsters have gotten a very false view of family life from television. They've seen such programs as "The Brady Bunch," or "Leave It to Beaver," which is enjoying popularity again as a result of reruns. The picture drawn is of the happy family, where there are no arguments; no serious problems; and certainly no separations, divorces, or death. Homelessness was unknown, and, like death, surely would never be the subject of one of these episodes. When unpleasant family situations are shown, they are generally in programs that do not appeal to young people.

In real life, when a family upheaval occurs, the girls and boys in the family experience great pain and become very upset. They often carry that upset over into the classroom and become disruptive. Separation and divorce are most frequently accompanied by verbal and possibly physical abuse, and it is usually the mother who is the subject of that abuse. Youngsters carry that picture with them and at times strike out because of it. Far too often boys who have seen their fathers being abusive emulate that behavior. They will fight with classmates while in school, playmates on the street, siblings in the home, and , later on, their girlfriends and wives.

A few statistics show how true the cliche "times have changed" really is. In 1900 there were 55,571 divorces in the United States, and in 1970 there were 708,000. By 1988 that number had risen to 1,183,000 per year.

There is no information available regarding children involved in divorce in 1900, but in 1950, the first year for which statistics were available, 299,000 children below eighteen years of age were involved. By 1970 that number had risen to approximately 870,000 per year, and in 1986 the number had grown even further, to 1,064,000 per year. These statistics do not take into consideration those young people involved in families where the parents have separated or where there has been a death in the family.

These are the youngsters who are in our schools and in our classes. Is there any wonder they are different from those of yesteryear? As Bob Dylan once wrote, "The times, they are a changin'." They certainly are, and that has changed our work considerably.

At one time we believed that parents were the teacher's essential ally. Without question, some still are. However, today we cannot count on every parent because many are very busy or totally involved in working out their own problems. Their children go to school, and they feel it is the school's responsibility to educate their youngsters. These mothers and fathers have given up almost any responsibility they may have had. This is especially true when families are disrupted and the parents are involved in separation or divorce, or when one parent is confronted with the death of a spouse. We cannot expect much help from parents when a family is homeless and lacks one of the very basics of life.

This is certainly not to say that the teacher should not try to contact parents and should not try to involve them in the education of their children. However, it would be unrealistic to expect the parents to give much attention to schooling when the family is in a state of disruption.

## HOW CHILDREN ARE AFFECTED BY FAMILY DISINTEGRATION

It is often difficult to find out why a child is being disruptive. Is it because of family disintegration? As mentioned in the previous chapter, you may learn a great deal by having your youngsters write compositions. Sometimes the material that is revealed comes as somewhat of a shock. This happened to one fourth-grade teacher when she gave the topic, "What I Did During My Easter Vacation."

One youngster wrote about her parents separating. She actually had to help her father, whom she loved dearly, move out of the house—and, she was sure, out of her life.

Should any child confide in you in this way, be very sure to stress the fact that anything he or she has told you is confidential and that you will keep the secret. This is essential if you are to be of help to such children, who are often really in grave distress.

Many children have been sheltered from family problems, and when the disintegration of the family comes out into the open they are shocked, and some become angry. That anger can easily manifest itself in the classroom, for the girl or boy is often afraid to let it out at home. Your quiet conversation with him or her, on a one-to-one basis, can often help to avert some of that anger.

## CHILDREN NEED ASSURANCE THEIR PARENTS STILL LOVE THEM

When a family is disrupted by separation or divorce, the children desperately need assurance that their parents still love them. "My father wouldn't have left if he loved us," a ten year old confided. "He's supposed to play baseball with me, and now he can't." How does one reply to a child who says something like that? Yet we, as adults, must reassure the child, for nothing is sadder than to feel unloved.

I recall telling this boy his father would still play baseball with him, but that he had to wait until his father was able to do so. This did happen. Perhaps I was lucky that the situation did go that way, for it could very well have been different. However, as a teacher, one must have confidence and act on the assumption that parents do love their children.

There are times, though, when parents are not able to express their love to their girls or boys because marital breakups or the death of a spouse have had profound psychological effect on them. Margo, an eighth grader, came to the guidance office looking very unhappy. "My father left us, and my mother never talks to me any more. She used to be so much fun, laughing and joking. Now she walks around in a daze, or she just stares into space," the girl said softly.

The counselor explained to Margo that her mother was very traumatized by her husband's departure and that she needed help from her children until she recovered. "But she does love you," the counselor reassured the child. "Wait and see."

It took several months before Margo's mother recovered, but bit by bit she overcame her sorrow and was able, once more, to hug and kiss her children, as she had before the breakup.

Youngsters can understand difficult concepts, such as psychological causes for behavior, if those concepts are taught to them on their level of understanding. An angry boy or girl can comprehend the concept that he or she is being disruptive, or "acting out," in school because of events occurring within his or her family.

I recall one youngster, after I had been rather unpleasant with his class early in the day, saying, "Oh, well, she had a fight with her husband this morning." I answered, "I have to admit it. You're almost right. The argument wasn't with my husband. It was with my son."

## CHILDREN BELIEVE THEY CAUSED THEIR PARENTS' DIVORCE _

"I did it," Orin shouted. Every child in the class looked at him, for this was an unexpected outburst from a normally quiet child. Then he ran from the room. Fortunately, a teacher was walking in the hallway at the time, and stopped the distraught youngster as he ran for the stairs. She quickly guided him into an empty classroom and let him sob for several minutes. She then questioned him, but he didn't answer. She tried again and again. Finally he murmured, "They're getting a divorce. I know I caused it. I've been bad. I don't listen, and I talk back."

Orin was taken to see the guidance counselor immediately, and his parents were sent for. It was only after he was reassured by both of them that he was not the cause of their problems did he accept the fact, but even then it was with uncertainty.

When their parents separate or divorce, many youngsters, such as Orin, feel very guilty. While most of the time these feelings are unjustified, there are cases where the parents actually instill a sense of guilt in the child.

A parent may be very upset and violently angry, and scream at his or her children. What is a child to think if his or her mother shouts, "I hate you. I wish you were never born," or words to that effect? Because the outpouring of anger is directed at the child, he or she assumes blame, while the overwrought parent is reacting to his or her other problems. The boy or girl then reacts by becoming angry and often by becoming disruptive in school. This child may also get into fights with his or her friends, as Bonnie did.

This little girl, a fifth grader who was very small for her age, almost blinded one of the girls with whom she had been playing. The incident was clearly no accident.

"How do you feel now?" the counselor asked her.

"I wish I didn't do that," Bonnie replied tearfully. "But I didn't think. I just got real mad and hit her. I didn't mean to hit her in the eye, though."

To Bonnie, this type of behavior was all too familiar, for she had been witnessing it for months. "Think about it," the counselor told the child. "If you had counted to ten, would you have hit her?"

"I guess not," Bonnie answered, again crying. "And I wish my father and mother would stop hitting each other."

"We can't stop them, Bonnie," the counselor pointed out. "But we can show *you* that hitting other people is not the way to deal with them."

The story doesn't end so quickly. Bonnie cried for hours that day and afterward sought out the counselor frequently. She found some emotional support, which helped her handle what to her were difficult situations.

Tragically, the divorce took a long time to come through, and the children were witnesses to many fights, but because Bonnie, and subsequently her brother, received help, they were able to stay on an even keel and were not disruptive in school.

We have worked with many youngsters who felt they were to blame for their parents divorcing. Yet in only two cases did a parent actually tell a child that he (in both cases it was a boy) was to blame for their problems.

It is extremely difficult to really convince a child that he or she is not responsible for the breakup. In most cases the youngsters were willing to speak with a counselor but did not want their parents to know they had done so.

One of the things I found that seemed to make a difference in the children's attitudes was the simple question, "Do you think yours is the only family in which there is a divorce (or a separation)?" Almost invariably, the youngster would answer yes. I would respond by saying, "That's absolutely not so. There are many families in the same situation, even among the kids in this school." That always seemed to make the boy or girl feel better, and, of course, it was, unfortunately, the truth.

## WHO WILL TAKE CARE OF ME? _____

Youngsters are also concerned with a very basic question when parents are divorcing: "Who will take care of me?" (This is even more true when a parent has died.) Girls and boys realize their inability to provide the things they need to live the type of lifestyle in which they have grown up. They understand the need for money with which to buy life's necessities, and that one of the roles of the parent is to supply these things. When a parent leaves the scene, through divorce or death, the fact that the parent has been supplying these things becomes increasingly clear.

Yet this is one of the fears that is usually not discussed. We once heard a conversation that brings this out, although the speaker, incredibly, was a twenty-two-year-old woman. Her father mentioned he had an insurance policy that would adequately take care of his wife. The daughter immediately asked , "But who's going to take care of me?" This is unusual, but it is typical of the reasoning of a child. Worry and anger can cause a boy or girl to become exceedingly disruptive.

## ENCOURAGE YOUNGSTERS TO SEEK HELP

"Jack is driving me crazy," his teacher told the guidance counselor. "He's getting worse and worse, and I can't do anything with him." Because she was speaking to the counselor and not in any way gossiping, she continued. "I know his parents are getting a divorce, but they haven't been together for months. Jack seems to be acting out more and more."

Whenever you have a child in this situation, a child who is acting out, he or she should be referred to a guidance counselor. Like Jack, he or she may be suffering a great deal, and, as we've said, possibly blaming him- or herself. In fact, if you are aware of this type of family disruption, you can take steps to prevent the child from becoming disruptive. Encourage the boy or girl to speak with the school guidance counselor. Another path he or she can take and that might be more comfortable since it is away from the school, depends on whether the family is being seen by a social service agency. If so, the child might see a counselor or social worker on the staff.

As his or her teacher, speak to the youngster confidentially. Point out that helping people get through bad periods in their lives is one of the main functions of guidance counselors or social workers, and that there is no reason the boy or girl should not seek this type of help.

You may initiate this process by calling the child aside, but not when he or she is being disruptive. At another time say, very quietly, "It seems to me there is something really bothering you. Is there any way I can help you? Or would you rather speak to the guidance counselor?" If the girl or boy agrees, you could then help by setting up an appointment.

Many youngsters have no idea that talking about a problem can help solve it. If a solution itself is not possible, speaking about it can make one feel better. If you can get the idea across, that knowledge can help the child throughout his or her life. You may point out that talking to a friend or family member can be helpful as well, but that a counselor is a person who has been trained to be helpful and who probably has a great deal of experience guiding people.

## DEATH OF A PARENT

James, a thirteen year old, has a reputation for being "just impossible." He would tell his teachers off in no uncertain terms whenever he had the desire to do so, and in language that made him unique in the entire school. If an adult came close to touching him, he would shout, "My father will come up to this school and beat the hell out of you. You just wait."

Attempts to contact his mother were made many times, but she was not to be found because she seemed never to be at home. She worked, and it seemed she worked twenty-four hours a day. James's behavior became worse and worse. Finally, a telegram was sent, and she came in to see the principal. Her first statement was, "James hasn't been the same since his father died two years ago."

A check of the boy's records revealed the truth of her words. James had never been a problem until the fifth grade. Right after his father died in an automobile accident, he had suddenly become upset as soon as anyone spoke to him. The anger he felt at this loss manifested itself in this way. He was sent for psychotherapy, which, in time, helped improve his behavior. His cursing decreased and almost stopped once the root of the situation was uncovered.

Of course you would recommend that a child whose parent had died be seen by a guidance counselor. In the event that none is available, it should be suggested to the surviving parent that the boy or girl might benefit from this type of help and that it can be obtained from a social service agency.

## HOMELESSNESS

It is incredible that in the United States, the richest country in the world, there are people who are without one of the basics of life, a home. According to the Children's Defense Fund's publications, "Children 1990: A Report Card, Briefing Book, and Action Primer" and "S.O.S. America! A Children's Defense Budget," one in four homeless people in cities is a child.* Every night an estimated 100,000 children go to sleep homeless. Federal funding for low-income housing has been slashed by more than 80 percent since 1980. (* It depends on who estimates the number of homeless; two sources are quoted here.)

It has been estimated by the National Coalition for the Homeless that there are three million people who live in cars, under bridges, in train stations, in shelters, and on the streets.

Homeless children do attend school. Unfortunately, it is often painfully obvious from the poor condition of their clothing and the lack of cleanliness just who they are. Living in a car is hardly conducive to proper grooming.

Even when homeless youngsters are befriended by their teachers or by the members of the Parent Association and supplied with clothing and other needs, these youngsters have problems. Those who live in shelters report that their things are often stolen from them. Then too, girls and boys want to be exactly like their peers, which is usually impossible because they cannot afford the clothes and various other things most other youngsters have and that they take for granted. Is it any wonder that possessions, or lack of them, cause anger and consequent disruptive behavior?

Another problem the homeless face is that they frequently move from place to place. These youngsters may have made friends, only to have to leave them when the temporary place that has served as a home no longer suffices.

Fortunately, many schools, such as those in New York City, serve both breakfast and lunch, so that homeless children are assured of a decent meal during the school year. But while this is beneficial as far as it goes, it surely doesn't supply enough help for the homeless family.

## WHAT CAN A TEACHER DO FOR A HOMELESS CHILD? _____

What can a teacher do for a child living under such conditions?

1. The first thing is never, under any circumstances, reveal to him or her that you are aware of this. Girls and boys are very sensitive to being in this type of situation or, indeed, to any situation that makes them different from other youngsters. This is easily understandable.

2. Make time during the school day for all of the youngsters in the class to do their homework while in the school building. How could one expect a child to work on homework in a shelter or a place that barely serves as a home? Offer the child the use of the school library after dismissal, if this is permitted.

3. Should the child lose his or her textbooks, try to supply others as unobtrusively as possible. The same is true of writing equipment, note-books, and so on.

4. Speak to the guidance counselor and ask him or her to find some social services for the family. Do this without mentioning anything to the boy or girl. The counselor should communicate with the family by sending a note to them with the child, since an address is rarely available.

5. If the need for clothing is apparent, ask the guidance counselor to consult with members of the Parent Association. However, it is crucial that the homeless child not be named, for if the situation became public knowledge, the child would be hurt immeasurably. This discretion is absolutely essential.

6. Be especially understanding when this youngster does not behave perfectly. He or she is growing up under extremely difficult circumstances.

## DISRUPTIVE BEHAVIOR MAY COME FROM HURT FEELINGS _____

Some youngsters will fight at the drop of a hat. Disciplining them in the old sense, by punishment, doesn't work. In fact, if anything, it will frequently make their behavior worse. It is very important that you determine why that boy or girl (and it may surely be a girl as well as a boy) is so belligerent. Sometimes the cause seems far from serious to us, but not to that youngster. A case in point is Charles.

Boys who are small for their age often have problems. Such a boy was Charles. It was said he had an extremely "short fuse." He would take on any sized boy or girl, and it really didn't matter whether he won or lost, as long as he got into a fight. His astute teacher wondered about this, for here was a child whose baby-blue eyes and round face gave him the look of an angel. Yet scarcely a day went by the first two weeks of the term without Charles hitting someone—this while the boy was in the third grade.

The teacher had tried to solve the problem, for Charles's disruption was causing the class to lose valuable time. "What can I do with that boy?" he contemplated. Suddenly, he had a thought, and he realized wherein the problem lay. "Charles," he asked, "what do they call you at home?"

"Pee Wee."

"And your friends, what do they call you?"

"Pee Wee."

"Do you like it? I'd hate it if I were you."

The child's face lit up. The teacher continued, "When I was your age I was even shorter than you are. I wasn't as strong (Charles squared his shoulders), and I was always called 'Shorty.' I hated it. I squirmed. I got furious. Then I started telling everyone, 'My name is Donald. You can call me Donald, or Don,' and they did. It was that simple."

The boy looked at his teacher. "You mean I could say, 'My name is Charles, not Pee Wee, but if you want to, you can call me Chuck.'"

"Exactly."

Again, not 100 percent improvement immediately, but 50 percent at least in this child's behavior. And by the time he reached the eighth grade, he rarely fought at all, although he was still short for his age. At his request, his name, on his diploma, read "Chuck."

We cite this anecdote to show that all disruptive behavior is not from serious causes. In this case, by realizing Charles had a problem, his teacher helped solve it and improved the climate for learning in his classroom. Talk to the child to find out, if you can, whether the cause of his or her disruptive behavior can be changed, and if you can possibly help, of course do so.

In many situations, parents who are separating or divorcing do not speak nicely to their children. The children are upset, and it shows. By your manner, your attitude, and your concern, you can teach lessons that can last a lifetime.

If you have a child who is caught in this situation, work out a way in which the child can have a few minutes with you for a one-to-one talk. Even if the youngster doesn't wish to confide in you, just making him or her feel that you care and want to help may modify his or her behavior. Far too often parents don't find the time to do this, and through a tete-a-tete, especially with his or her teacher, a child will feel special. We heard an eighth-grade young man say he had never been spoken to by an adult the way his teacher had spoken to him, and he emphasized the word *never*.

## HELP CHILDREN OVERCOME FAMILY DISINTEGRATION

1.  Be sure you have set up your rules and regulations as suggested in previous chapters. These are particularly necessary when there are girls or boys in your class whose lives have been disrupted. By stressing rules you supply the structure and stability these youngsters need. When they are disruptive, you can remind them of the rules and show them that they are not observing them. It is strongly suggested that you combine this with the following item.

2.  Again, as previously suggested, set up a reward system. When a family is disintegrating, very little is happening that is pleasant for the youngsters. Since children need something to look forward to, but that something cannot be too far in the future, the rewards should be simple and awarded on either a daily or a weekly basis. This system works two ways: It helps the youngsters improve their behavior, and it also gives the "good" kids something to look forward to.

Don't let them know in advance what the reward will be or when it will be given. Just announce, "This is reward time," and vary the reward to make it exciting.

What can the rewards be? You may wish to give out trinkets, which you can obtain from a wholesale distributor at nominal cost. Or a reward may be a trip to get ice cream, or to a pizza parlor. (This would be a once-a-week, or once in two weeks reward.) You might show a mystery video or read ghost stories. Games such as spelling matches, or physical games such as foot races or soccer or volleyball games are possibilities.

One very resourceful teacher used her videorecorder, and took pictures of her class frequently. Then she would show them as a reward. Another traveled extensively during her summer vacations, and took many pictures and bought inexpensive trinkets. She used these for rewards, and, incidentally, because she really used her travels in her teaching was able to claim her trips as income tax deductions. Her children took home souvenirs from Mexico and even from Egypt, which they loved and treasured and which had cost their teacher very little. You will think up many ways to reward the youngsters, once you set your mind working in this direction.

3. Teach your youngsters how to keep a journal. Since they may be living in a situation that is chaotic, they can benefit by having some sort of outlet for their emotions. In many cases there is no one with whom they feel comfortable discussing their family problems. This is particularly true of boys, but many girls react in the same way. It is as if family problems are deep, dark secrets that must be kept hidden from everyone. Talking with a counselor or teacher is the last thing in the world they want to or will do. Yet they do need some sort of outlet.

An excellent one is keeping a journal. It is an unusual youngster who has ever even heard of a journal or of writing in one, and yet this is not difficult to do and can be very helpful. One starts with an empty notebook, reserved just for this purpose.

As you describe just what a journal is, point out at the very beginning of your discussion that whatever is written in it is for no one's eyes other than the individual writing in it. Explain that in their journals, people write about the events of the day or week. Say, "You can write in your journal any time you feel you want to. You can also include any ideas or things that interest you, and very important, you can write about the way you are feeling."

"This way you can put down on paper thoughts that you can't tell to another person and that can't hurt anyone. Your secrets are not in danger," you might tell them, adding that the journal must be kept in a place that is not accessible to anyone else. "Obviously this is important," you point out to the boys and girls. "You have to find just the right place to keep it."

When you bring this topic up, suggest it to the entire class rather than just to the youngsters whose families are disintegrating. Give an example, a fictional one that you, yourself, write. It should be similar to the one a youngster in your class might keep.

You might bring out the fact that many famous people kept journals, some from the time they were very young. One example is Leonardo da Vinci, whose journals had pictures of his inventions, including a machine that could fly, and a parachute.

"While most of us aren't inventors, perhaps you might come up with something that should be recorded, and you will do just that in your journal. This is something many adults wish they had done," you point out.

Stress, once more, the need for the journal to be kept in a private place, where no one else is able to read it.

## TEACH YOUR YOUNGSTERS TO GET ALONG WITH OTHERS

As teachers, we often assume our students have learned how to get along with others, and yet this is something that is not in the school curriculum. It is assumed the youngsters will learn this at home, but parents who are separating or divorcing are hardly concerned with this aspect of their child's education. This is especially true of disruptive youngsters.

One of the most successful techniques for teaching girls and boys how to cooperate is through the use of playlets that they compose themselves. First, have the "actors," among whom you would include your disruptive youngsters, act out scenes that illustrate noncooperation. These scenes might take place in the schoolyard, in the lunchroom, in the playground, or at home.

Next have them act the same scene, showing cooperative behavior. Encourage the youngsters to "let themselves go" and to make the scenes as realistic as possible. After they've done this, discuss the need for cooperation and what the youngsters did as they illustrated it.

At their level of understanding, show the girls and boys how to negotiate and how to make compromises. Point out that this is necessary if one is to get along with others. Then have them do the same type of playlet illustrating these concepts.

Another technique you might use is to have each youngster give an example of how he or she has been cooperative. Next, have each one give an example of noncooperation. Do not allow anyone to be judgmental, but have each child say how his or her behavior might have been changed so that no differences arose. Have them give examples of how they might negotiate or make compromises. This will indicate if they, and especially the disruptive youngster, have understood the points you made.

## LISTEN CAREFULLY TO WHAT YOUR CHILDREN TELL YOU

Waldo was a very difficult little boy, for he would do his work and present no problem for much of the time, but there would be days when he was extremely disruptive. "I couldn't figure out what was happening," his teacher commented.

"Then one morning when he started the day by fighting with a little girl, I called him up to my desk to speak to me. 'What is it, Waldo? What's the matter?' I asked in a quiet tone of voice.

"'Nuttin',' he answered. Suddenly I had an idea. I asked him, 'Waldo, what did you have for breakfast this morning?' The child looked at me, but didn't answer. I asked again, and again no response. Our school has a breakfast program, but I didn't remember Waldo taking part in it. Once more I asked, and this time he blurted out, 'We have nuttin' to eat. My pappy went away and my mama has no money.'

"'Why don't you have breakfast with the other boys and girls?' I questioned.

"'They won't give me any,' he replied.

"Sure enough, I checked into it. Waldo's mother had not signed the paper that gave permission for him to take part in the program, and so he was excluded. It was simple to change that. She didn't speak English, and when we had someone explain to her that her child would be given breakfast, she was very appreciative."

How different the outcome of this incident might have been had his teacher not been perceptive.

We are getting huge numbers of children who are the sons and daughters of recent immigrants in our schools, and the language problem is a very real one. People who don't speak English often experience difficulties in the course of their daily lives.

We recall one case where a teacher, after speaking with a child, referred the child to the guidance counselor, who was able to arrange for financial assistance for the family. This was for the Spanish-speaking widow of an Army man who had died in action.

Children with autocratic parents are often terrified of them. Jonas, a small, red-haired, mischievous boy, told his teacher, tearfully, "I can't go home with this report card. My father will beat me up." It was entirely possible, since the parents were in the midst of a very ugly divorce. The mother had left the father because he had physically abused her. Incredibly, he had been given custody of the boy.

The matter was handled by the principal. He asked the father to come in to see him and told him what a fine son he had. "This report card isn't too good, but his teacher assures me the next one will be better." The father got the message that there was concern for his son, and when the child received his next report card, he did not react the same way.

## Child Suicides

Child suicides, too, are a possibility to be considered. *If a child makes a threat of this nature, don't take a chance ignoring it.* He or she may never take any such action, but you cannot judge this yourself. Discuss the remark with the guidance counselor or with your principal, and then tell the child that one of them will have to talk with his or her parents. *A remark of this type should never be ignored.*

We were discussing this with an experienced teacher. "Never, in all my years of teaching, have I had this happen," he said. "I don't know how I would react." About a year later he ran into our office, saying, "I'm so glad we had that talk about child suicides. John Doe just told me he's been thinking about it. I'm really upset, but I can just imagine how I would have been if we hadn't talked about it." There are many reasons a child might make this threat, among which family disruption or homelessness is certainly an important one. But no reason negates the seriousness of it.

## PASSIVE DISRUPTION

In our typical "happy homes," there are often serious clashes of personalities, which become worse and worse with the added stress of family disruption. Then, too, there are the added problems brought about when parents are overly permissive. Their children seem to have difficulty coping with the rules and regulations of the school situation and become passively disruptive.

Little chubby Billy, a first grader, brought candy and cookies to school each day. An overweight child, he was supposed to eat these only during lunch. However, he proceeded to consume them all morning (and he had an abundance that would have lasted most children a week). When told that he could not do this, his reply was, "My mother lets me." His teacher tried, very sweetly, to explain that this was against the school rules, but Billy refused to stop. It was only after his mother came into the school and told him, while his teacher listened, that he could not eat while he was in class that he tried to control himself. Persistence on the part of the teacher finally won out, and Billy had to "starve" until lunch time.

While this appears to be trivial, it is an indication of the type of child who is defiant in a passive way. This type of disruptive behavior cannot be ignored because if it is, the teacher loses control of the situation and more serious disruptive behavior often follows.

When you suspect this is happening, it is important to show that you are aware of it and will not tolerate it. You have rules and regulations to fall back on, and since you have already made sure they are understood by the youngsters, you can use them.

An eighth grader who often got into difficulty with her classmates came to me complaining about a boy who had never been in trouble before.

"He's taking my things. He took my dessert at lunch, and he took my pen when I wasn't looking," she reported.

"Are you sure?" I questioned, for the young man was not one who had previously gotten into difficulty. "Oh, yes," the girl replied. "He's a sneak. He does things and no one catches him." When other youngsters were questioned, they agreed, even though they were all aware that the girl herself presented problems in class. The boy was new in the school, and after I spoke to him the incidents ceased. He had done things like that because he had not been caught, and once he was, he stopped. He was almost typical of the passive disruptive youngster.

## USING SPORTS, MUSIC, OR CRAFTS TO HELP THE CHILD

Girls and boys need something that can absorb some of their energy. The school band; the chorus; the baseball, basketball, or track teams; the cheerleaders; or the art department can all be of use with youngsters whose lives are disrupted because of family disintegration and who are disruptive in the classroom.

Energy that is used to disrupt a class can be turned to constructive purposes if the child who lacks self-control can be placed in an environment where his or her talents are recognized. When a family is in turmoil or is homeless, parents are, understandably, too upset with their problems to take the time to be supportive of their youngsters. The child, who may feel guilty and blame him- or herself for the breakup, loses self-esteem and often with that self-control. Such was the case of a seventh grader named Danielle.

Danielle would not or could not, it appeared, keep quiet while in class. She loved to sing, and sing she did, when there was work to be done. Yet she didn't want to be part of the school chorus, when that was suggested to her. When questioned, it was discovered her greatest desire was to be a cheerleader. Since 99 percent of the girls want to be cheerleaders, this was no surprise.

Danielle was given a card (a "conduct card") on which her behavior, every period, every day, had to be indicated by each teacher. If she could improve her behavior for two weeks, she could then audition for the cheerleaders. She understood she had to learn self-control and that if she "made the 'leaders'" she would not be permitted to resume her constant disruption of her classes.

Danielle did manage to control herself and was accepted for the cheerleaders. How long this would have continued was difficult to say, for when her parents separated, her mother moved away, taking her cheer-leading daughter with her.

Like Danielle, some of the most disruptive youngsters are those who are unable to achieve academically. By taking part in any of the activities listed above, they are motivated to change their behavior. We've seen this happen time and time again.

When a school offers extracurricular activities after regular school hours, it can serve as a haven for youngsters whose homes are unpleasant or lonely because of the disintegration of their families. The gymnasium may take the place of the kitchen or living room of an empty or embittered dwelling. There is vitality and excitement to be had through sports of all kinds.

Disruptive youngsters should be encouraged to take part in sports, for it gives them the opportunity to vent their frustration in an acceptable way. It is better for them to kick a soccer ball than to kick another person. I recall, on one very difficult day, being told by a fellow guidance counselor, "Go out and hit a tennis ball around. You'll feel better." I followed his advice, and it worked. It usually does with youngsters as well.

It's important to try to find the exact outlet that the disruptive boy or girl will enjoy. Boys often take to the suggestion of sports, be it baseball, basketball, track, or soccer, as will some girls. However, music and art both offer similar opportunities, and they too offer relief from frustration and anger. One sixth grader told her music teacher during an after school session, "I can't be unhappy when we sing such good songs."

## CONCLUSION

During the times in which we are living there is much family disintegration due to separation, divorce, death, or homelessness. The children involved in families with these problems are, too often, involved and faced with situations that are very difficult for them to handle. Some boys and girls carry this frustration into the classroom and become disruptive. Their burdens are too much for them to carry.

It is important for teachers to understand the trauma involved and to assure the boy or girl in this situation that he or she is still loved by his or her parents. This must be done in private, of course, on a one-to-one basis. Children often believe they have caused their parents to "split" and are guilt ridden. They may have seen violence and imitate that type of behavior in class. Probably the most important of their worries is, "Who will take care of me?"

When a youngster disrupts your class, and you suspect it is because of family disintegration, encourage the child to accept the help of a guidance counselor. The same is true if a boy or girl must face the fact that one of his or her parents has died. This is the most traumatic experience a child may have.

Homelessness is something that very few teachers can truly comprehend. However, there are many children in our schools who are in that situation. They must be helped in every way possible, and we must start by empathizing with them and providing help by allowing them to do their work in school and by getting aid for them whenever possible.

There are techniques you may try to help youngsters involved in family disintegration. Keeping a journal, which can serve as an outlet for their feelings, is one. Another is teaching lessons on cooperation, negotiation, and compromise. Still another is getting disruptive youngsters involved in sports programs.

When boys and girls are disruptive and family problems are the reason, all of your teaching skills are called for, for this is an extremely difficult time for the youngster, although he or she may be reluctant to discuss it. Your friendship and affection can do wonders for a child in distress, and you may be sure a child involved in a disintegrating family is in distress.

# 14

## CHILDREN LIVING WITH SINGLE PARENTS, STEPPARENTS, OR IN FOSTER HOMES

As we mentioned in the previous chapter, the times have changed considerably, and in no area more so than in the single-parent family situation. In 1960, the Department of the Census reported 4,494,000 "Families Maintained by Women, with No Husband Present." By 1975, the number had grown to 7,242,000, and by 1986 there were 10,211,000 in that category.

According to the 1988 report, more than 13,500,000 children under eighteen live only with their mothers. On the other side of the coin, 1,807,000 live with their fathers. Statistics are not available for the number of children in stepparent families and in foster homes. These children, then, are among the youngsters in our classrooms and are among those who are disruptive.

There is no parent who is more determined to have her or his child do well in school than the single parent. However, when a child lives with a single parent who works, it is very difficult to bring that parent into the school should that child be disruptive. This is surely understandable, but parental cooperation is necessary in cases where a youngster does not follow the rules of the school.

If you have a boy or girl who is being disruptive in your class, try, by every means you have at your command, by every method and device you know, to get that child involved in his or her schoolwork. Perhaps you can do this by talking with the youngster and by being supportive.

Many children are reluctant to discuss family problems, but some will reveal their situations. If there is some way in which you can offer help, of course do so.

Should it be necessary to see a working parent, try to reach him or her by telephone or by letter and schedule an appointment at the parent's convenience.

Perhaps the parent is having difficulty with the child. We have seen both mothers and fathers, when called into the school, throw their hands into the air and say, "I can't do a thing with that child. He (or she) is impossible."

Should that happen to you, immediately set up a meeting with the guidance counselor. He or she may try to work with the parent. If necessary, he or she might send the parent for family counseling. Every parent must learn to set limits for the child so that the boy or girl knows exactly what is expected of him or her. However, it is not your function as a teacher to suggest the family get further help. The guidance counselor should do this.

Many times a child who is troublesome in school will react well to the counseling situation, for both the parent and the youngster learn from a professional who is an "outsider" what can be done to help the situation, both at home and in school.

## HOW TO HELP "LATCHKEY" CHILDREN _____

Harry comes to school with a string around his neck, to which is attached a house key. "I'm big," he says proudly. "I have a key to get into my house." Harry is in the second grade, and he isn't big. He lives with his mother, who is a single parent, and she has told him that he must go into the house when he gets home from school. He can watch television until she gets there, which will be about two hours later.

There are many, many latchkey children. Some live with both parents, both of whom work during the day. Harry's mother has set limits for him. The seven year old may live by those rules, whereas older latchkey children may not. As youngsters get older they are anxious to experiment, which may cause many problems.

If you have disruptive children in your class who are latchkey children, you must, without pointing them out, stress safety rules in your teaching. Many children are curious and like to experiment, some disruptive ones even more so. Playing with matches, for example, has caused the deaths of many children who were left without adult supervision.

The danger of fire can be taught very effectively by showing videos and referring to films that the child may have seen, such as *Backdraft*. A trip to the local firehouse may be very effective. There the men and women on duty can discuss the subject. They can show the equipment they need to put out even a little fire and what can happen to a child caught in a fire as it spreads and gets bigger and bigger.

Never allowing strangers to enter the house is another point that you should teach. It is to be hoped that the child's mother or father has discussed this already and that you are reiterating it, but it cannot be repeated too often.

If a parent doesn't allow a child to have his friends in the house when the parent is not there, this rule should be covered. Many times what a teacher says seems to have more weight than the words of a parent.

Every child should be taught how to call the police or the fire department if he or she should need help. It's possible for kindergarteners to learn this, and there have been cases where this has proved to be lifesaving.

Often events written up in newspaper articles can be used to show how vital it is that all youngsters understand the dangers that are ever present in their home environment.

## USING COMMUNITY RESOURCES

Bobby was so cute and pleasant it was hard to understand why in the classroom he was very disruptive. His mother couldn't believe it, saying, "He's just as good as can be at home. He helps me with the dishes, and he straightens up after he's been playing." (We have encountered this situation many times. There are youngsters whose behavior changes radically when they are in school. We've also encountered the situation going the other way, when parents are the ones who find the child disruptive.) Bobby was transferred from one class to another, with no improvement in his behavior.

One day a speaker from the Boy Scouts came in to talk with the youngsters. Bobby listened carefully, then asked if he could join the Scouts. "Of course," responded the speaker. "Boys from seven to ten can become Cub Scouts, and from eleven to seventeen they can be Boy Scouts." He couldn't know why the boy was asking this question, because Bobby was sure his disruptive behavior would keep him out.

This is one of those success stories we hope for. Bobby became deeply involved in the Cub Scouts, and his behavior improved dramatically.

Will it work with your disruptive youngsters? You never know until you try. There are many organizations and community centers where a child may get the attention he or she needs and not seek it from his or her teacher by being disruptive.

## THE NEED FOR A MALE ROLE MODEL _____

In many homes where there is no father, grandfather, or other male role model, someone is surely needed to serve in that capacity. This may be a teacher or a guidance counselor, a coach, or someone else in the school situation. Very often the youngster finds some way in which he or she can be close to a man. (Girls, as well as boys, need male role models, but the need may not be as great.)

It is interesting to see the way in which the youngsters seek to fulfill this need. "Can I work for you?" a boy named Frank asked the principal of the school. This request was made soon after the boy had been called into the office for being disruptive and had been placed on detention. The gentleman was very surprised, but as he tells it, "I think I was flattered. Of the men in the school, Frank picked me." (There were only a few men on the staff, but that didn't matter.) Frank became the official "gopher" and had a wonderful time. Of course, the stipulation had been made that should the boy become disruptive, that situation would be canceled immediately. Frank straightened out in school, for he gained not only a male role model but status as well.

One excellent organization that helps youngsters is Big Brother/Big Sister. There are branches of this organization in many areas. They are listed in the telephone directory, along with the name of their community, as for example, Big Brother/Big Sister of New York.

Lasting relationships have been formed between the boys and girls and their big brothers or sisters. In some cases, entire families become very close.

Other organizations, such as church and community groups, can possibly offer help in this regard. Male guidance counselors frequently become role models. This is fine if the relationship with the youngster can last for a year or more. If, for example, the family is prone to move frequently, then the change can prove traumatic for the boy or girl. Any relationship of this type should be for a long period of time.

## DIFFERENT CULTURES, DIFFERENT SITUATIONS, CHILDREN WITH PROBLEMS _____

Among the immigrants who have come to the United States a situation exists that was unknown in their country. For example, in Miami are many people who have settled here after leaving Cuba. Since divorce is extremely rare there, its commonness here opens new vistas for some of the men.

When husbands realize the mores of this country are very different from those of their homeland, they quickly adopt new ways. In some cases the man will leave his family and marry a new wife. He doesn't see his children, and, indeed, doesn't want the responsibility. The mother is left to raise the children, and, in many cases, the children are angry. This anger carries over into all aspects of their lives, including school, where they become disinterested and disruptive.

One of the ways in which these young people are helped is through bilingual teachers and counselors, who work with them, often on a close basis. Since the teachers are aware of the difference in the two cultures, they are able to discuss what is happening. One of the ways the young people can be reached is by explaining that what has happened in their family has happened in many others as well. While it is no solution, this does seem to help.

## WORK WITH THE DISRUPTIVE CHILD OF THE SINGLE PARENT

One important aspect of teaching is the ability of the teacher to make his or her pupils feel safe. In the case of the single parent, this can be most important. Picture it for yourself. The child goes home to an empty house. Not always, but often, the parent who returns home is harried and impatient. If there is more than one child in the family, there are added responsibilities, unless these are turned over to the children.

In one case that came to our attention, the youngsters were given chores, all listed on the family bulletin board. They were content to do them, and their mother was able to come home to an orderly house. When one of the children, the youngest, told his teacher he had chores to do and enumerated them, he beamed with pride.

Teachers can use this point and discuss it with the youngster who needs to hear it. "You have a big advantage. You can help with chores, and by doing this you are learning to take care of yourself and to be independent. You will be far ahead of a kid whose parents do everything for him (or her)." This can be a big step toward improving the youngster's self-image. When a child is disruptive, he or she may need to hear comments like this to improve his or her self-control.

Children of single parents may not have anyone to help them with their homework. In some schools aides are available to do so, or you may have to assume this role. While the rest of the class is at work, you can question the needy youngster and help where necessary. In some cities, homework aid is available by telephone. If your community offers this, make the child aware of it.

Of course, the need for you to serve as a confidante is always present when a child is disruptive. The question "What's buggin' you today?" is good when you ask it with a smile. It is not too serious and may be tossed off by the youngster, or it may be taken seriously. "I hope you can forget the problem for now and do your work," you would add. This way you are not ignoring the boy or girl's feelings, and you are giving him or her a chance to tell you about them if he or she so desires.

Another technique, and one that may supply another confidante, other than yourself, is to ask each girl or boy, not just the disruptive ones, to find some individual who can help him or her with homework. By requiring the entire class to do this, you do not single out any youngster who is a latchkey child. Have each youngster bring in a note signed by the person who will be helping him or her and checking the work. This may be an older sibling, a neighbor, a friend, or a member of a community service organization. In this way, you make sure the youngster is in close contact with another person, and this individual will become part of the child's support system.

Disruptive youngsters often do not really know what is bothering them. The problems are below the surface, and since they are painful, they don't come out. What does is behavior that shows lack of self-control.

Mr. X. was a teacher who was very in tune with his classes. One boy commented to me that his language arts class was the highlight of his years in intermediate school. This was noteworthy because this youngster had been a discipline problem in many of his classes. Of Mr. X. he said, "He understands us. He knows some of us have problems, and he always says, 'You're smart enough to solve them. Try really hard. If that doesn't work, then just let them go.'" The youngster added, "I do that, and it works for me."

## PROBLEMS WITH ADJUSTING TO FAMILY CHANGES _____

When youngsters go through a period during which their parents are being divorced, they experience great pain and may well become disruptive in school. As a general rule, the chaos and bad feeling cannot be hidden from the members of the family, and girls and boys react to it.

Youngsters have to adjust to new living conditions after the divorce, as they find themselves living with one parent or sharing their time between the two. Many times the youngsters become used to having the one parent they live with to themselves, and they become quite possessive. Each child in this new, smaller family has his or her role. The fact that this family is small usually makes daily living easier than when it was larger.

When a single parent remarries, a whole new period of adjustment on the part of the children is required. One new person is entering the family constellation, and he or she may bring along children of his or her own. A new family is formed, with stepparents and stepsiblings. Things suddenly become very different for the children of each parent.

The anticipation of having new brothers or sisters may be very pleasant, but when the event comes to pass, the story may be entirely different.

According to columnist Dr. Joyce Brothers, "Having stepsiblings forces children to reevaluate themselves. This can be troubling and often sets off intense rivalries and jealousy. Adults should never assume that just because they love each other, their children are also going to be great buddies. Friendship and respect will take a great deal of time and effort."

## GIVE ATTENTION TO THOSE WHO NEED IT

Disruptive youngsters are those who usually crave attention, and if they can get it in acceptable ways, their needs are fulfilled. Children in a new stepfamily may feel ignored.

While you teach language arts, you can use certain devices that draw attention to each child. One of these is by having the class write and produce plays. When a child is "on stage," he or she is the center of attention in a cooperative way, rather than a disruptive one.

One of the plays that is valuable in terms of young boys or girls who are in a stepfamily situation is *Cinderella*, but with a definite twist. Have the stepmother be very nice to the child, helping her rather than being cruel to her. The story is not quite as dramatic, but it can be very effective. Since her stepmother is so good to her and tells her, "Cinderella, you have to be home by midnight," the youngster wants to please her. From that point on the story can be the same. What could be more effective than having the disruptive child be Cinderella or Prince Charming?

This type of play might lead to a class discussion of kindness and cooperation, always valuable under any circumstances.

With older boys or girls, a technique might be a debate on the presentation of the family on television. Is it portrayed realistically or not?

The composition technique we have mentioned previously is always valuable. Possible topics include, "My Family and How We Get Along Together" or "How Do I Cooperate With My Family, and What Could I Do to Improve My Contribution?" Whenever you use this type of composition, have the youngsters list some ideas on the board. This serves to "jump start" the thinking process.

## CARRYING PROBLEMS FROM HOME INTO SCHOOL IS COSTLY

"I can't get along with that guy. He's mean, and I hate him." This was Ron, a twelve year old, who thought he was an adult and deserved adult privileges, speaking of his stepfather. "He won't let me stay out as late as my friends," Ron added, "and he thinks he knows it all. I liked it better when it was just my mom and me."

Ron decided that he didn't have to go to school. When brought in by the attendance teacher, he was rebellious and disruptive to the point where his teacher called in the parents. She was surprised to meet the stepfather, for he seemed anything but authoritarian.

"I've been trying to be pleasant with Ron," he said, "but he is very difficult. I thought we'd be friends, but that seems to be impossible."

Not impossible, but very,very difficult. However, Ron had said he wanted to graduate with his class, and when the fact came out in the interview that he was being held back, he announced, "But my friends are all graduating." That realization made Ron alter his behavior. He came to school for the rest of the year and did graduate with his class.

To the teacher's knowledge, the situation at home did not improve very much. However, Ron realized he was hurting himself, not his stepfather, by not attending.

In Ron's case, the idea that he wouldn't graduate penetrated very quickly. Many times it does not. Young people think they can go their merry ways without penalty. This concept, in their minds, has to be changed before they will change.

Of course, not every disruptive youngster cares, but a surprisingly large number do. Surely, no teacher would ever say this if the youngster wasn't in danger of being held back, for if one threatens and cannot carry through, it can be disastrous in terms of the future.

## COMPOSE PLAYLETS FOR SELF-EXPRESSION

To encourage self-expression you can utilize the playlet technique, for it does supply an excellent vehicle for expressing oneself. It is, for instance, particularly valuable to draw out the very quiet child as well as the disruptive ones.

To use this technique, begin with a discussion of the situation. Set the tone somewhat this way, saying, "There are many problems people have—lots and lots of people. Let's act one out. We can start with a scene at the dinner table. The family is just getting ready to eat."

Next, choose children to play the roles. If you have youngsters who are particular discipline problems and have problems because they are in a stepfamily situation, be sure to use them.

Have the girls and boys compose the dialogue as they go along. Encourage them to really express themselves—to really throw themselves into the play. Help them "let themselves go" in the various parts. When the subject has been exhausted, discuss the playlet. What particularly important points did it make? Was it of interest to the audience? How might it be improved?

By this method, you can show the universality of problems, a concept that is of great value in the changing world of today. Family problems are well handled by this technique, as are those arising from puberty and developmental changes.

We recall one playlet that dealt with a new family, consisting of stepmother, stepfather, and eight new stepsiblings. (In our school, we had one such family with twelve children. Each parent "contributed" six.)

The playlet was structured around lateness—getting out of the house in the morning on time. From this, it moved to the use of the bathroom—ten people and one bathroom, to be specific. The "family" sat around and talked about their problems. The seventh graders were well aware of the difficulties presented. One of the boys suggested they draw up a time schedule. Others objected, but since no one could suggest any other *feasible* possibility they decided to try it. (Remodeling the house to include a new bathroom was suggested, but the "children," realizing their "mother and father" could not afford this, vetoed it immediately.)

In addition to the solution to the problem, the playlet also addressed selfishness and the consideration of the rights of others. It was time exceedingly well spent, with realizations of concepts brought home to the youngsters.

An interesting aside: One of the usually disruptive girls came up to the teacher after class and said, with great pride, "I'm going to go home and tell my family to do this."

Not all playlets will solve specific problems, but they do enable you to bring out points that would otherwise be difficult to teach. By showing that everyone has problems, youngsters can see that they are not alone, which helps them accept their situations and possibly realize the situations aren't so bad after all.

## FOSTER CHILDREN AND THE DIFFICULTIES INHERENT IN THE SITUATION

Timmy, a foster child, was in the eighth grade. He had a pattern of behavior that was almost routine. He would be sent out of class to the assistant principal every Monday morning because he had gotten into a fight. He was always furious. Then someone noticed that this same fighting occurred when school reopened after a holiday during the week.

When questioned about his fighting, Timmy refused to say anything. The foster parents would make appointments to come into school but did not do so. Finally, after they were informed that the boy would be suspended, the foster mother appeared.

"I can't understand that boy," was her first comment. "We try to do everything we can for him." Indeed they did, for Timmy was always well dressed and seemed to have spending money. Then his foster mother added, "His real mother comes to see him every weekend and every holiday." That was the clue.

When the assistant principal asked him a question about his mother, Timmy broke down completely. "She doesn't want me," he literally screamed. "Why does she come to see me and bother me? I hate her! I hate her!"

It was not that Timmy's birth mother did not want him. She was a very young woman, and she felt she could not give him a stable home life, and that he was better off in a foster home. Actually, nothing was further from the truth. The boy took out his feelings of rejection on teachers and other youngsters.

When his birth mother realized she was actually, but unwittingly, causing Timmy's belligerence, she promised she would try to arrange for him to live with her. He didn't believe her, and the fighting continued. When his mother ultimately did manage to have him live with her, Timmy's anger slowly disappeared, and he fought less and less, and finally not at all.

Not all foster children react in this way, but many have problems and are disruptive. The basis for this is their insecurity, for many have been shunted from one foster home to another. This type of instability often leads to the youngster being transferred from one school to another.

There are those times when foster children get little love and affection, for they have been taken into people's homes because they want the money paid to those giving foster care. (In 1990, close to $800 million was spent in New York City alone for the care of foster children. This is an increase from $320 million spent by that city in 1985. The increase is due to the crack epidemic and the removal of babies from crack-addicted mothers.)

Foster children, we have found, react especially well to teachers who interact with them on a one-to-one basis and who show they really care about them. This is particularly true when the girl or boy has not been able to form close friendships because she or he has been moved from foster home to foster home.

One technique that may help such youngsters is to have the class do group work. By placing the child with girls or boys who are sympathetic and understanding, it is possible that the "new" youngster will make friends. Creating teams and again causing the boys and girls to come into close contact with one another is worth trying, for here proximity may help promote close relationships.

## AVOID COMPETITION AMONG STEPCHILDREN OR FOSTER CHILDREN

Parents sometimes encourage their children to compete against one another. The effects of competition depend on the relationships within the family. If they are good, the competition can be healthy. The same is true of the classroom, where competitive games can work well to bring interest and excitement into the educational process. However, in stepfamilies and foster families, competition can be disastrous.

Dr. A. was a highly successful dentist. He was a widower with one son when he married a woman who had two boys from her previous marriage. Dr. A.'s son was of average intelligence, while the new Mrs. A.'s sons were very bright.

When Mrs. A brought her sons in to be registered in school, one was placed in the same class as Dr. A.'s son. It didn't take long before the newly arrived boy began to excel. The other youngster became annoyed and proceeded to start fights with his stepbrother. The parents did not know of the situation until it spilled over into their home life.

Dr. A. requested that his stepson be transferred to another class. This caused still more animosity, but he reasoned his son had been in that class first and should not be removed. The new boy had his class changed and was very resentful. Although he did well, to our knowledge the two boys never became friends. The problems between them continued as long as we knew the family.

Children do not like to be placed in situations where they feel inferior, which is exactly what happened with Dr. A.'s son. Should you use competitions, be sure that no one feels he or she is "dumb" when the competition is over.

When you know that some of the youngsters in your class are not as competent as others, and you set up a competition, equalize things by giving some of the slower children some advance credit so that the others don't have an advantage.

## BELIEVE WHAT CHILDREN TELL YOU

Years ago we heard of a teacher who had written on the board during Open School Week, "If you don't believe what your children say about me, I won't believe what they say about you." At the time it was considered very clever, for often the tales children told were considered to be stories they had concocted from their imagination. Today we know better. Perhaps some were fictional, but surely not all.

Hundreds of thousands of stepparents and foster parents are kind and loving, but there are also the other kind. Molestation does occur within step- and foster families, as it does within all types of families.

This has always been true, but since child abuse was not acknowledged by society at large, abuse in the past could be carefully hidden away. Make no mistake, much is concealed today as well, although the climate for revealing such behavior has changed. One only has to read the newspapers or listen to news reports to be aware of this. And many cases don't make the headlines.

Should a child tell you a story that seems unbelievable don't, under any circumstances, ignore it. Should a little one tell you, "My uncle touched me," or "My grandfather," or "My stepfather," refer it to the guidance counselor. This is true of little boys as well as little girls. Should you see signs of neglect, as well as bruises or signs of violence, don't hesitate for a moment to refer the youngster for help.

In 1965, a twelve-year-old boy came to me. (I was then an intermediate school guidance counselor.) "My landlord is killing me," he said. Then he added words that, I confess, shocked me. "He won't even use vaseline," the child said, almost crying. He was being molested, sexually, by the fifty year old man who owned the building where the family lived.

The boy went on to tell of this abuse, which had made him extremely nervous. He could not function in school, and he thought all the boys and girls knew what was happening to him, although, of course, they did not. He was often absent. However, one day he had heard me tell the youngsters that if I could be of help to them, they were to come to me. "I'm new at this job," I recall telling them. "I'm anxious to do a good job. If you have a problem, I'll try to help you with it." I had told this to every class and was actually trying to sell my services.

After listening to this child's tale of horror, I asked him, "Does your mother know about this?"

"No, I can't tell her," he answered.

"We'll have to, if I can help you," I told him. I had to persuade him; he was sure his foster mother would blame him instead of the adult.

We did manage to get help from a social service agency. The family moved into another dwelling, and the boy was sent to another school. But that isn't the end of the story. I would get "regards" from this boy as the years passed. It had been a thrill the first time I heard from him—until I learned that he was in a mental hospital. To my knowledge he has spent much of his life there—the result of the abuse he has suffered.

## FOSTER AND STEPCHILDREN NEED TO HEAR PRAISE _____

As adults, we know how we react when we are chastised or, just the opposite, when we are praised. Youngsters who are in stepfamilies, and surely those who are in foster homes, need very much to be told they are worthwhile human beings and that they can do things right. This is true from the time these boys and girls are very young until they are adults, and even then, the same concept applies. At times these children are disruptive because they are seeking attention.

Disruptive youngsters are often insecure. The ego structure of a child who is insecure is very fragile. It is a very wise foster parent or stepparent who can help the child develop self-worth and self-confidence. If you, as the teacher, can work to help the child feel important and self-assured, you can make a big difference in the child's life.

That is not easy when a child is constantly being disruptive. You cannot ignore that behavior, and you have to rely on your rules. You must insist, without hostility, that they be observed. However, you can set up situations where even disruptive boys and girls can be successful and praiseworthy.

There are very specific activities that will accomplish this. Nonrepresentational art projects are one example of work that you can praise wholeheartedly. It may be because the colors are good, or the shapes are interesting, the scene is attractive, or the drawing or painting is good.

What compliments can you give to a boy or girl? Perhaps he or she has beautiful eyes, or a nice smile, a pleasant manner, or good speech. More important, is he or she cooperative and willing to help others when necessary? Does he or she have good manners, or is he or she fun to have around? Was he or she disruptive, and has his or her behavior improved?

If you can find characteristics to praise, you can make the child feel good and help his or her self-confidence develop. You might share these thoughts with his or her parents. Of course, you would not restrict your words only to stepchildren or to foster children, but you would make these comments to every child in your class, and all would benefit.

## CONCLUSION _____

Years ago, the typical American family was thought to be two parents and their two children living together in peace and harmony. Today the situation is far different. Many youngsters live with single parents or with stepparents or in foster homes. They number in the millions, and it is a very unusual classroom where there aren't some of these youngsters. Possibly because of their family situations, some of them may be disruptive. Should you need to communicate with any of their parents, you will find a letter more effective than a note or even a telephone call.

You may have one or more "latchkey" children in your class. Teaching and stressing safety in the home is very important to these youngsters. Experimenting with fire is a constant danger, and if you are able to get across to the children that they are never to do this, you may possibly save a life.

Disruptive youngsters often need male role models, and if so, community resources such as the Boy Scouts, or the Big Brother/Big Sister organizations can supply this. The role may also be filled by a member of the church or a guidance counselor. When youngsters who are immigrants are learning English, bilingual teachers and counselors can be of great help.

Specific techniques for working with the disruptive boy or girl include a policy of strict adherence to the rules and giving these youngsters meaningful chores. Of course, offering to act as confidante is extremely important.

There is a definite period of adjustment for a child when a parent remarries or when the child is placed in a foster home for the first time, or moved to another. Disruptive behavior is often the result. This can be helped by carefully listening to the child and allowing him or her to express his or her fears. One of the ways in which you can allow for self-expression is by having the children do playlets, composed by themselves.

It is vitally important that you listen to your children carefully, for among stepfamilies and in foster homes, as in other families, there is always the possibility of child abuse. Should you have any reason to suspect this, be sure you make your referral immediately. Most of the time children have trust in their teachers, and by seeking investigation or aid, you will make a huge difference in a child's life.

# 15

## WORKING WITH DISRUPTIVE STUDENTS WHO JUST DON'T "GIVE A DAMN"

Have you, in your class, youngsters who are disruptive for no other reason than that they don't care, that they just don't "give a damn" about school, about education, and about their future lives? As a result, they will ultimately probably be a part of one of the very serious problems our nation faces—the large number of young adults who graduate from high school but who are not educated.

Often these are the girls and boys who, while in elementary and intermediate school, refuse to take part in the educational process. They have no serious problems of the type we've described in previous chapters, and they are of normal intelligence, but they have no interest in the work going on in the classroom and in getting an education. Teaching them requires a great deal of effort.

These youngsters are often street smart, and they may do enough work just to get by, but no more. They have their own agenda, and if that involves being disruptive then so be it. It often does. What can you do to change this "don't give a damn" attitude?

### BE KIND, FIRM, AND FAIR

"Don't touch me," the little boy said, within hours of the first time the young teacher met him. He was in her second grade class. "You can't touch me," the child repeated, with great hostility. What was this teacher to do?

Her answer came from Mrs. X, an experienced colleague who was her mentor. "The first time this happened to me, I almost hit the ceiling. I became so angry," she told the young teacher. "I thought, 'Who does this brat think he is anyway?' I was a brand new teacher, right out of college, and this was what has been called my 'baptism under fire.'

"I tried being tough, and we had a very difficult year. I was miserable, and I'm sure the kids were too. Then during summer vacation I had occasion to speak to a woman who had been teaching for many years. Her advice has helped me, and I've never forgotten it."

Mrs. X. was happy to share what she had learned. "I've found that this type of child is already angry at the whole world, even though the child is so young. To make him or her, and it can be a her, angrier gets you nowhere."

"The next year one child said those exact words to me. I decided to try being just the opposite of angry. 'Of course I won't touch you, but I want you to know you're welcome in my class,' I told the youngster. Then I added, 'I hope we'll get to be friends.'"

"What happened?" the young teacher asked.

"I ultimately won the little boy over. I think making him a monitor was one of the turning points. However, the teacher who had him in the third grade used a different approach, and sure enough, the anger came out again."

"So," continued Mrs. X, "I've learned that being kind, combined with firmness, works well for me."

As we have said before, one must always remember that children sometimes mistake kindness for weakness, so the kindness must be tempered with strength. This applies to youngsters of all ages. Anger and hostility are the teacher's enemies—in him- or herself, as well as in the children.

## USE THE MONITORIAL SYSTEM AND MAKE YOUR TEACHING INTERESTING _____

At the beginning of this book are our suggestions for a monitorial system, which involves giving every child a specific job. Virtually every boy or girl will be pleased with this, especially when the jobs are changed frequently. A "don't care" youngster often cannot believe that he or she is being trusted with responsibility.

Even those youngsters who are blasé become involved in the classroom situation as a result of being monitors. Some have never had this honor given to them, and because of its newness it has a favorable effect. This division of labor makes your life easier and gives you the opportunity to praise even the boy or girl who makes a show of not "giving a damn." It may help to change their attitude, which is, of course, what you are trying to accomplish.

It almost goes without saying that the more interesting you can make your teaching, the more chance you have of reaching these youngsters. You will find some ideas in this chapter and other chapters that we believe you will find useful.

One intermediate school teacher was able to teach even the most recalcitrant group of youngsters. He found he could work with them and get them to work. "I would tell them, 'I think you kids are great. You keep me on my toes. I know I have to do a good job to keep you interested. You know what good teaching is!'"

When one or several of the youngsters became disruptive, he would say, "I guess I'm not doing a good job today." The rest of the class would clamor, "Yes you are," and the disruption would stop almost immediately.

"I can't believe it," this teacher told a colleague. But the youngsters were right. This gentleman's teaching was a reflection of the hours of planning and preparation he put into his work. He would divide the forty-five-minute lesson into three parts.

"I sometimes think of this as a three-ring circus, except my rings would be one at a time. One part of my lesson might be written, another discussion, a third reading, but not necessarily in that order. Or I would have a debate, or a filmstrip, or a video in a lesson to vary things. I'd change the order to make the class more interesting. Then, of course, there were games and quizzes for review. Variety made the period go quickly, and the "don't care" kids would often get involved. Not always," he was quick to point out, "but often."

## IS READING THE PROBLEM?

Are your "don't care" kids behaving this way because they can't read? This is always something you have to look into, for it never fails to be a possibility. Use diagnostic materials early in the year to determine this.

As you probably have experienced, all too often youngsters who haven't learned to read or who are sufficiently behind to have problems are promoted. The lack of this skill causes all sorts of difficulties. If you have youngsters whose attitude is "devil may care," it is worth checking their records as well as retesting them. The "don't care" attitude may well be a coverup for feelings of inadequacy.

If they have a reading problem, remedial work may be the key to changing their behavior. This is very often the case, for people actually reach adulthood having gone to school, even graduated from high school, still functionally illiterate. May we say that no teacher has been able to get through to them, to make them understand the importance in their lives of reading.

## HOW DO YOUNGSTERS DEVELOP THE "DON'T CARE" ATTITUDE

Children even in the earliest grades may have already begun developing the "don't care" attitude. They may have gotten it from their older siblings or from the older boys and girls with whom they associate. "I hate school," one seven year old was heard to say.

"How can you say that?" her teacher inquired. "You're just beginning to come to school."

"That's what my sister always says," the little one answered proudly.

Another cause of this attitude may come from the youngster having watched and become enamored of television. This presents a problem because viewing the screen does not require any active mental participation. This habit of passivity is a great barrier to learning.

The child watches you, without concentrating, as if you were on a screen, making no demands of him or her. The material you are teaching just goes over the child's head and soon he or she falls behind. It is then that the "don't care" attitude begins to develop. It gets worse and worse as the youngster doesn't understand what it is you are teaching to the class currently because he or she has never mastered the necessary background material.

Television programs, and films too, frequently present the school situation in a very negative light. What an adult may view as ridiculous, a child sees totally differently and accepts as the truth. A perfect example is the film *Problem Child 2.* Because it has the word *child* in the title, parents think it is suitable for youngsters. Nothing could be further from the truth. Teachers and principals are portrayed as fools, and even as being immoral. It is difficult to bring home to the youngsters that this film is not true to life but is an attempt to be funny. We found it very sad to see our profession so denigrated by an insignificant, disgusting film.

Television programs may be wonderful and offer intellectual stimulation, but those kinds do not have the popularity of one such as "The Simpsons." This show was described in *Time* magazine, August 27, 1990, as "the Fox network's enormously popular cartoon family show." Bart Simpson is drawn to be ten years old and was made the hero because he is an underachiever. His face can be seen on everything from beach towels to the ubiquitous millions of T-shirts. This family of cartoon characters is crude and argues constantly, and Bart is incorrigible. The kids love him, and his hairstyle, with his long hair standing on end, was copied almost immediately and became a fad.

Older siblings or friends, movies, and television, are three of the influences that may cause the development of the "don't care" attitude, of which Bart Simpson may be considered the archetype, although the attitude existed long before the cartoon character. He is merely a reflection of it.

## HOW TO PREVENT THE "DON'T CARE" ATTITUDE _____

It is our firm belief that, down deep, youngsters want to do well in school. They may cover up this desire because they feel inadequate and unable to function on the level asked of them. If you can speak with them privately, on a one-to-one basis, you can possibly help change their negative attitude. This is not easy to do, but if you are willing to try, it can be done.

Possibly there is a specific problem, and if you determine what it is, you may be able to effect positive changes.

"I think you have the potential for doing better work," you say to the youngster. He or she may well look at you blankly because *potential* is a new word. Explain it, and go on. "Is there any particular area where you would like just a little bit of help?" you ask. "Sometimes even just an hour of help can make a difference," you tell the child.

I recall one incident which illustrates this. A fourth-grade teacher commented to her supervisor, "Carmine is getting out of hand. He was a little bit of a nuisance at the beginning of the year, but now he's very disruptive. He makes noises and disturbs the others, and he will not do his work."

"When did you first notice this?" the supervisor asked.

"Just after the Thanksgiving holiday, I think," the teacher replied.

"Try talking to Carmine. See if he will tell you what's happened. He may be able to."

When the teacher spoke to the boy, he wouldn't answer her at first but just stared ahead, She prodded him, and finally he said, "I can't do my arithmetic. I was absent for two days, and when I came back, I didn't know what to do."

Sure enough, that is exactly when the youngster started to act up. The problem was solved by an hour of "catch-up" work. Carmine ceased making noises and settled down.

Too often it is one child who starts the disruption and others follow. It's important to nip any misbehavior as soon as it occurs. Speak with each child, and when help is needed, supply it. You may ask the parents to assist you in this, but you can't count on them, for they may feel inadequate. This is especially true of arithmetic skills. Furthermore, many mothers and fathers are too busy to take the time to do remedial work with their youngsters. As one told a teacher, when the suggestion was made that she work with her son, "That's your job. You get paid to do that. I don't." Most parents don't react that way, but many, while their intentions are good, can't help or don't follow through.

But supposing a youngster doesn't give you any information. When you ask if he or she needs help, suppose there is absolutely no response. Your next step is to draw on your knowledge of the boy or girl and try to build on his or her strengths.

"You're so good at spelling," you say. "Your written work is sometimes excellent." You can almost see the child's attitude, for just one minute, change. Continue this line of talk for a few more minutes. By speaking in this way, you can often reach a child whom you thought was not reachable.

## POINTING OUT A YOUNGSTER'S STRONG POINTS _____

Perhaps it is some aspect of his or her personality that you can point out. "You get along so well with people," you tell the youngster. Or, "I notice you seem to be the leader of your group of friends. Leadership quality is very important, but you need an education to use it in the future," you point out. "Won't you put your mind to that and give it a try?"

Always be honest, but particularly with youngsters who are "street smart," for if you embellish the truth, they will know it immediately and label you a phony. You don't want that.

Young women, I have found, are often very much into the fads of dress and coiffure. "You are really fashion conscious, aren't you?" I asked a fourteen year old. She was a year older than most of the others in her seventh-grade class. She seemed to feel she had to show what she thought was her maturity by being nasty to her teachers.

When I sat down and discussed the fashion industry with her, her eyes opened wide. "I think you'd enjoy a career in that field," I said to her. She looked at me, absolutely incredulously. I don't think any teacher had ever spoken to her about her future or taken her seriously. I continued, "You might be a fashion coordinator, for example." She, of course, had no idea of what that meant, but after I explained it, she was very thoughtful.

"Do you think I could do that?" she questioned.

"If you get your education, you could," I replied. "You'd probably have to go to college," I added.

"Me go to college?" The youngster laughed.

"Why not?" I continued. "You have the brains, if you would work at it. Think about it." We left it at that. Years later, when she graduated from high school, this young woman came back to visit me. "I'm going to FIT (Fashion Institute of Technology)," she said, beaming at me, then recalled, "You gave me good advice. I came back to tell you. Thanks."

If you can discover a talent of any kind, it can give you some leverage when speaking to a youngster. Building on that can possibly help stop him or her from being disruptive.

## COMBATING PEER PRESSURE

Once a youngster is of intermediate school age, and possibly even younger, there is no one who can influence him or her more than his or her peers. Peer pressure is one of the dominant factors in young people's lives. It is almost as if it is life-threatening if they don't conform to the mores of their age group. You need no further proof of this than to observe the manner of dress of boys and girls. This may even be true of little ones in the second or third grade.

There are groups of youngsters who make it a point to look down on girls or boys who do well in school. One sixth grader told his grade advisor, "Please keep my name off the honor roll. If I'm on it my friends won't even talk to me."

The grade advisor confessed to a colleague, "In all the years I've been in the school system, I've never heard that before. But I've seen kids go along just beautifully all year and then mess up on their finals. I wonder now if that was intentional." He commented further, "I tried to show the honor roll refuser how foolish this was but it didn't work. I also tried to keep his name off, but when I took it to the faculty committee, they wouldn't go along with me. This kid would never have anything to do with me after that."

Of course, here too a one-to-one discussion is virtually the only approach that offers any hope. However, one should never say anything in any way derogatory about other boys or girls.

"I hear your friends are giving you a hard time because you're getting decent grades" is definitely a "no-no." Saying "I think your friends are a great bunch of kids" is also not good, unless you can be sincere when you say it.

## DEAL WITH THE SHOW-OFF

How many times have you had a disruptive youngster who is behaving this way for effect—who is simply playing to the crowd by showing off?

Weight lifters often show off their muscles, and many youngsters show off their big mouths. Should this happen in your class, never laugh (even if you have to try very hard not to). Say to the boy or girl, in almost a whisper, "I'll speak to you later." Then discuss the fact that rather than showing himself or herself to be a worthwhile person, he or she looks stupid. You might say, "The class thinks you're a clown. Do you want to be thought of as a stupid person who fools around, or as someone who's smart? It's up to you to decide."

One of the most effective ways to handle a show-off or other disruptive youngster is more serious. Don't do this until you are "at the end of your rope." You may say, "I know you are in this class, but as far as we are concerned, you cease to exist. You are not part of this group. Nor will you be until you change your behavior entirely." Follow this up by ignoring the culprit, by not even looking at him or her. This approach has proved to be devastating even to the most recalcitrant youngster. I have seen it actually bring tears to a boy's eyes. No one wants to be told they no longer exist.

## TEACH THE VALUE OF EDUCATION _____

When youngsters are disruptive, they take up an inordinate amount of class time. In effect they are thieves. If you can persuade the other boys and girls in the class of this, you can use peer pressure in a positive way. One of the most honest ways to reach the "don't care" youngsters is by the use of facts and figures. "You may not realize it now," you may say, "but your education is worth a fortune to you. It can make the difference in your life—will you be rich or poor? Let me show you some statistics." You can then show them, in terms of dollars and cents, the value of education.

The figures that follow were for the years from 1970 to 1989, and were supplied by the U.S. Department of Commerce, Bureau of the Census.

The figures are the medians of a sample survey. This means that half of the people in the group cited earned less than the number indicated, and half earned more. However, the figures enable us to make comparisons in regard to the amount of education.

A man with eight years or less of schooling earned $17,555 per year, while a woman earned $12,188. With one to three years of high school, a man earned $21,065, while a woman earned $13,923. When a person graduated from high school, a man earned $26,609 while a woman earned $17,528.

With one to three years of college education, a man earned $31,308 while a woman earned $21,631. A male college graduate earned $38,565 while a woman earned $26,709. With an additional year of college, a man earned $46,842 while a woman earned $32,050.

These statistics are from a totally unbiased source. They may be used as a basis for lessons in virtually any subject area. It should be pointed out, too, that women can go into fields where their salaries are the same as those of men if they do the same job. Teaching is one of them.

If you are teaching in the intermediate school, you can show your youngsters how close they are to high school graduation. You can do this by selecting an event which happened six or seven years ago which they will remember, and then pointing out that, in the same amount of time, projected ahead, they will be at the point where they have to decide on their future education.

Many youngsters may think that the salaries mentioned are huge amounts of money. It's then that you have them discuss this with their parents. They have to be shown just how much or how little the dollar actually buys. Have the boys and girls question their parents about the costs of food, housing, clothing, medical care, education, entertainment, and insurance. This will then give the figures more meaning. *Ask the youngsters not to question their parents about how much money they earn.* If they do, this can cause problems for you. The subject is to be discussed in the abstract.

The youngsters may ask their parents, "How much must a person earn to live comfortably?" You may wish to say, "This is a confidential talk between you and your parents, and we will not talk about it in class. It is to give you a realistic picture of the cost of living."

I recall a chance meeting with a young man who had been in my eighth-grade class some years before and was a typical "don't care kid" who had been very disruptive. In fact, I didn't recognize him, he had changed so much. We had time to talk, and he suddenly demanded, in an angry tone, "Why didn't you tell us how much money we have to make to get married? My girlfriend and I want to, but we can't afford to. Rents are so high it would take almost everything we make to get an apartment, and we're both working." It was then that I decided to become a guidance counselor and stress this very important aspect of education.

If you think about it, you will realize many, if not all, of your disruptive youngsters will be the ones who will make no effort to prepare themselves to earn a living. If you can impress this fact upon them, perhaps you can change their behavior and their future lives. The tragedy is that many have never had role models who go to work every day. They have not experienced a person getting up in the morning (or at any time during the day) and preparing to leave for a place of employment, or returning home afterward. Can you explain this to them in a way that will change their perception of the world? Surely it is worth giving it a try.

## CITING THE PEOPLE KIDS CONSIDER TO BE HEROES _____

Years ago, teachers spoke of heroes whom they hoped served as role models. However, the heroes they spoke of were usually historical figures. I recall having one class read a story about Nathan Hale. Without question the story of this young school master and his deeds will inspire these kids, I thought. I was teaching eighth-grade language arts at the time. I have to say that, if the story had any effect, it was one that they wouldn't reveal. "Man, he's dumb," I'll never forget one boy saying. "They weren't paying him enough."

Cynical? Absolutely, and many of the youngsters of today are equally so. For ten years, the World Almanac has held an annual poll of students in grades eight through twelve. They were asked to select those individuals in public life they admired most. The schools chosen to participate represented a geographic cross section of the United States.

The Top Hero in 1990 was one of our nation's leading basketball players, Michael Jordan. Not only is he one of the best, but he has gained fame and fortune outside the basketball court by his many endorsements. In a tie for second place were businessman Donald Trump and President Ronald Reagan. In third place was actor Tom Cruise, and in fourth, again a tie, were Eddie Murphy and Bill Cosby. Most of these men, and there were no women among the Top Ten, were athletes or entertainers, not statesmen or other movers and shakers of world events. However, we can still use this information for our purposes. Let's look at Michael Jordan, for example.

In *Business Week* magazine recently, an article appeared about this young man. However, he was pictured, not on the basketball court, but in a three-piece suit, smoking a cigar. Jordan is, indeed, a business man, for his earnings off the court far exceed those he is paid as the star of the Chicago Bulls. He earned $10 million in 1990 through his endorsements and his outside activities, such as speaking before groups and running a basketball camp. He will receive $3.5 million per year for five years for playing basketball, according to his recent contract.

Youngsters, even in the intermediate school grades, are already aware of the huge salaries paid to entertainers and sports stars. It is for this reason, as well as their expertise, that they are respected. Such individuals can and do influence boys and girls. When one of them can be seen on the television screen saying "Stay in school," and they do this often, it carries more weight than when you or I say it. When the message is longer and the person talks about the need for education, so much the better.

Principal Arnie Magenheim of Public School 39, Staten Island, about whom we have already written, has brought many celebrities to his school to talk to his girls and boys. He wrote letters inviting stars from many different fields, and they sometimes accepted his invitations. The impressions made on the youngsters, especially the "don't care kids," may be long-lasting. One never knows just how or what will reach a particular youngster, but virtually any idea you may have is worth trying. This is where your creativity is needed and may help you change "don't care kids" into interested youngsters.

In the August 1988 *Reader's Digest* there is a group of articles under the heading "Escaping the Underclass." The first is by the widely read syndicated columnist William Raspberry, titled "It's Up to You." His thesis is that it is necessary to "make our youngsters understand the critical importance of individual exertion by showing them examples of people for whom exertion has paid off and by making certain that their own exertion is rewarded, beginning in the very earliest years." A youngster from San Francisco, Orenthal Simpson, was able to spend a day with a man who was his hero, baseball great Willie Mays. Orenthal, at the age of thirteen, was already a fine athlete. However, he was a member of a gang, and he and his friends would steal bottles of liquor so they could party. A youth counselor, realizing Orenthal's potential, arranged for the boy to spend just an ordinary day with Mays. "I had an entirely different outlook on everything after that day with Willie Mays," Orenthal recalls.

"That day with Mays made me realize that my dream was possible. Willie wasn't superhuman. He was an ordinary person, so I knew there was a chance for me." Orenthal became a famous football player, better known as O.J. Simpson.

Not all youngsters can spend a day with a famous person, but perhaps you and I can help them realize that they, too, can be successful in one way or another.

## NEWS EVENTS CAN BE USED WITH "DON'T CARE KIDS" _____

Many of your youngsters, almost surely the "don't care kids," will be tempted to experiment with drugs or alcohol. Since the drug epidemic has spread all over the country, it reaches into every school and every level of society. The "don't care kids" are particularly influenced by their peers, and since they are not interested in school and have "turned off" to education, they are especially vulnerable.

What can you as a teacher do in the area of drug education? Your daily newspaper can be used to bring reality into the classroom. In some areas of the nation, for example, drug dealers are seen as big shots. They drive fancy cars, flash huge rolls of money, and wear expensive clothes and jewelry. This is what the youngsters see. What they don't see, as a general rule, are the dealers in prison uniforms, or being murdered. When this bit of news appears in the media, it is well worth taking the time to discuss it with your class.

Sadly, many of the "don't care kids" are so impressed by the affluence of the dealers that they totally ignore the down side. Yet it is there, very much so, and it is one of the aspects of life that should not be ignored. Far too often the media glorify the drug purveyors, even making them sound like royalty by calling them "drug lords." As educators, we should add their demise to our teaching, and the simplest and best way is by using the printed media to convey the message.

Do all drug dealers get caught? Of course not, but many do, and they can serve as examples. You need not be reluctant to discuss topics such as this. You will find your youngsters will be very much interested, and you can never tell, but you may actually save one of their lives by this discussion.

## THE "DON'T CARE" YOUNGSTERS OFTEN GROW UP TO BE POOR CITIZENS

We live in a nation for which our youth are willing to go to war, with the ever-present danger that they will be wounded or killed. Ask almost any young person if he or she is willing to fight for his or her country and the answer is rarely anything but yes.

Yet the "don't care" attitude extends to one of the very basic concepts on which the United States as a democracy is based. This is voting. It is a sad fact that even in a presidential election, 50 percent of those eligible do not vote. "I don't have the time," some Americans will say. "I couldn't get there," is another common excuse, referring to the place where they have to go to vote. What flimsy excuses these are! The true cause, of course, is general apathy.

During and after World War II, there were many protesters contending that if at age eighteen a person was old enough to fight, he or she was therefore old enough to vote. It took until 1971 for the Twenty-sixth Amendment to the Constitution to be ratified and to become law. But today, many young people do not exercise this right. In the year immediately after the law went into effect, the percentage of people voting dropped from the previous year, and it has continued to drop since. In 1972, the percentage of people who voted was 55.2; by 1988 it had dropped to 50.1.

As teachers, we should discuss voting, showing that it is a duty as well as a right. If you begin your discussion by asking if your boys or girls would fight for their country and then extend that to voting, you may be able to reach some of them. Unfortunately, this attitude often reflects that of the parents and is difficult to counteract.

Another way to stimulate an interest in voting is to have the young-sters debate the qualities of the candidates who are running for office and then actually have "elections." This gives the girls and boys the opportu-nity to "vote" for the candidate of their choice. This technique may be used for local and state as well as federal elections.

## "DON'T CARE KIDS" SOMETIMES REFLECT THEIR PARENTS' ATTITUDES

Mr. R came into my office blustering. The gold chain around his neck gleamed against his sunburned skin. In another mood, I thought, he'd be a handsome man, but in this one he surely wasn't.

"Why did you need to see me?" he almost shouted. "My kid's okay. He's a good boy. So what if he hates to come to school? He helps me in my place, and the customers like him." Mr. R. seemed genuinely annoyed that we were anxious to get his son Richard to attend school regularly.

After speaking with him, it was easy to understand his son's attitude. This boy was growing up in a home in which no one understood the value of education. It was no easy task to get Mr. R. to see this.

"Look at me," he said proudly. "I'm doing okay, and I never went past the eighth grade. I know enough to run my business. I've had to enlarge it twice," he added. Mr. R. owned and operated a very successful restaurant and bar and grill. "Richard has been a big help to me," he pointed out, and he went on and on.

What do you do when you have a situation like this, one we might call "dealing with an uncooperative parent? "Certainly, tact is essential in any interchange with such a person. First we pointed out to Mr. R. that he was breaking the law if he allowed Richard, a sixth grader who happened to be big for his age, to work in the bar, where liquor was sold. We told Mr. R. that he could actually be brought up on charges. He claimed he did not know this.

Next I attempted to show him that he was really cheating his son. "Richard has a good mind," I said. "He deserves a chance to develop it." Then I asked, "Don't you agree?"

This time Mr. R. did agree, and it was this approach that won him over. It may be necessary to use different arguments, but if you can change the attitude of this type of parent, you have taken the first step to changing that of his or her son or daughter.

There are parents who will side with their children under any circum-stances, and these are more difficult to win over. I recall spending hours trying to enlist the cooperation of a single mother. She refused to accept the fact that her daughter was doing no work whatsoever. I was not able to convince her, and though the girl went on to high school, she never graduated. As has been said, in many different circumstances, "You can't win 'em all." We try, but we have to keep that in mind too, and accept defeat gracefully.

## SHOW THAT *YOU* TRULY BELIEVE IN THE VALUE OF EDUCATION

As teachers, we do have the opportunity to reach and teach our students, if for no other reason than we spend a good deal of time with them. We can usually have some influence, even on the "don't care kid," by showing our sincere belief in learning. We should, however, be very specific in presenting our reasons. What essentially does education do for us? Why should a youngster try to learn as much as possible while he or she is in school? Here are some reasons, and you will probably think of others as well.

Education helps you earn a better living. We have already given some statistics proving that, which may possibly have some influence over the "don't care kid." Even young children can understand the need for money and that the more educated you are, the better your chances are to earn more.

What isn't so obvious is the fact that education adds greatly to one's intellectual life. It provides interests and enhances one's curiosity. Many a person has selected a career because he or she was exposed to the subject area while in school. Hobbies too are often a result of an interest developed as a young person. Reading for pleasure, for example, has become a way of life for some adults. This interest was born of exposure to literature as a young person.

The study of history, geography, and current events goes a long way toward making every person a better citizen and a more intelligent one. This can benefit one when it comes to paying taxes, for example. One gains some understanding of the workings of the three branches of the government. These subjects also encourage one to study foreign languages and to travel. The latter has proved to be, for many people, one of the great joys of life.

The majority of our youngsters will, in the future, become parents themselves, and even "don't care kids," when asked the question, "How do you want your kid to do in school?" often answer, "Not like me." This short question can bring home to some youngsters their own shortcomings. (Of course it doesn't have to. I've had boys tell me, "Not me, I'll never have kids.")

Another aspect of education that may have an effect on youngsters when pointed out to them is that it helps people to better express themselves. One's speech is very often an indication of the amount of education he or she has had.

A little girl aged eight, and apparently a "don't care girl," once asked me, "Can you help me talk better?" When questioned, I learned her grandfather, whom she had never seen, was coming to visit the family, and the child, young as she was, wanted to make a good impression on him. Instant improvement was needed, which presented a real problem. I though about it and then pointed out she could try to say "asked" instead of "axed," and could stop saying "ain't." I added that I was trying to help her "speak better" rather than "talk better." She was very pleased and really did try, but the most important benefit of all was that she changed and developed a desire to learn.

Be honest with your youngsters. Think about it, and give your reasons for everything you say, but be sure that you don't reveal personal information. We recall being told by one sixth grader, "That teacher is dumb. Why does she tell us about her husband's underwear? She even tells us the size."

But by telling your students about books you've read, about places you've visited, about sports you've participated in or observed, and even about your relationships with people, you are showing them how you have grown and developed. By sharing your interests in this way, you may possibly change a "don't care kid" into a youngster who is, at least, willing to learn. It's surely worth a try.

## CONCLUSION

Of all the youngsters you must reach to teach, among the most difficult are those we have called "don't care kids." Allowed to go along with that pattern of behavior, they may do enough work to get through, but no more. They are truly a challenge to us as educators.

Such youngsters will often be disruptive, frequently trying to anger their teachers. To respond in like manner allows them to call the tune. If you can react without hostility, with pleasantness but with firmness, you have a better chance of reaching them and changing their previously disruptive behavior. Building on their strengths can encourage them and can help them develop self-confidence. This can have a positive effect on their entire outlook and on their behavior in school. As you work with "don't care kids," try to determine the cause of their negative behavior. If necessary, as soon as possible get or give them remedial help. Peer pressure is, at times, a cause of disruptive behavior, as is the desire to show off. Once you realize that these are the causes, you can work to eliminate them.

Many youngsters, especially the "don't care kids," have no concept of the financial value of education. It is almost our duty as educators to teach them the "financial facts of life." Boys and girls often have heroes, and these individuals can be our allies in our attempts to get through to our students. News events, even those of a negative nature, can be powerful teaching tools. As we teach our young people, we can work toward making them better citizens and encouraging them to vote. This can be tremendously important to our nation and its future.

We at times may encounter uncooperative parents. It's important that we get their cooperation, for their negative attitudes often create a "don't care kid." As an adult, you can use your own experiences and feelings to show how valuable your education has been for you. Where other techniques have failed, this one may prove successful.

# 16

# THE SERIOUSLY DISTURBED CHILD

Probably the most difficult problems you will face in your teaching career are those presented by seriously disturbed children. It has been estimated that ten percent of our population falls into this category. (In previous years these people would have possibly spent some time in mental institutions, but since the advent of new medications this is no longer true.) However, in the classroom, these are your "impossible children," the ones you cannot understand—or reach.

## HOW TO RECOGNIZE THE PSYCHOLOGICALLY DISTURBED CHILD

How can you recognize these youngsters? Often they perform bizarre acts, which you realize immediately are "way out." "This child is out of his mind," you think. "I'm afraid he's mentally ill." Unfortunately, you are probably right. But he or she is in your class, and you must cope and help him or her adjust to the school situation—if that is at all possible.

When you have a girl or boy whose actions are very different from those of the other youngsters, you may suspect that he or she is seriously disturbed. (Incidentally, a child who is a genius may also display eccentric behavior, but it will be obvious to you that this is a child of unusual intellectual ability. His or her actions, while unusual, will not be destructive.)

Let us discuss some cases that, while they are comparatively rare, are encountered in classrooms from time to time. One or more may seem familiar to you. We have known children, for example, who claim they talk to God and are answered. One such young girl would recount long stories about her conversations. She was constantly asking for forgiveness, and it would be an agonizingly long time for her before it was granted. Yet the actions for which she asked to be pardoned were events of everyday living—"little white lies," for instance. This is, in our culture, paranoic behavior. Other seriously disturbed youngsters have heard voices or hallucinated.

Another form of paranoia is illustrated by the boy who complained to his teacher, "They're after me. Everyone in this class hates me." When questioned, the youngster maintained that every boy and girl he knew, in school and out, felt the same way about him. These feelings of persecution make it difficult for the child to function in a class situation. He or she may fight these "enemies" or hide from them, but enemies they are—to his or her disturbed mind.

Climbing is normal for young children, but in a playground situation, not a classroom. Witness the seventh grader who crawled along the lighting fixtures and on the window sills, laughing uproariously as he went. The child who completely isolates himself or herself, while not usually a discipline problem, should be considered a sick child. Very often he or she appears angry if approached by his or her classmates.

One of the saddest cases we ever worked with was a teenage girl who at times would place her chair in a corner of the classroom and suck her thumb. If other children spoke to her, she used extremely foul language in reply. She paid absolutely no attention to the teacher's words when she was behaving this way and in fact responded in the same manner to her. On other days she would be pleasant and would really try to cooperate.

One day, in the cafeteria the girls in her class ran screaming to the teacher in charge. There were hundreds of youngsters having lunch. "Look at ———, look at ———" they shrieked. The sight was unbelievable, for the poor, sick child had permitted her menstrual blood to cover her skirt and her chair. Moreover, she was laughingly parading around, almost proud of herself as she showed her skirt.

When a child's actions are so out of the ordinary, there is a very strong possibility that he or she may be mentally disturbed.

## BIZARRE ACTS AND HOW TO HANDLE THEM

What do you do if you have a youngster who behaves in a bizarre manner?

1. Check his or her records to see if there is any previous behavior of a similar nature. Very often you will find there is.

2. Speak to previous teachers, asking them if incidents occurred in their classes and, if so, how they handled them. This can be most helpful, for you can learn, in this way, what might set a youngster off. We know of youngsters who cannot be screamed at. If a teacher raises his or her voice to such a child an altercation is sure to start. This child must be spoken to in a very soft voice.

3. After an incident, when the youngster has calmed down, talk with him or her quietly, asking "———, why did you do that?" Give him or her a chance to explain to you, but then say softly and gently, "But you know we have a rule. You can't do this. It endangers you and the other youngsters in the class. No one can break the rules, and you can't. Promise me you will try not to."

Of course, you are aware of the fact that such children cannot control their behavior, but you should make them aware of the rules. Keep referring to them. Stress fairness—that the rules apply to everyone.

4. Send memos to the guidance counselor and to the principal detailing incidents that concern you. This makes the administration aware of problems that exist and that may become more serious in the future. If this pattern doesn't continue, so much the better, but if it does, then the administration has been forewarned.

One third grade teacher sent such a memo, which said, "I've noticed Jerry Jones likes to light matches. I found him playing with a package and confiscated it. He brought another one in today." Several weeks later there was a fire in the boys' lavatory. Jerry was, of course, suspect. A number of boys were questioned, and he was identified. It had been his teacher's short note that had alerted the administration to Jerry's behavior and to the danger it presented.

5. Discuss the child's behavior with the guidance counselor. Because he or she may already know the youngster, the counselor may be able to make suggestions. He or she may know if the child is already receiving therapy from a psychologist or psychiatrist. Often a surprisingly large number of children in a school are receiving such treatment.

Should you learn that this is the case, do not mention it to the child or to anyone else. We had one teacher who learned of the therapy and told another teacher, who mentioned it to the child's parent. A very ugly situation arose. "This was supposed to be kept confidential," the youngster's mother shouted. She threatened to sue the school but never did. However, the anguish could easily have been avoided.

6. After a second incident (or even the first if it was serious) write the parents a note or telephone them, but set up an interview. Make them understand that this meeting is very important.

Try to learn from them whether the child behaves unusually at home. Some parents may not be quite open with you, but others may. The information they have to offer can be of great help. Particularly, try to find out if the girl or boy has been seen by a psychiatrist, a psychologist, or a psychiatric social worker. Of the three, only the psychiatrist is legally permitted to administer any type of medication. Has the child been given any?

7.   Be fair but firm with this type of child. He or she needs to know the rules of acceptable behavior. Tell the youngster, for example, that you will have to be in touch with his or her parents whenever he or she doesn't follow those rules. If any child doesn't follow the rules, he or she may lose his or her monitorial status.

Try not to lose your patience , but let the girl or boy you consider to be seriously disturbed know that your limits cannot be ignored by anyone. Never threaten to do anything you cannot do. If you threaten but don't follow through, the youngsters will comprehend this immediately. (They may be slow in other things, but they understand idle threats.)

8.   Whenever you have a child with a serious behavior pattern, take the other youngsters into your confidence. This is most effectively done when the troubled child is absent. You may say to the youngsters, "I know each of you is interested in helping Mary and helping me and the rest of us as well. By being friendly to her and by trying to understand her, perhaps you can get her to see that the rules we make are for the benefit of everyone, including Mary, and that it's necessary for her welfare and everyone's that these rules are obeyed."

Add very fervently, "I think you girls and boys can do more than I can to help her." We can almost guarantee, in the light of our many years of experience as teachers, that the youngsters will be willing and eager to help you. We have seen cooperation "above and beyond" in just these circumstances.

An example is the case of the girl in the cafeteria mentioned above. The other girls in the class had befriended her, and the reason they had run for the teacher in the cafeteria was to save the troubled girl embarrassment.

## THE FRUSTRATION OF WORKING WITH SERIOUSLY DISTURBED CHILDREN

Have you ever felt you were taking two steps forward and then three back? The feeling of frustration is utterly depressing. So it is when you work with the seriously disturbed child. You talk to him or her, you reason, you do not lose patience. You even grow to love the child. Then, like a bolt from the blue, he or she is at it again. He or she screams invectives at you—when all you did was ask him or her to sit down and do some work.

What should you do? Send a monitor to the guidance counselor or the principal for help. There is, after all, the possibility this child may become violent. Meanwhile, wait until he or she has calmed down. Then, and only then, speak to him or her very quietly. If the boy or girl is agitated, think of a quiet place out of the classroom and take him or her to it yourself. (Leave the class president in charge and notify a neighboring teacher that you are doing so.)

Here is where your self-control is very important. Don't respond by screaming back at the child. When you ask, "What happened?" invariably the answer will be, "I couldn't help it." And the truth of the matter is that he or she really couldn't. We have heard this statement hundreds of times over the many years we have been educators. To a person who had control of his or her actions, it is very difficult to fully comprehend it. But if you consider the child to be mentally ill, perhaps the concept will be easier to grasp.

Another case serves as an example. Julie was a lovely girl—lovely to look at, that is. She entered our school in the sixth grade, and it came as a distinct shock when youngsters reported she bit them for absolutely no reason. She also loved to swing the handbag she carried—and she swung it as if it were a weapon. It always made contact with another youngster's anatomy—usually a girl, and usually her head. (One term she broke six handbag handles.)

Her teacher and the guidance counselor both tried to work with Julie. One day when her teacher questioned her, talked to her, and listened to her, the girl replied, "I like you a lot. You're nice to me. If I could stop myself, I would. But I just can't. I can't help it." Julie was ultimately transferred to a special school, and we lost track of her.

The most you can ask of a seriously disturbed child is that he or she try to obey the rules, and that by trying to do so, he or she can please you. And don't expect more, for you will be doomed to disappointment. Your task is to teach such children, but if they have their own demons, your task is surely made infinitely more difficult. Proceed from day to day, accomplishing as much as you can without becoming frustrated yourself. This is, indeed, very taxing, enervating work.

## THE DIFFICULTY OF COMMUNICATION

Some seriously disturbed children are very verbal and are able to communicate easily. Others, and this has more frequently been our experience, seem to have some difficulty speaking and are leery and afraid to tell you too much. This is almost for fear of giving themselves away. However, establishing rapport with them is essential to their functioning passably in your classroom.

We've already mentioned the value of having your youngsters write an autobiography for you. Even children in the third or fourth grade can give you some information about themselves. This autobiography will probably be a help with these troubled children. However, be sure you do not single out any child by requesting that he or she be the only one to write it. Read the disturbed child's autobiography carefully, and you may then use it as a point of departure to involve the child in conversation. He or she can surely tell you something about himself or herself.

Telling uncommunicative children about yourself is a good ice-breaker. Be careful, though, that you do not say anything that does not bear repetition, for what you say will probably be repeated far and wide. Talking about your interests and hobbies can prove of interest to the youngster, even the seriously disturbed one. If you can find a common interest, a meeting of the minds, this can be a great help.

We know of one teacher who used his tropical fish to reach a very difficult child. The boy became interested in the care of these fish, and the teacher wisely placed the class aquarium under his care. The threat to remove the youngster from this position of importance helped keep the youngster on an even keel for most (but not all) of the school year.

## REFER THE CHILD TO THE GUIDANCE DEPARTMENT IMMEDIATELY

Whenever a child exhibits strange or unusual behavior and you feel he or she may be mentally ill, discuss the case with the guidance counselor. This person is trained to identify serious problems and refer them to the appropriate agencies for assistance. The counselor, hopefully, has the time to work with the child on either a temporary or a permanent basis and to develop a one-to-one relationship with him or her.

It may be necessary, too, to remove the child from the classroom at times. One method is to send the child to the counselor's office. This procedure should have been set up in advance and be done only with the consent of the counselor. The last thing you want is to send or take the youngster there and have him or her returned to you immediately. He or she may need that cooling off period. This is especially true of the mentally disturbed child, who may flare up quickly and then cool down almost as quickly. He or she, however, does not belong in your classroom when all of this is going on.

## THE IMPORTANCE OF EARLY IDENTIFICATION _____

It is often possible that youngsters who are seriously disturbed may be helped through medication or various forms of psychotherapy. However, these boys and girls must be identified first. Parents, of course, are the logical persons to see such illness but are too often ashamed to admit the problem and to seek help. The child's teacher is next in line. It is his or her task to refer the youngster to the guidance department or if there is none to the administration, as we have already suggested.

The teacher, however, should not be the person to suggest any sort of help, because doing so may be bitterly resented and set up barriers to teaching the girl or boy. A parent may respond to a teacher's comment with words such as "You think my child is crazy" and become furious. Further-more, while teachers frequently have taken courses in psychology or guid-ance, they do not have an adequate background to make judgments, but surely they should discuss problem children with the school's personnel who are trained to recognize mentally ill youngsters.

After youngsters have been referred to the counselor, they may be sent to the latter for special testing to determine the seriousness of their behavior. A number of tests are available for this purpose. However, it is still the teacher who is in the "front line" in spotting the seriously disturbed child.

If you notice a child who exhibits any of the patterns we have men-tioned in this chapter, keep a very watchful eye on him or her, after you have made the necessary referral to the guidance counselor. It is also essential that you keep an anecdotal record of the child's actions in the classroom. Without this record you are almost lost. Make note of the incident as soon as you possibly can. If you must, wait until the end of the day, but do it then. You need not write a long report; the date, a simple account of what actually happened, and what you did in response are all that is necessary, but these facts are very necessary. They supply a picture that the counselor and/or the therapist who is working with the child needs.

These notes are not to be seen by the parent. They are for professional use only. You may, if you are asked to do so, discuss what they contain, but no parent should be privy to everything you write. Of course, you would not make value judgments, although this might be difficult to avoid.

I recall having one boy who loved to walk on the fluorescent light fixtures. I was terrified. It took every bit of self-control not to call him a lunatic or put that in my notes. Nor would that boy come down when told to do so. He was removed from the class and later put on "home instruc-tion" because his actions endangered not only the boy but the other youngsters as well. Incidentally, he never fell, and he did this walking several times before he was taken out of the class. He would climb up, very quickly, while I was writing on the board. I'd look up and there he was. The other boys and girls were speechless. We, they and I, were very lucky that no one was hurt.

## WORK WITH THE CHILD IN THE CLASSROOM

Here are some suggestions of techniques that may be of help to you in your classroom.

1. Separate the seriously disturbed child from children with other behavioral problems and also from youngsters who are easily led. By changing everyone's seat frequently you can place your troubled children among those who will pay them a minimum of attention. Often the immediate environment stimulates the seriously disturbed child and a change can help, but while this may appear to be the answer, the improvement rarely lasts.

2. Give your class a great deal of written work, but be sure it is work they can handle and that they enjoy doing. Consider all of their abilities and, if you are able to, utilize them. There are things that every child can do, such as drawing posters, and they will feel satisfaction if their work is exhibited. You might find topics the youngsters are interested in and help them make dioramas illustrating them. Most children are fascinated by prehistoric life. Dinosaurs are as real to them as elephants and a lot more interesting.

Often disturbed youngsters will enjoy working with their hands, doing painting or possibly carpentry. Almost every youngster can have fun with clay. Perhaps it will serve as an outlet for the disturbed child's emotional strain. Working with one's hands is considered to be highly therapeutic.

Making papier-mache requires tearing up newspapers. If you have a child who needs such activity because he or she is upset, have him or her actually make confetti-sized bits—if he or she is willing to do so. Other youngsters may prefer doing calculations—adding, subtracting, or even multiplying or dividing. If a child gets satisfaction from doing them, that's fine. Still others derive comfort from penmanship drills. This is an almost lost practice but can prove to be a valuable one.

It is possible that the disturbed child will enjoy writing short paragraphs, and this activity too can prove to be worthwhile.

3. Physical education can prove valuable too, providing the class does not become overstimulated. Baseball and volleyball can provide fun and at

the same time serve as an emotional outlet for many youngsters. Simple calisthenics can be done in the classroom, but you must be sure every child has medical permission for this.

4. It may prove helpful if you give the seriously disturbed youngster a daily report card, to have signed by his or her parents. (If the child has more than one teacher, each should sign the card.) In so doing, you are able to keep the family informed of the girl's or boy's actions from day to day. In the event that the youngster has to be removed from school, the parents cannot claim they were not notified of his or her behavior.

However, you have to be very careful that the report is completely truthful. If your comments do not reflect the actual situation, they are of little value. As is very often the case, a seriously disturbed child may have one serious incident and then appear to be transformed. If this is really the case, that is truly wonderful. However, several months later another outburst may occur. Unless the parent is informed by you, he or she will never hear about it and think his or her child is "doing fine." Then if serious action must be taken by the school, the parent is shocked by it. He or she is entitled to be informed, and by your doing so you are helping everyone concerned.

5. Keeping an anecdotal record of the behavior of the seriously disturbed child is the task of the teacher in the elementary school. If the youngster is in the intermediate or junior high, the homeroom teacher may be responsible for this, or it may be kept by the person in charge of discipline, the administrator, or the guidance department. It is essential, though, that someone keep it—and keep it carefully, for without such a record, it is often impossible to exclude a very ill child from school.

The guidance department should be kept informed, for, hopefully, the counselor is working with the child and with the family as well.

6. We have previously discussed helping your students develop a success pattern, and it is in no situation more important than with troubled children. Their self-esteem may well be at a low ebb and sorely in need of nurturing and development.

Find jobs they may do and give them work you can subsequently exhibit, and you may see improvement in their behavior.

7. Watch, Watch, Watch! If you have a seriously disturbed child in your class, try to watch him or her. Of course, you cannot possibly have your eyes on the girl or boy all of the time, but it is well worth scheduling your time. Do as little clerical work as possible while the class is in your room. We have found that relatively few serious incidents occur when the teacher is actively supervising the class. You may not be speaking, but your watchful eye can prevent many outbreaks, particularly by disturbed children.

A seventh-grade teacher, Mr. Q., saw a boy take a knife from his pocket, open it, and place it inside his desk. But Mr. Q. did not see this action by chance. He constantly kept his eyes on this boy—for this youngster had given many clues to the seriousness of his problems.

Mr. Q. went up to the boy and very quietly asked him for the knife. The boy complied, and the teacher told the child to see him after class. He then discussed the school's rule in regard to knives and told the youngster his mother would have to come to school to retrieve it. Of course the boy did not deliver the message, but Mr. Q. called her in, and the child never did that again. However, the boy lost control one day, screamed and ranted and raved, and ultimately was placed in a special class.

8. Remember, many seriously disturbed children have very short attention spans. It is exceedingly difficult to keep them interested for long periods of time. However, you might wish to try some sort of programmed material with them. It is not essential to purchase expensive equipment to do this. You will find there are a number of products available, similar to workbooks, that may prove of value. Even the conventional form of workbook can be useful if used judiciously and for short periods of time.

9. If a child in your class has been seen by a physician and medication has been prescribed, the task of making sure the boy or girl takes it may very well fall to you. Far too often effective medication may remain at home, where it will do the child no good.

If you are sure medication has been prescribed, ask the parents if they would like you to see to it that their child takes it. Discuss this with the school nurse. Perhaps it can be arranged to keep a portion of the child's prescription at school in a locked cabinet. If the parents agree, arrange to say to the youngster, very quietly, "It's time for you to take your medication." If the youngster is old enough, you can use a signal such as "It's time for you to go to the office for me." This signal might be preferable to a sensitive child.

We were, at one time, very skeptical about the use of medication, but we have seen many children unable to function without it do very well when it is taken conscientiously. We've even said, "Mary, did you forget to take your medication today?" because the change in Mary's behavior was obvious. Medication may not be the answer to all serious problems but surely it has great value for some.

No teacher is in a position to recommend medication. This must come from a physician. However, the school administrator may suggest the parent take the child for a complete physical examination and explain his or her behavior to the doctor. Very often he or she will understand the situation and prescribe the necessary medication. This is surely worth a try, for many youngsters have been enabled to function reasonably well—but only if and when they take the medication.

## MAKE COMING TO SCHOOL A PRIVILEGE

Many people believe children would rather stay at home than attend school. (This may be true if they sit glued to the television screen, but after a period of time that, too, palls.) It has been our experience that if school attendance is regarded as a privilege rather than forced on youngsters, they react entirely differently. In the case of the seriously disturbed child, his or her actions may necessitate suspending him or her for short periods of time. Often suspension can be the action that will cause the parents to have the child examined by a physician.

On other occasions, parents have been asked to keep the child at home. While not a formal suspension, this threat of action may be sufficient to modify the child's disruptive behavior. "If your child had a cold, you'd keep him at home, wouldn't you?" one administrator asked, then added, "Well, he needs a cooling off period so that he will realize attending school is desirable and that by his actions he is jeopardizing his right to attend." Unfortunately, this is often necessary to protect the other children. No teacher can say this, but administrators can and at times do, depending on the rules of the school system in which they serve. We have found that with certain children this action has a noticeably favorable effect on their behavior. Particularly in the intermediate school they enjoy socializing with their peers.

## HELP THE CHILD ADJUST

Some seriously disturbed children are, almost by definition, unable to adjust to the classroom situation. If you can work with them, helping them see the reasons for obeying rules and helping them alter their behavior to fit into the school's society, you are doing the most effective teaching possible.

Many of these children have never had to live by rules or have been unable to do so. Their environment has adjusted to them rather than they to the environment, and faced with school, they have no background for living by rules.

Learning about youngsters from their previous teachers and from their parents may be of great help in this area. Developing rapport with youngsters, always important, is even more so with these girls and boys. You may have to teach them just what rules are.

To what specifically do we refer when we use the term *adjustment?* Adjustment implies cooperation and consideration of the rights of others.

It implies compliance with rules made to protect everyone in the school, and above all it means the ability to show self-control and self-discipline. It's necessary, though, to remember that, particularly from these children, one cannot expect perfection. All one can ask of them is that they learn what self-control and self-discipline are and that they try and try again to achieve these goals. There are times when they "forget" and when it seems impossible that they are able to do so, but other times when you will see progress.

## BEWARE OF LABELS

A case in point: Jennie had been in four state mental hospitals for periods of three months to two years. She was considered to be mentally ill. A very serious girl, she rarely smiled, had no friends, and managed to alienate the youngsters in her class by the tough way in which she spoke. She was placed in an intermediate school but told she could be suspended at any time if she became involved in any fights. She always seemed to manage to avoid them, but she made other youngsters feel very uncomfortable. "Yes, ma'am" or "No, ma'am" were her customary responses. She dressed in a manner that was definitely unfeminine, and people were afraid of her for, with her record of hospitalization, it was assumed she was dangerous.

One alert counselor decided to delve more deeply into the case. She interviewed Jennie's mother and found her to be a hard, brutal woman who believed children were placed on earth to serve their parents. Since Jennie's father had deserted her at the time of the girl's birth, she was especially bitter toward men and toward this daughter, because of her father. The girl was an actual slave, and she constantly ran away from home. For this, her mother had had her institutionalized four times!

Jennie, in spite of the manner she affected, was not aggressive. The counselor discussed her case with the girl's teachers and informed the mother that what she was doing was child abuse and that she could be subject to family court action. The teachers changed their attitudes toward the girl and began to show interest and sympathy for her. With their help and the work of the counselor Jennie changed. She graduated from intermediate school and she had learned a little about relating to human beings and trusting them. The guidance counselors at the high school she was to attend were notified, and from her very first day, Jennie was given the attention and support she needed.

## EXCLUSION FROM SCHOOL

Many seriously disturbed youngsters, such as those mentioned in this chapter, have proven unable to function in a regular school situation. They have been placed under home instruction or in special schools. However, this is done only after working with the youngster and after much psychological testing. The teacher's role in this is to supply the anecdotal information necessary, showing the child's behavior pattern and illustrating the problems the child has manifested. Each incident should be dated and, as has been pointed out, the action the teacher took should be noted.

Far too often, before a child is excluded from school, he or she must perpetrate some drastic misdemeanor, which establishes him or her as being a seriously disturbed or mentally ill child. Generally, it is the culmination of repeated antisocial behavior. It is the signal that our efforts, however great, have been defeated.

## PREVENTION OF ANTISOCIAL BEHAVIOR

How much better it would be if our combined efforts can serve as preventative medicine that will preclude antisocial behavior that is so often detrimental to the child and to society as well. The task of working with a disturbed youngster must fall to everyone—to the youngsters in his or her class, to the teachers, to the guidance counselors, to the supervisory staff, and to the parents and other members of the boy's or girl's family. It is possible that someone in the family constellation, other than the parents, can effect changes in the youngster's behavior. It is not terribly important who specifically this person is, as long as he or she can influence the boy or girl. Sometimes sisters and brothers are willing to take on this role, and some have proved to be extremely helpful. They must be shown, however, that punishment can sometimes be more harmful than one might imagine.

Very often the young person's friends can have an even greater effect on his or her life than adults. A friend will frequently be very eager to help. This requires discussion with that friend and apprising him or her of the entire situation. However, before the aid of a young person is enlisted, one must be sure that he or she will be an influence for good, working in the right direction.

## CONCLUSION

Working with the seriously disturbed or mentally ill child is one of the most difficult aspects of our profession. Children who act in bizarre fashion fall into this category.

To work with a child of this type, who may or may not try to tear your class apart, find out as much as you can about him or her—from records, from previous teachers, from the guidance department, and from his or her parents. After an incident has occurred, notify the mother and father. In your treatment of the youngster be firm but fair. Remember, though, that you cannot expect too much because often the child is incapable of refraining from misbehavior. Try to get through to him or her and to establish rapport, but do not expect miracles.

In the classroom, separate him or her from other behavioral problem youngsters and from boys or girls who are easily led. Find work they will enjoy and in which they can be successful. You may wish to give them a daily report card. If you do, make sure that you do not omit incidents of both good and poor behavior. This will give the parents a true picture of their child's behavior in school.

Keep an anecdotal record of all of the child's activities so that should it be necessary to take further action, the principal is able to do so. Keep a watchful eye on this child to preclude serious difficulties.

Every avenue of approach should be tried to assist the seriously disturbed child—for because of the seriousness of his or her problem, he or she needs all the help possible. In school he or she needs, more than anything else, your patience, your understanding, and your affection.

Always keep foremost in your mind the fact that this is a sick child, a troubled human being. In the future, he or she may function in society or become a burden on it, depending on the amount of education he or she has been able to receive, regardless of his or her mental illness.

We have seen some seriously disturbed youngsters adjust to school, learn, and do well because of the efforts made by dedicated teachers who were able to take into consideration the children's strengths as well as their weaknesses, and their value in society in spite of their unfortunate handicaps.

# 17

## NEGATING SOME OF THE VIOLENCE ALL AROUND US

The world in which we live seems to be becoming more and more violent every day. Consider these statistics: According to the 1988 Uniform Crime Reports of the Federal Bureau of Investigation, in 1987 there were 172 murders and non-negligent manslaughter arrests of youngsters under fifteen years of age. For the under-18 age group, there were 1,514 murders and manslaughter arrests. For youngsters under fifteen years of age the total of crimes including murders, forcible rape, robbery and aggravated assault, burglary, larceny, and motor vehicle theft was 456,722, while for the under-18 age group, the total number of crimes was an incredible 1,381,909.

In that article it is stated that, according to the Center to Prevent Handgun Violence, 10 children a day are killed with handguns. According to the Children's Defense Fund, about 135,000 children bring guns to school every day. In 1987, black fifteen- to nineteen-year-old males were ten times more likely to be killed by violent means than white males in the same age group.

In an editorial in New York City's United Federation of Teachers' newspaper of April 29, 1991, was the following report: "The day after General Colin Powell told students at Morris High School about the importance of education, sixteen-year-old Jason Thomas brought a .25 caliber automatic pistol for an unsanctioned show-and-tell at Morris. A friend accidentally shot him in the neck.

"Jason told police he needed the gun for 'protection,' a sign of the drugs, guns, and violence that grip parts of the city—the very culture that the chairman of the Joint Chiefs of Staff had warned the students about."

Later in the article it is stated, "At least 12 students have been wounded or killed in or around schools since September 1990."

## THE VIOLENCE OF WAR

All of our youngsters are growing up seeing violence around them. What is more violent than war? In the Persian Gulf War, as in previous wars, the bloodshed was seen constantly on the television screen. The adults in the family would be watching the news intently, and while the children may not have appeared to be watching, they still saw much to trouble them. What to a youngster could be more frightening than war? Can anyone ever forget the sight of missiles flying toward their targets and the devastation they caused?

In some cases the war came much closer to home. Many of the children attending Principal Magenheim's Public School 39, Staten Island, have parents who are in the armed forces, and they were justifiably very frightened. "What do you tell a child who comes to you and asks you 'Mr. M., is my father going to die?'" This happened more than once, the principal reported. The casualties the United States suffered were low, but not low enough. The deaths of the Americans and Iraqis were seen by the youngsters on the television screen, at times in very gory detail. Memories of this stay with the boys and girls.

## TELEVISION PROGRAMMING IS OFTEN VIOLENT

As if this were not enough violence, there are television programs and films, videos, and video games, that are based on themes involving bloodshed. An article in *Time* magazine, of October 15, 1990, stated that the average child will have watched five thousand hours of TV by the time he or she enters first grade, and nineteen thousand hours by the end of high school, more time than he or she will spend in class. Newton Minow, director of the Annenberg Washington program in Communications Policy Studies of Northwestern University, pointed out that "by the time a child is 18, he or she has seen more than 25,000 murders on television."

Yale psychologist Jerome Singer has done research that has shown that prolonged viewing by children of violent programs is associated with more aggressive behavior, such as getting into fights and disrupting the play of others.

## VIDEO GAMES AND FILMS ARE MODELS OF VIOLENCE

Even youngsters are aware of the violence found in videogames. In "Zillions," a Consumer Reports magazine for children, youngsters were asked whether they believed video games contributed to aggressive behavior. One boy responded, "Violent games imply that violence is okay. The effects may show up in the way a person handles things in adult life." Another child said, "Video game violence may be okay for kids who can play and still understand that violence is stupid and useless. However, not everyone can see the difference." Still another youngster commented, "A game has to be 50 percent violent to be fun."

Music videos such as those made by the group Guns 'n Roses and 2 Live Crew use words that are clearly violent. The latter have made rap recordings that can hardly be healthy for young people. They carry the message that women are to be used for sexual purposes and abused in violent ways. This in the name of entertainment.

When it comes to films, it seems the more bloodshed the film has, the bigger the box office gross. In 1990, two of the films nominated for the Academy Awards Best Film of the Year were *Godfather III* and *Goodfellas*. Both were filled with shootings galore. Even films such as *The Terminator*, which to an adult are fantasies, to a child may be very real.

## YOUR CLASSROOM CAN AND SHOULD BE A SANCTUARY

We've already mentioned principal Arnie Magenheim and P.S. 39. During the Persian Gulf conflict, in a very prominent place in the office of the school, he had posted a large sign with only one word on it, REASSURE! It was there for good reason. In that school there were approximately one hundred youngsters whose fathers are in the U.S. Navy. Many of them were serving on the missile carrying cruiser, the *USS Normandy.*

"We have no guidance counselor," the principal pointed out. "Each teacher has to play that role." Not only do the teachers act in that capacity, but so does the principal.

Another child, a fourth grader, said in front of his whole class, "They're going to drop bombs on Staten Island." Children were very much aware of what was going on.

Mr. Magenheim's word *Reassure!* applies in virtually thousands, and possibly millions, of situations, however. Even without war, there are countless numbers of violent situations, and because it is often the school, and only the school, that offers a sanctuary, we must, as educators, use this opportunity to do what we can do to negate the violence that surrounds us.

Mr. Magenheim suggested to his teachers to show the youngsters on a world map just how far away the Persian Gulf is from the United States. "How long do you think it would take a ship to get there?" the teachers asked, and then talked about the great distance.

As a teacher, if you keep the word *reassure* in your mind, you will find you are doing just that over and over again.

(While it isn't really germane, I feel I must add that when the Persian Gulf conflict was over, Mr. Magenheim had a parade in which the men of the USS *Normandy* were honored. The captain of the ship was the Grand Marshall, and every child in the school participated. It was a wonderful celebration by the children of the end of the conflict, a celebration they will never forget.)

## WHEN CHILDREN BELIEVE PREDICTIONS OF APOCALYPSE

Periodically there seem to be people who claim to be ministers and prophets and who predict the world is coming to an end. In my years in the school system this happened three times. We saw youngsters in the seventh grade, mostly girls (and I cannot say why), who were totally taken in by this and who were very frightened. While this type of thing may seem to be ridiculous to us, these youngsters were in great need of reassurance from us, for they were not getting it anywhere else. (Their families, the girls told us, believed the forecasts were true and were equally upset.)

It's interesting to note that even though the end of the world did not come to pass on schedule, the youngsters were still convinced that this would happen some time in the future. They could not be told, simply, that this was ridiculous. We decided the science classes would be the logical time to work on the problem. The teachers were briefed and then taught a nonscheduled lesson in geology, dealing with the age of the earth, four and a half billion years, and the huge number of changes it has gone through. (They were careful not to say anything detrimental about those preaching the end of the world, for that would have alienated the youngsters.) The lessons did calm the children down a bit, and they even learned a little geology.

We have already discussed the possible violence that may have affected your girls and boys because they have seen it on television. It is sad to comment, but often that violence may be much closer to them. It may well be present in their homes.

## USING SKITS TO HELP CHILDREN COPE
## WITH ALCOHOLIC PARENTS _____

Unfortunately, there are many parents who abuse drugs or alcohol, and when they do, they frequently become violent. How can you reassure children when this happens? Rarely will they even tell you about it. However, if you can teach the youngsters to avoid antagonizing the person who is "under the influence," you can help those children immeasurably. This is a good time to make use of the playlet technique, already discussed in previous chapters. Another technique is through the use of skits.

One guidance counselor, who discovered this situation was quite common in her school, developed skits and worked with the language arts teachers as they had the skits performed. The skits showed how much worse it was for a child to "fight back" against an alcoholic parent than to try to get out of the room or to at least keep quiet and not answer back. Those youngsters who had never been exposed to family violence of this type learned about life and the problems other children have. It was made very clear that no child was ever singled out or embarrassed in any way. The discussions afterward were based on the characters in the skits and never about any person in particular.

There is a magnificent film, which we highly recommend to every educator. It was first a play, written by a teacher, Paul Zindel, and for which he was awarded a Pulitzer Prize. The play and the film are called *The Effect of Gamma Rays on Man-in-the-Moon Marigolds*. The story concerns a very unhappy mother and the role a teacher can have in influencing a child's life. The film is available on video and is very well worth your taking the time and the effort to see.

## USING LANGUAGE ARTS CLASS
## TO COMBAT VIOLENCE _____

There are many ways in which language arts can be used to negate the effects of violence, depending, of course, on the ages and level of understanding of your students.

One technique that has proved to be very effective, and that boys and girls enjoy, is monitoring television programs for violence. Here is the way it was done by one class as an experiment.

Each youngster was given a television station to monitor. Then he or she was to check the listings in the newspaper for the programs that might have violence. (Obviously "Wheel of Fortune," for example, does not, but news programs almost always do.) Then they were to watch those that they thought might have bloodshed. They were to count the number of times a gun was drawn or any type of violence was shown. This was to be done for a week, and then the results were tabulated. The arithmetic calculations were done, comparing the number with the statement made by Newton Minow, that by the time a young person is eighteen, he or she has seen more than 25,000 murders.

After this, violence was discussed in terms not only of television but of "real life." The teacher brought in articles from the local newspaper, showing just how prevalent it is. Next and most important was further discussion of the topic, "What can we do to prevent violence in our own lives and in those of others?"

One of the girls was overheard to say, "I never realized there was so much violence right around us." Her friend agreed, saying, "I never thought of it that way."

This lesson was used with eighth-grade classes, and one of the songs they sang at their graduation ceremony was "Let There Be Peace on Earth." That is the title and the first line of the selection. The second line is, "And let it begin with me." This too was the basis of discussion, as the youngsters were asked such questions as "How can you do this? How can you bring peace to your immediate environment?"

## SHOW THAT FILMS ARE UNREAL

The lives portrayed in films are not real, nor is the violent behavior portrayed in them, and yet there are youngsters who imitate it. One of the ways in which this can be brought out to the boys and girls is by having them watch a film that has violence. If you can show it on video, you can stop the film when you get to the credits, which will enable the boys and girls to read the list of stunt men involved. (We used the film *Die Hard*, and the list was extremely long.) The listing is usually at the end of a film. Discuss what stunt men actually do to create nonreal violence when a film is made.

It is vitally important that young people understand that what they see on either the big screen or the television screen is not the way in which most real people behave. Films such as the *Rambo* series or *The Terminator* are completely fictional, as are a host of other films that feature shootings and bloodshed.

After discussing this, one way in which you can get your students to react is by having each one write a short paragraph describing a scene in a film or television program that they realize now is not true to life. It may be assigned by saying, "How about doing some debunking on our own. You've learned just how much fakery is used in making films. Now select one you know is not real and write about it." Have them read these paragraphs aloud, which will lead to further discussion. You will probably find that your boys and girls enjoy this activity.

It is unlikely that your girls and boys have seen a film called *The Cook, the Thief, His Wife and Her Lover*, but we mention it here to point out just how violent a film can be. This film includes, besides other horrendously brutal acts, cannibalism. Yet it was highly praised by many critics and actually called "brilliant" by some. This is an indication of the type of people producing and making movies and the type of violence that is promoted to the general public. Is it any wonder that there are so many murders, and mass murderers, in our society?

It is very possible that a youngster might see *The War of the Roses*. His or her parents might rent it because it is available on video and has been touted as a very fine film. What would that child think? Here is a married couple who, literally, kill each other. Couldn't that youngster imagine that his or her parents might do the same thing? This is especially true if the youngsters have heard their parents quarreling. If we can show our boys and girls that films are not to be believed, we can do much for their healthy emotional development. We can do this by full discussion.

Even films that are ostensibly for children can have violence in them. Some little ones seem to know when a film will upset them. One four year old absolutely refused to see *The Little Mermaid*. "I'm afraid of the witch," she said, adding, "I saw her picture in the book." Her six-year-old sister tried to convince her that the witch wasn't real, but the younger one would have none of it.

The extent to which violence is part of our lives can be seen even in the comics. We saw one little one cry bitterly when a cat pounced on a mouse, and this was in a cartoon. Trying to convince this child that the film wasn't real was very difficult.

## CONVEYING IDEAS OF THE VALUE OF LIFE

Young people rarely have an understanding of the value of life. You can help them gain this, and it is most important that they do, by reading material that brings this out. One source is the *Reader's Digest*. Rarely is there an issue that does not have a story of a person's heroism. Here is one example.

In the June 1991 issue is an article, condensed from *Life* magazine, titled "Lee Atwater's Last Campaign." Lee Atwater was dying of a brain tumor at the time he wrote the article, and his last days were very precious to him. He described them magnificently. Here is the last line, "There is nothing more important in life than human beings, nothing sweeter than the human touch."

Scientists have worked and are working relentlessly to develop ways to preserve and to improve human life. In the July 1991 issue the story of "The Doctor Who Conquered a Killer" describes Dr. Holmes Morton and his truly remarkable work. He became very interested in metabolic diseases and went to do research in Philadelphia. There he first saw the illness he later was able to diagnose and later cure, an obscure disease now called glutaric aciduria.

In the October 1989 issue of the *Digest* is a condensation of the book *The Steven McDonald Story.* Steven had been a New York City policeman when he was shot. After fifteen months in various hospitals and although paralyzed and wheelchair bound, he has managed to lead a life that is truly an inspiration to others.

The magazines and newspapers you read will give you more material that will enable you to bring out other concepts, such as perseverance, the desire to be of service to other human beings, and, of course, the value of life. However, after students have been exposed to this type of reading matter, the ideas just mentioned have to be brought out and clarified, or your young people may possibly miss them.

## USING TELEVISION FOR CONSTRUCTIVE PURPOSES _____

Many parents are well aware of the fact that their youngsters watch too much television. However, it is an undeniable fact that everyone, adults and children, does watch television. Ninety-eight percent of U.S. households own at least one television set. How then can television viewing be made constructive as far as youngsters are concerned?

One successful teacher decided to do just this. She compiled a list of programs that she felt were of value to youngsters. She duplicated it and sent it home to the parents. She suggested they might want to limit their children to viewing only these programs rather than permitting them to watch any program that was being shown. Then, to motivate the boys and girls, she asked them to view specific programs.

"After you have watched the program," she said, "we will have a contest. Anyone who answers every question correctly will receive a prize." (This lady gave prizes often. She had, at the beginning of the year, found a distributor who sold trinkets, and she had bought dozens of them. "The cost is very little, compared to the results I get with these little things," she commented.)

The youngsters watched nature programs and programs of scientific interest. One day she suggested that if anyone wanted to, he or she could take some notes and use them to answer the questions. These fourth graders learned almost immediately that it was easy to write a few words to help them remember important points. "I found that by the end of the year I was asking what I considered to be quite sophisticated questions. Many of the children were able to answer them and were quite proud of themselves for being able to do so."

## TEACHING AN UNDERSTANDING OF THE VIOLENCE BEING DONE TO THE ENVIRONMENT

In my home community, Staten Island, New York, there is a street called Old Town Road. On the corner of that street and Richmond Road are two magnificent trees, estimated to be over one hundred years old. Old Town Road was to be widened because it is a heavily traveled street, and the trees were to be taken down. Strong community protest had the desired effect, and the trees stand there today, a monument to the residents who did not want to see this type of violence done to the environment.

The cutting down of trees is one of the things that detracts from the quality of life. Trees, during the process of photosynthesis, put oxygen back into the air, and all living things require oxygen to live.

At the time of this writing there is controversy over a very important situation in Alaska. It was the cover story in the *New York Times Magazine* of August 4, 1991, entitled "The Great Alaska Debate: Can Oil and Wilderness Mix?" We quote, "The coastal plain of the Arctic National Wildlife Refuge may contain vast amounts of oil, but many fear that drilling will destroy America's last frontier." This area is particularly important because it is the place where caribou go to have their calves and is the home of other species of wildlife. These, it is feared, will be destroyed by the drilling. Is this considered to be violence to the environment? That seems to depend on one's views.

Until now, the Wildlife Refuge has been protected by law. However the president of the United States is very emphatic in his support of drilling and threatens to veto any energy bill that does not include lifting the restriction.

It is possible for public pressure to prevent violence. An excellent example of this is the action taken by the tuna canning industry. Tuna fishermen would catch large numbers of dolphins along with the tuna in their nets, killing the dolphins as a result. The companies purchasing the tuna were pressured by the public, and they in turn forced the fishermen to change their types of nets so that the dolphins were protected. To show how important this was there is an indication on tuna cans that the fish were caught under conditions not dangerous to dolphins.

This is just one of the many ways in which environmentalists have been able to protect the environment. As our young people learn more about this and become involved in it, they will be able to work hard to eliminate this violence and create a better world.

## VANDALISM IS THE RESULT OF VIOLENCE _____

Vandalism is definitely a form of violence. It occurs frequently in many of the major cities in our nation and in some smaller communities as well. The use of paints of various kinds to deface buildings is extremely common, particularly in the big cities. Called "graffiti," it defaces buildings, trucks, trains, and walls, and can be seen almost everywhere. If we, as educators, do not discuss this negative behavior, who will? The same is true of littering, for that is just as unsightly. It is also far more serious, for it may breed insects and encourage the spread of vermin and rats in the neighborhood.

More serious are garbage cans being thrown over or gravestones being desecrated. When an incident of this type occurs, you may want to have a speaker come to your class to discuss its seriousness. Your police department may be able to supply one. When these events are ignored, they often multiply, for the "copy-cat" principle goes into effect. You cannot expect parents to talk about such things with their youngsters. They may, but far too often they do not.

Furthermore, it is frequently the disruptive youngsters in your class who engage in such activities. If they can be shown how bad the effects are, they will possibly think twice about what their friends suggest. They should be shown that what they think is "fun" is really far from it.

At times this type of behavior leads to other types of undesirable behavior. One incident brings this out. Police in a small city were trying to learn who was responsible for the bones of animals that they discovered in a secluded vacant lot. When the culprits were found, they turned out to be high school freshmen. One told the detective on the case that he and his friends had been turning over gravestones and gotten bored with that. From that they "progressed" to killing stray cats and dogs. The youngsters were put on probation, but their parents were sufficiently upset to take steps. They greatly limited their children's free-time activities, and the youngsters were carefully supervised.

Does this event happen in every community? Of course not, but acts of vandalism do occur in many places, and far too often they are not reported. The youngsters are not caught or punished, and they go on to other things that always seem to be of a negative nature.

## THE DANGER OF HANDGUNS _____

One of the major problems today is the ease with which guns can be acquired. In one community of 400,000 people, of all sixteen to eighteen year olds arrested, one in five was booked for criminal possession of a weapon. However, there, as everywhere, guns are not the only weapons. BB guns, bats, golf clubs, tire irons, pipes, and handmade devices are all used.

Handguns are a menace in every community in the country. Adults are buying them in huge numbers, and according to the Children's Defense Fund's "Children 1990: A Report Card, Briefing Book and Action Primer," about *135,000 children a day bring guns to school.* In one incident recently, a kindergarten child brought a gun to school in his lunchbox. Fortunately, no one was hurt, for the teacher was able to handle the situation. It seems the little boy's mother had put the gun there!

The United Federation of Teachers of New York City has proposed an educational campaign to prevent violence in the schools starting in the elementary school and has secured private funds to run it. It is hoped that the Board of Education will have it in place in September 1991.

The Center to Prevent Handgun Violence has published statistics in this regard: that handguns kill 10 American children each day; that at least sixty-five students and 6 school employees were killed with handguns in U.S. schools and 201 wounded between September 1986 and September 1990; that 242 hostages were held at gunpoint in America's schools during those years.

It is more likely that it is your disruptive students who will become involved with guns. It is absolutely certain that they will deny any interest in handguns. However if you are able to work with your class, showing them how great the chances are that *they themselves will be hurt or killed by guns,* you can possibly make a difference in their lives. Here too a speaker from the police department can point this out very graphically.

There are signs that a child may be on the road to becoming involved with guns. A teacher may see these signs and hopefully will recognize them. An astute social studies teacher sent me a composition on which were drawings of guns, many guns. The boy who had drawn them was a constant discipline problem, and she had written "I bet he'll kill someone some day."

I called the boy into my office and said I realized he was having difficulty in his social studies class. He agreed. I then talked with him, but not about the drawing. Rather we discussed what he expected to do with his life, what he "wanted to do when he was an adult."

"I want to be a mercenary," he said. I recall being very surprised that he knew the word but questioned him further. "I want to fight, and I can get into a foreign army when I'm eighteen," he told me. "I can go fight and make money at the same time." He had learned about mercenaries from his father.

We kept close tabs on this youngster, and I saw him from time to time when he was sent to me because of his behavior. His parents never responded to our requests that they see me. The boy did manage to graduate, and no one heard of him until five years later. Just before he was to celebrate his eighteenth birthday, he was shot by a friend to whom he was showing a gun he owned. His father had bought it for him!

Incidentally, he was not the only youngster who "doodled," drawing guns, knives, and so on.

**It is entirely possible that a girl or boy may bring a gun into your classroom. In the event that this happens, do not do anything to even indicate that you are even aware of the situation. If you see the gun, then you cannot ignore it, but the procedure is the same. Do not do anything to excite or challenge the youngster. Do not try to take the gun away. If you can do so, very quietly notify the principal or another administrator. Make every attempt you can to follow a normal routine until you can send for help.**

**Should the bell ring and make it necessary for you to dismiss the class, hold them. Make some excuse, but keep the class with you until help comes to see what is wrong.**

The child with the gun may have no intention whatsoever of using the gun but may have brought it to "show off." It is very dangerous to react to its presence with anything but calm. Of course this is easier said than done, but it is the only way to handle a potentially dangerous situation.

## DEALING WITH WEAPONS SUCH AS KNIVES

I have not personally dealt with guns, but I have on several occasions had children bring in knives. One, brought in by a seventh-grade girl, was a bread knife, fifteen inches long. I was alerted by a boy in her class. As assistant principal, I supervised one grade, which usually consisted of eight classes. I always told the youngsters in "my grade" some words usually credited to Edmund Burke: "All that is necessary for evil to flourish is for good men to do nothing."

The boy who came to me said, "Can I tell you something?"

"Of course," I replied.

"So-and-so has a big knife," he said. "She's threatening people."

"Who's she threatening?" I questioned immediately.

"Me," he said. And she had.

The principal was out of the building, so I called the girl into my office and spoke to her, as I said above, very quietly.

"What's happening, honey?" I asked her. (I often called the girls "honey.")

"Nothin'," she answered.

"You know we're friends, aren't we?" I asked.

The girl responded yes, because I had, indeed, befriended her on several occasions. She tended to get into fights and I had smoothed the way to her being accepted again by the friends with whom she would fight regularly.

"I heard you have a knife in your bag," I told her. She carried a large bookbag, although rarely were there books in it. "May I have it?" I asked quietly.

"Okay," she answered, then asked, "Can I have it back at three o'clock?"

She handed me the knife before I answered. Then I said to her, "Honey, I'm afraid you might get into trouble with this, so I have to keep it until your mother comes in to see me."

I kept her in the office until dismissal time. Before the child left I was able to contact her mother and the youngster was permanently suspended from our school. She was referred to a special school and for therapy.

I was unfortunate in that the principal was out of the building at the time the boy came to me with the warning but fortunate in that I had that type of relationship with the girl.

On two other occasions I took knives from boys who were referred to me. I mention this to show that I am writing from my experiences and not from any advice I have read. I am sure that in all three cases it was the relationship I had with these intermediate school youngsters that enabled me to achieve the results I did.

It was school policy for the assistant principals to be in the cafeteria when our grades were eating. I would walk around, chatting and joking with the youngsters, and got to know many of them that way. Of course, I knew many of the disruptive ones because they would behave the same way in the cafeteria.

Whatever the situation, whenever an adult loses his or her cool, the disruptive youngster wins. By being calm and collected and speaking softly and persuasively, you can accomplish far more than if you were to berate or shout at the boy or girl.

## WHAT YOU CAN DO IN YOUR CLASSROOM TO CHANGE YOUR DISRUPTIVE YOUNGSTER BEFORE HE OR SHE BECOMES VIOLENT _____

Once more, we have to repeat a point we have been making throughout this book. Human beings crave attention and approval, and this surely includes the child who is disrupting your class and who, in fact, may well be headed on a path to violent behavior. He or she probably is acting out to get attention not given at home.

By befriending the disruptive child you may be able to change his or her behavior. By speaking with him or her on a one-to-one basis as often as you can and developing a relationship, you may be able to strike a chord that will work what may seem to be a miracle. We've seen this happen time and time again.

You may find this youngster is very angry and is in need of counseling. If this is the case, then speak with him or her about making a referral and try to convince the boy or girl of the value of "speaking to someone who may be able to help you." Youngsters, we have found, react very badly to the word *psychotherapy*, or *psychiatrist*, or *shrink*, but there is no problem with the word *counseling*. In fact, it is important to repeat "counselor" several times, so there is no question about the referral being to a "shrink."

## ENLISTING THE PARENTS' COOPERATION _____

Children are influenced by their teachers. This is particularly true of those in the elementary schools, but even older boys and girls can be reached by our words. Be sure that what you say is of value to them. If you have tried to reach the child in a one-to-one situation and haven't been able to do so, your next step is to contact the parents. When you feel the need for their cooperation because the boy or girl seems to have a serious behavioral problem, don't hesitate to ask to see them.

In this era, when many families have problems, when there are single parents, when there are two parents but both are working, it may be difficult to enlist the parents' aid, but speaking with them can often be achieved if you will work around their schedules. Try very hard to get a personal meeting rather than speaking to them on the telephone.

You might first say to the parent, as we have previously suggested, "Both you and I want the same thing. We want your youngster to get a good education. I'm sure you agree with me about that, don't you?" It is extremely rare that a parent will give you an argument about that.

Before you mention the problem that caused you to request the interview, make mention of one or more of the youngster's good points. You may be hard-pressed to think of any, but try hard. Then continue, "I believe your son (or daughter) may get into serious trouble if his or her behavior doesn't change." You may say to the parent, "I can see that he (or she) is going in that direction" and then give your reasons. Very often one of the indicators of trouble ahead for youngsters is their choice of companions. You can surely mention this to the parents, but never name names. The parents may know whom you are talking about, or it is their business to find out.

Perhaps you suspect the youngster is carrying a knife but have no proof. Discuss that in the abstract. "There are some youngsters who carry knives," you say, and then add, "I don't know if your son (or daughter) is one of them, but I believe you would want to investigate this possibility."

**Do not appear angry or hostile to the parents.** It is entirely possible that their boy or girl has been a thorn in your side for weeks and weeks, but you cannot show that. What you have to show is a sincere interest in helping the child, and in that way you will be helping the parents as well.

I recall one mother who finally came in to see me after many requests. She spoke no English but had brought an interpreter with her. Her son, a big boy for his fourteen years, had been annoying girls, and his behavior had gotten to the point where he might prove dangerous to them. Through the young interpreter I told the mother what was going on.

Her son had been seated in an outer office. She asked that he be called in, and he was told to sit down at the table. (I always use a conference table rather than a desk and chairs.) His mother asked him if he had actually done what was discussed, and the boy admitted he had, and showed no remorse or embarrassment. The mother took off her shoe and hit him with the high heel a number of times. What a change in the boy's attitude that produced! His mother's visit definitely had the desired effect. Although he continued to annoy the girls, he did so only verbally, and never again with any physical action.

## CONCLUSION

How regrettable it is that violence is spreading in our society at a tremendous rate and in our schools as well. It is important that we, as educators, do all we can to stop it. By doing so, we are helping not only ourselves but our nation as well.

Our youngsters are surrounded by visual reminders of violence. The televising of events of the Persian Gulf War brought it into our homes on a daily basis. This frightened the boys and girls, who had never been exposed to what they realized was real fighting before.

The television screen is filled with stories of bloodshed and murders. Research has shown that violent programs are associated with youngsters' more aggressive behavior. Videos and films seem to feature aggression. Actress Shelley Winters was quoted in *Parade* magazine of April 21, 1991: "I get scripts all the time, but not many good roles come along. . . . I don't want to do violent films, don't even want to see them. . . . Violent movies have a numbing effect on children. They see them and they don't believe in death." Video games and music videos are more examples of the violence that permeates our society.

Not only do youngsters see violence in the entertainment media, but far too often they experience it at home, with parents who are sadistic or who are under the influence of alcohol or drugs.

Whatever you can do to make your classroom a sanctuary, free from all violence, is worth doing. As one principal told his staff, it's necessary for you to reassure the girls and boys constantly, for they are subject to all sorts of violence.

To show just how much violence there is on television, you may have your students monitor the programming and then discuss their findings.

Skits may be used to teach youngsters to deal with aggression from parents by not fighting back or antagonizing them.

Youngsters often have no idea of the value of human life, and this can be brought home to them by having them read materials that emphasize this. Such material is often published in the *Reader's Digest*.

Television viewing may be used constructively by having contests after the youngsters have seen the programs you deem of value to them. Damage to the environment is a form of violence, and this concept, too, can be taught. In our own environment, vandalism may be considered a form of violence, and our girls and boys should be encouraged to fight against it.

The presence of handguns in the classroom is a menace that may present itself in any community. Should one of your youngsters bring a gun to school, it is essential that you handle the situation as calmly as you can. By speaking very quietly and not challenging the boy or girl, and by sending for help, it is probable that no one will be hurt.

Informing parents when you feel a disruptive child is on the path to violence is absolutely essential, and you must try to enlist their aid by speaking with them in a friendly manner.

As educators, our influence counts in the fight against violence. We must use it.

# 18

# A SELF-ANALYSIS QUESTIONNAIRE FOR EVERY TEACHER

Dear Teachers,

If you feel you'd like to do some self-analysis, the following questionnaire may prove helpful. *This is for your eyes alone,* to help you understand your areas of strength and become aware of areas in which you may want to make some changes.

Teaching is extremely taxing work, and in the last four decades it has become more and more difficult. For this reason it is often discouraging. Our sole purpose with these questions is to assist you, to aid you in seeing how you can improve your professional life. It is not meant to be critical in any way.

As I reread these questions after years of additional experience, I'm afraid they may sound pompous. If they do, I beg your forgiveness. It is just that I hope I can help you. I truly believe in the tremendous importance of education, and I feel that we, as teachers, have been given a very "bad rap."

As we have already mentioned, our society has gone through four revolutions since the end of Word War II. There was the sexual revolution, which changed our mores tremendously. The same may be said for the women's revolution and the black revolution. The technological revolution has changed many of the ways we do things. The original writing of this book was on a typewriter, while today it is on a computer. But not one of these revolutions has helped educators, and those that weakened the family have caused, I believe, disastrous results.

Of course, answering this questionnaire will require your time and effort. We have attempted to give you an objective picture of your teaching—of the techniques and methods you use, and of their effect on your youngsters. You will be considering too the boys' and girls' reaction to you, as a person, and yours to them.

When you've completed the questionnaire, you can note the methods you have not tried, and implement them if you think they are valuable.

## STRUCTURING YOUR CLASS SITUATION _____

1. In what ways have you indicated to your youngsters, what, specifically, you expect of them in terms of work and in terms of behavior?

2. Have you held class elections and established specific duties for every class officer?

3. Have you developed, with the children, a specific set of rules and regulations for use within your classroom?

4. How have you discussed with the youngsters the rules and regulations of the entire school?

5. Have you established a monitorial system—so that every child is a monitor?

6. Have you seated the children so that each child knows which seat in the classroom is his or hers?

7. Have you seated the children with problems close to you? Have you separated those who tend to talk to one another often?

8. Have you reviewed the fire drill procedures and insisted on compliance with them?

## DEVELOPING RAPPORT WITH YOUR YOUNGSTERS _____

1. How often do you greet your children with a smile?

2. How often do you engage in small talk with them or discuss their personal affairs? Is this with the same child or with different children? With boys as well as girls?

3. How do you encourage youngsters to discuss their problems with you?

4. Do you treat every child the same way? Do you allow some youngsters to do more work for you than others? What is the effect on the other children?

5. In what ways have you attempted to draw out the quiet, retiring boy or girl?

6. Do you have a supply of pencils, pens, and paper on hand for the children to "borrow"?

7. How often do youngsters stop to talk to you?

8. Many of the girls and boys in your class have outside interests—hobbies, possibly jobs, and so on. Of how many are you aware?

## LEARNING EXPERIENCES YOU ARE GIVING YOUR YOUNGSTERS _____

You may wish to check your planbook for answers to the following questions. Another technique is to tape-record one of your lessons and review it at your leisure. Best is a combination of both.

1. How have you linked your lessons with the children's lives? Is there some connection between them and the lessons you are teaching?

2. Is the technique you used in today's lesson similar to the one you used yesterday? To the one you have planned for tomorrow?

3. Do you lecture?

4. Review several of your lessons. Do they have a variety of experiences within each one?

5. Have you given your class assignments they are to do "on their own"?

6. Have you discarded any lessons because you felt they did not interest the youngsters?

7. Have you tried to diagnose the skills the boys and girls are lacking?

8. Have you taught them those skills—whether they are in reading or arithmetic, or social studies or even legible penmanship?

9. How have you helped the children develop good work habits?

10. Have you taught your students how to study—taught them actual study skills?

11. Is the pace of your lessons too slow or too rapid?

12. Are most of your youngsters actively participating in your lessons most of the time?

13. Have you refused to accept inferior work from any child—or have you settled for it?

## TEACHING SELF-CONTROL _____

1. Do your boys and girls feel you can control the class? Do you feel you can?

2. How do you handle children who call out—who are noisy? Do you ignore the situation? If not, how do you handle it?

3. Do you give the youngsters enough work to do so that their minds are occupied? Their hands? How often do you give them a "study" period?

4. Do you start working immediately, or do you wait for the children to get quiet?

5. Do you help the individual child while the rest of the class is working?

6. Do you set an example by your personal behavior? For example, do you frequently lose your temper?

7. Have you changed the youngsters' seats so that the troublesome boys and girls are not seated together?

8. Have you enlisted the aid of the class officers and really utilized their services?

## DEVELOPING RAPPORT WITH THE PARENTS _____

1. What steps have you taken to get to know the parents of the children you teach?

2. Have you learned about the special problems the individual child may have?

3. Have you met with the parents and discussed working with them for the benefit of their child?

4. With how many parents have you established some parent-teaching program? What success have you had with this?

5. Have you, in conducting parent interviews, approached the parent with some good aspects of his or her child's behavior?

6. How would you approach an irate parent if the occasion arises?

7. How do you request an interview?

8. How do you communicate with parents through the report card?

## WORKING WITH TROUBLED OR TROUBLESOME CHILDREN

1. Have you discussed their behavior with them personally, on a one-to-one basis?

2. Have you tried to show them how their disruptive behavior is wasting valuable class time?

3. Have you tried to determine specific learning areas in which each individual is deficient?

4. How have you tried to help with these deficiencies?

5. Have you attempted to learn of personal problems which each disruptive youngster may have?

6. Have you made any referrals to the guidance counselor?

7. Have you consulted other teachers to try to learn how to "reach and teach" these children?

8. How have you attempted to help disruptive children gain a positive image of themselves and increase their self-worth and self-confidence?

9. Have you tried to get from these children the promise that they will try to do their work carefully?

10. In what ways have you shown these youngsters warmth and affection, so that they know you care about them?

11. Have you considered the possibility of physical problems affecting any of these children, and have you checked into this?

12. Have you shown your willingness to forgive? After reprimanding a youngster, how do you show him or her that bygones will be forgotten?

13. Have you kept notes (from which you will be able to write anecdotal records) that can be used to help the therapist to better understand the child in question?

14. How much do you rely on one child in the class for errands and such work? On several? On the entire class?

15. What specific steps have you taken to supply the hyperenergetic child with work suitable for him or her?

## CONCLUSION

After you have answered some or all of these questions, please keep one fact in mind. It's one that is easily forgotten. No teacher is perfect, as no human being is perfect. But we believe teachers can improve their work and can make great strides forward. We have seen this happen literally hundreds of times. Far too often teachers have no concept of where they are going wrong or what mistakes they are making. That is the real purpose of this self-analysis. Make your self-appraisal and at the same time you will get ideas about techniques to try and methods with which to experiment.

You should become a pragmatist, constantly experimenting with new ideas, for this will help you grow professionally. Without experimentation, one stagnates, and if you become bored, most assuredly your boys and girls will be too. The key to teaching is getting and holding the children's interest—but that must include all of the children, the disruptive ones as well as the well adjusted, the slow as well as the bright. The teacher who can interest all of the children will have far fewer problems in the classroom. Pupil behavior is poorest when teaching is dullest—in any school, with any child. The time you spend preparing lessons that the youngsters will enjoy is far more valuable than time spent in disciplining.

With troubled children, however, you must try to understand them and help them. For some, your classroom must be a refuge from the ills of society—a haven, if you will, from the abuse to which they may be subjected at home. When a child is disruptive and lacks self-control, the best way you can change him or her is by trying to find the cause. If he shouts or punches, if she is playful, or only "fooling around," the reason may be because this youngster has never been taught otherwise. If you are able to teach self-control to this boy or girl, you may change his or her entire future life. If a youngster daydreams, it may be because the work being done in school holds no importance or interest for this boy or girl. Whenever there is a child misbehaving, try to find the reason for it.

Most important of all, be the type of person the children will wish to emulate. Far louder than words, your actions indicate what you are as a human being. If you are fair, your children will learn to be fair. If you are unpleasant, that too, unfortunately, will be copied. You have to remember that you are always "on display."

Every educator must be engaged in a never-ending battle. Today that word is almost never used in connection with the schools. Our president has asked that this be a "kinder, gentler world." But our battle is against ignorance and against superstition, against fear, and against prejudice. These are our enemies, and the weapons we use to fight them are compassion and knowledge, affection and intellect. And the development of our youngsters into thinking, feeling, functioning human beings is the prize we are all fighting for.

Because a troubled child is so often a disruptive child, it is up to us to try to teach self-discipline to this child and to every child. The teacher's work is critically important, for it is on you (not the superintendent of schools, not the supervisors in the schools, not the counselors, not anyone else, except possibly the parents) that the future of this nation depends. What can ever be more important?

If in some small way we have been of help to you with this book, that is, indeed, a great privilege.

# INDEX